Frames of Deceit is a philosophical investigation of the nature of trust in public and private life. It examines how trust originates, how it is challenged, and how it is recovered when moral and political imperatives collide.

In politics, rulers may be called upon to act badly for the sake of a political good, and in private life intimate attachments are formed in which the costs of betrayal are high. This book asks how trust is tested by human goods, moral character, and power relations. The author explores whether an individual's experience of betrayal differs totally from that of a community when it loses and then seeks to recover a vital public trust.

Although this is a work of political philosophy it is distinctive in examining three literary texts – Sophocles' *Philoctetes*, Shakespeare's *Troilus and Cressida*, and Zola's *Thérèse Raquin* – in order to deepen our understanding of the place of trust in morality and politics.

This is a book of interest to moral and political philosophers as well as to literary theorists.

Frames of deceit

Frames of deceit

A study of the loss
and recovery of public
and private trust

PETER JOHNSON

CAMBRIDGE
UNIVERSITY PRESS

Published by the Press Syndicate of the University of Cambridge
The Pitt Building, Trumpington Street, Cambridge CB2 1RP
40 West 20th Street, New York, NY 10011–4211, USA
10 Stamford Road, Oakleigh, Victoria 3166, Australia

First published 1993

Printed in the United States of America

Library of Congress Cataloging-in-Publication Data
Johnson, Peter, 1943–
Frames of deceit : a study of the loss and recovery of public and
private trust / Peter Johnson.
p.   cm.
Includes bibliographical references.
ISBN 0-521-43193-X
1. Political ethics.   2. Trust (Psychology)   3. Politics in
literature.   I. Title.
JA79.J63   1992
172 – dc20   92-17105
                                                   CIP

A catalog record for this book is available from the British Library.

ISBN 0–521–43193-X hardback

For my nieces and nephews

It is a big affair our Trust.

F. W. Maitland,
Collected Essays

If anyone, then, is to practise deception,
either on the country's enemies or on its
citizens, it must be the rulers of the
commonwealth, acting for its benefit;
no one else may meddle with this privilege.

Plato, *Republic*

Wilt thou make trust a transgression? The
transgression is in the stealer.

William Shakespeare, *Much Ado About Nothing*

Contents

Acknowledgments

I would like to thank Steve Buckler for many stimulating discussions at various times and places about the dirty hands problem; Liam O'Sullivan for a conversation during the writing of this book, which encouraged me to continue; my wife, Sue, for her close and critical involvement with the book from its inception; the readers for Cambridge University Press for their helpful suggestions; and Mrs. Jean Ballard for efficiently transforming the manuscript into a legible form.

Introduction

When I began writing on the problems of political morality, in *Politics, Innocence and the Limits of Goodness*, my main interest was in how certain moral dispositions such as moral innocence might disqualify themselves from political engagement. The relation between morality and politics I saw not as a framework of principles providing a necessary constraint on politics, but as a case of moral character engaging with political demands often in circumstances of great urgency and strain. My view of those who might be described as unreflectively good, that is, those unaware of potential betrayal and hence the need for caution and prudence, was that they were capable only of a sort of hopeful trust, both in others and in the way things turn out. If moral innocents experience trust in this half-seen way I wanted to go on to ask about those who are not moral innocents how in fact they learn to exercise trust, particularly in situations where other people's intentions are often opaque. My attention turned, therefore, to the relation between trust and dirty hands. I wanted to see how it is possible for trust actually to be given to those who are likely to be called on to act badly for the sake of some political good when the chances are that those who are doing the trusting will be the victims of those actions. And to ask whether trusters base their trust in the moral character of officeholders, in rules intended to govern the behavior of officeholders qua officeholders or in the specific checks designed to control their conduct in advance.

Further, I felt that it would be wrong to examine trust in

political life in isolation from the experience of personal trust. It seems to me that one can acknowledge the conceptual differences between trust in public and private life and still address the possibility that there are important features common to both, and, indeed, I would maintain that an individual's experience of being personally betrayed and trying to recover trust is not totally remote from what it is for a community to lose and attempt to reclaim trust. This is why I have chosen to examine texts, Sophocles' *Philoctetes*, Shakespeare's *Troilus and Cressida*, Zola's *Thérèse Raquin*, in which the public and private worlds – specifically how trust is tested there by human goods, power relations and moral character – exist in a complex relation one with the other.

The more I thought about this problem the more I became convinced that a theory which construes individuals simply as units of uniform psychology, abstracted from ideas of moral character and from the circumstances of their lives, is not going to be sufficiently refined. By contrast, seeing the giving or withholding of trust as a feature of *narrative* in my view enables us to grasp its intelligibility and at the same time focus on those actual gaps and interstices in conduct which often create the risks of trust and go to the very heart of its moral point. Literature, of course, fulfills this narrative requirement very well – my hope is that my treatment of these literary examples furthers the philosophical discussion too.

My actual route is first to examine the general problems associated with public and private trust (Chapter 1), then in Chapter 2 to explore moral character, in particular the "best dispositions" as a possible basis for trust, leading to a consideration of the very different strategy of grounding trust in well-founded structures of rationality (Chapter 3). The shortcomings I find in these approaches lead me to try to formulate in the following chapters an alternative understanding of trust in public and private contexts. Here I analyze moral and political trust, its loss and recovery, as a feature of narrative. So I delineate the origin of trust in different contexts (Chapter 4), its risks and rewards (Chapter 5), and its endings – in terms of forgiveness and forgetting (Chapter 6).

My intention is to develop three main points. First, I argue that it is a mistake to construe trust in political life as if it were simply correlative with something like discretion, merely the subjective view taken by individual citizens toward those who take decisions on their behalf. My line of thought is that the moral significance of trust is both wider and deeper than this would imply. That is to say, we do not simply trust political agents *not* to abuse their discretionary authority, but to *use* it prudently for the achievement of common ends. We do not just trust them not to put their own interests first, but to act positively, to exercise specific virtues of character to defend the way of life we value. With this emphasis on "positive trust" we see why it is necessary to place trust in political life alongside an understanding of the moral significance of trust and its risks in the face of transgression by the trusted.

Second, I interpret dirty hands problems as a species of dilemma. Here trust is clearly not free from risk, but my argument throughout is that this does not mean that trust is always to be seen as credulousness, a lazy faith in others which eliminates the need for thought or action. I argue that to see trust as a form of naïveté both in public and private worlds is to give unargued priority to the fear of being a dupe, is incompatible with any substantial sense of moral or political loyalty, merely assumes that the fault of misplaced trust is always to be laid at the truster's door and does not allow for the possibility that being trusted can sometimes make a difference to one's trustworthiness.

Finally, I concentrate on the uncertainties and frailties of trust, rejecting the view that the vulnerability to betrayal which is one of the risks of trust entails consequent withdrawal from the public realm if betrayal occurs. My point is that goodness requires such assaults if character is to be formed and if the virtue of courage in the face of disloyalty is to be developed. What controls the suspension of morality for the achievement of public and private goods certainly

3

places trust under great strain. Constraints may take the form of advantage, reward and benefit as well as threat; hands may be sullied by attempts to minimize the moral costs of blackmail, and also by the means necessary to reduce the fear of treachery and betrayal – a recognition that it may be necessary to lower one's sights is not always a surrender to full-scale pragmatism. Political action may be constrained as much by what has been entrusted to our friends as kept secret from our enemies. It is my view that the full intelligibility of trust – its positive strengths, its vulnerability – is best explored in narrative logic, against the background of the history of a life or a community. How trust displays itself, is tested, lost and sometimes recovered in moral and political contexts is my subject here. I begin with a discussion of the nature of public and private trust.

Chapter 1

Public and private trust

Show me the man who rules his household well: I'll show you someone fit to rule the state.

Sophocles, *Antigone*

Statecraft in modern states is not: what must one do in order to be a
minister, but: what one must do in order to become a minister. More
than that they do not understand, and consequently they use what
knowledge they have as a sort of introductory science, in order to
become ministers. In that way the state will inevitably break up, for
in point of fact nobody rules or governs.

Søren Kierkegaard, *The Journals*

If we cannot trust rulers when they appear to act well, how
can we trust them when we know they are acting badly? If
we cannot trust them when their hands are clean, how can
we trust them when their hands are dirty? In politics we
want rulers to be trustworthy, but we treat them as if "every
man ought to be supposed a knave, and to have no other
end . . . than private interest."[1] We want rulers to possess
the morality of doves, but we wish them to act as if they were
serpents. We want them to act well toward ourselves but
badly toward our enemies. We hope they are successful as
long as the benefit is ours and we are not the victims of their
success. They should be both lion and fox, honest and deceitful in turn for the protection and furtherance of our common
purposes. We wish them to be "trusting but not credulous."[2]
In political morality such ambivalences are endemic. What

kind of trust is possible in such a world? What notion of moral character would merit trust in circumstances of political complexity?

Moral character, trust, and political order often collide. Rule needs to be both effective and well intentioned: Neither impractical saints nor pragmatic gangsters provide a location for trust or a basis for political legitimacy. Trust may be a realistic policy in highly constrained circumstances or it may be dangerously ill-advised. A political order that aspires to public accountability must contain offices whose rights and duties are formally constituted and upheld. And yet in politics the roles of officeholders "are not fully scripted."[3] Trust in the context of discretionary powers "risks abuse of those and the successful disguise of such abuse."[4] There may be occasions on which legitimate political purposes can be achieved only by means otherwise regarded as morally undesirable. Here great strain is placed both on the formal conditions of officeholding and on the moral character of the officeholder. How does trust express itself in such circumstances? An attitude of comprehensive distrust toward those faced with morally difficult political choices may be sustained only through political inaction or hypocrisy. Equally, a policy of trusting in appearance may lead to disaster.

Machiavelli explores these intricate relationships in a notable passage in *The Discourses,* where he discusses the conduct of Piero Soderini after his appointment as Florentine head of state.[5] Soderini had been entrusted with the preservation of order and stability in the republic. Faced with the challenge of malevolent factionalism, he responded with patience and goodness. In trusting his enemies, he betrayed the trust of the citizens who looked to him for the maintenance of civil peace. In refusing ruthlessness and guile as instruments of policy in dealing with the faction, he failed to protect those who had no power to protect themselves. Character, trust, and necessity are all present in Machiavelli's reflections in this passage. Soderini displayed genuine virtue. He possessed virtues of character – patience and goodness. He had the political sense to recognize the need for prudence and action: Aware that the enemies of the republic were not impressed by goodness, he tried to bargain with them. Additionally, he faced a constitutional problem. The anti-republicans could be eliminated only by his assuming an extraordinary authority, which might have so alarmed the citizens that they lost faith in an office of great value to the republic, even though Soderini had no wish to use its powers tyrannically in the future. Machiavelli describes Soderini's viewpoint as "wise and good,"[6] but considers that he was fatally weak in dealing with his political opponents. Soderini faced a dilemma that many less reflective rulers might not have seen, or been troubled by if they had, but from Machiavelli's perspective it is not intractable. For Machiavelli the survival of the republic is paramount: "An evil should never be allowed to continue out of respect for a good when that good may easily be overwhelmed by that evil."[7] Soderini should have ensured that ruthless actions were seen in the context of his public reputation as a good and trustworthy man. He should have made it known that his actions were performed for the good of the republic and not for reasons of personal ambition. Constitutional arrangements should have been so regulated that "none of his successors could do with evil intent what he had done with good intent."[8] However, Machiavelli neglects important aspects of the relation between moral character and politics. A Machiavellian politician construes political morality as *raison d'état* – it refers to the measures that are necessary for the preservation of the republic. Politics is a consequentialist activity in which the achievement of the desired end leaves little room for moral doubts about the choice of means. From this perspective it is difficult to identify the specific moral problems facing political agents in those severe circumstances in which extraordinary measures may have to be employed. Here the demands of office may be seen as legitimate claims on personal moral values or they may be a stain on moral integrity, their fulfillment an indication of the presence of dirty hands. Machiavelli identifies politics as a realm of appearance. Rulers should be foxes when necessary, but "seem to be exceptionally merciful, trustworthy, upright, humane and devout."[9] Of course, dissemblance requires both that there are those who are deceived and that there are those who are nothing other than what they seem. But Machiavelli goes much further than this: "Men are so naive, and so much dominated by immediate needs, that a skilful deceiver always finds plenty of people who will let themselves be deceived."[10] The "always" and "let themselves" in this passage are instructive. If things were so, it is difficult to see how trust would be anything other than foolhardy or that a cautious distrust would not be the only rational policy for the prudent, the scheming, and the enlightened. Duplicity, then, is connected with necessity, and both are essential features of political capacity. Those who wish to rule in a republic should "be capable of entering upon the path of wrongdoing when this becomes necessary."[11]

To stress the capacity to rule, as Machiavelli does, distances ruling from the Socratic understanding of it as a skill exercised for the good of the ruled. For Socrates, rule is an expression of wisdom and judgment in accordance with the idea of justice. By contrast, capacity implies an image of ruling as a mechanism for the production of specific effects. In the absence of any reference to the nature of human agency and character it is difficult to see how capacity could include such moral qualities as fortitude, determination, and resolution. In the Machiavellian view, rulers are trusted if they possess the capacity to act in accordance with political necessity. In the Socratic view, trust in rulers is justified because ruling is a craft conducted by reference to standards derived from the nature of moral knowledge. The notion of trusting rulers implies that we have some conception of the kind of agency involved in being both the truster and the trusted. Utilitarian and contractarian accounts of agency emphasize powers and capacities. They stress the ability required to maximize utility or to make rational agreements that will be of mutual benefit. However, to describe trusters solely in terms of the rational capacity to further a moderate self-interest is to attenuate our conception of substantive human character and hence to say nothing about the state of mind that bestows trust or the moral qualities that may inspire it.

The giving and receiving of trust in morally complex political circumstances are both crucial and problematic. From the
Machiavellian viewpoint, trust seems mysterious and puz-
zling: In politics the trustworthy are precisely those we should
not trust. But why must it be the case that those who trust are
the foolhardy and the easily deceived? Is the moral value of
trust so easily diminished? Socrates associates trust with just
actions and policies, though his conception of ruling as a craft
assumes an agreement on rules, standards, and personal attributes that may not be sustainable. We are all too familiar with
the courageous defense of unjust causes, with intelligence
used in the service of evil ends, and we have suffered the
consequences of attempts to transform the world in the image
of ideology. The Platonic association of reason, justice, and
ruling might seem to provide a basis for trust in those who rule
in accordance with their philosophic natures by reference to
the form of justice and with the aim of sustaining the good of
the whole community. Nevertheless, even here Plato allows
for the telling of a noble lie by the guardians, albeit in the
context of the ideal state and with the common good of the
ruled in mind.[12] Plato may have thought of the lie as a kind of
treatment, in which case those who are told a lie trust in much
the same way as the ill trust their physicians to act in their best
interests even when what is prescribed to them appears harmful. In the *Republic,* trust depends on the natures of the trusted
and the trusting. And so it may be that Plato was not so much
thinking of rulers as experts, but drawing our attention to
what it means to act on behalf of others in a political community. In so doing he raises the possibility that one of the unavoidable features of politics is the need for concealment and
secrecy, and he is pressing us to consider how trust may or
may not survive such withholding.

In the political world outside Plato's *Republic,* however, it is
the ignoble lie that rules. Here, lies may be told to further
reputation, power, and interest. Awareness of such motives
puts us on our guard when deception is defended as the only
way of protecting or benefiting us. In these circumstances
the ruled may be justifiably concerned that they are being

exploited as a convenient means to the achievement of ends that serve the interests of others. They may suspect that they are victims sacrificed for political convenience. The question of perspective is central to problems in political morality, and it has been neglected by Kantian or utilitarian attempts to ascertain an impartial standpoint from which agent choices may be scrutinized. But who bears the burden of hard choices? What moral difference arises if we take the standpoint of the victims rather than a neutral assessment of outcomes? In *Les mains sales* Sartre poses the dilemma of a revolutionary party committed to the abolition of exploitation and deceit, but faced with using lies in order to achieve it. In one respect, the choice is between the good and the effective. More important, it is not that the means to be employed are morally neutral – that any methods can be used as long as they are technically efficient in achieving ends. In Sartre's play the proposed means are subject to the conflicting *moral* perspectives of the political agents involved. It is their contrasting moral standpoints that provide the focus for our ethical attention, a point stressed by Michael Walzer as crucial in understanding decisions made in dirty hands cases:

> His willingness to acknowledge and bear (and perhaps to repent and do penance for) his guilt is evidence, and it is the only evidence he can offer us, both that he is not too good for politics and that he is good enough. Here is the moral politician: it is by his dirty hands that we know him. If he were a moral man and nothing else, his hands would not be dirty; if he were a politician and nothing else, he would pretend that they were clean.[13]

To whom should rule be entrusted when such decisions have to be made? A utilitarian conception of ruling requires that it evaluate rival considerations in the light of their consequences for the general welfare. A contractarian theory requires that ruling is in accordance with principles of justice pre-agreed by rational agents who are moderately self-interested. In both accounts substantive questions concerning the nature of human character are addressed only after the priority of the rules of justice has been established. This means that dirty hands cases are problematic only insofar as they represent a failure in the application of an already agreed structure of moral reasoning. Political morality is construed not as the experience of tragic moral dilemmas but as a field of utilitarian or contractarian theorizing. The neglect of human character and disposition means that trust in rulers is understood by reference to the institutional constraints that have been placed on them and within which they have to act if rule is to be legitimate. We trust the constraints because it is through them that we hope to be protected if rulers act badly. In so doing we lose sight of the meaning of trust when it has as its object a friend, a compatriot, a stranger, or an enemy. We ignore, too, the complexities of trusting those with dirty hands, of putting our faith in the individual whose conduct "may be exactly the right thing to do in utilitarian terms and yet leave the man who does it guilty of a moral wrong."[14]

One response to this problem is to ask for a greater degree of explicitness in the way public actions are justified. Stuart Hampshire, for example, understands the special domain of political morality to be marked by a responsibility for policies that affect large numbers of people unknown to those who make them, by the actual or potential use of violence, and by a requirement in modern democratic politics to protect the interests of those one represents *in* representative roles that contain both rights and obligations.[15] Openness follows both from the idea of representation and from the consequentialist nature of modern politics. It is desirable that the ruled know which consequences have been taken into account and which set aside. Hampshire brings out the connection he sees between explicitness and trust. In modern democratic politics a political agent

> needs an endorsement that his policies are right from his followers; and he needs to be understood by his followers, who will otherwise tend to distrust him if they do not know,

or do not think that they know, how he thinks about substantial moral issues and what his calculations of consequences are.[16]

What provides the basis for trust here is not that we agree necessarily with decisions taken on our behalf, but that we follow the process of moral thinking by which they are reached. We trust the rules of the game, and so distrust is not our automatic response if we regard any particular outcome as undesirable. A public context of accountability provides an essential link between the moral character of rulers and the judgments of their actions and policies made by the ruled. But can the problems raised by trust in the circumstances of political morality be solved so neatly? Accountability may actually be at odds with the need for secrecy in certain political decisions where "publicity would preclude their success."[17] Political choices frequently involve consequences that cannot be retrieved, and "by the time citizens have a chance to review the decision, the damage may have been done."[18] The persistence of dirty hands in such circumstances revises the democratic conception of political trust. It is no longer sufficient to speak of trusting the institutional constraints on rulers; procedural rules governing the decisions of officeholders are now penetrated by ambiguity and uncertainty. A region of political choice is disclosed that may be explored in terms of the moral character of political agents. What conception of trust is appropriate here?

To be trusting in the face of concealment is not necessarily to trust blindly, but ignorance of another's political intentions gives trust a sharper edge and places it on the limits of moral advisability. Our attention is drawn to the contrasting moral attributes of the trusting and the trusted, and we are introduced to the complexity of thinking about trust as a relational good. Inescapably connected with risk, trust may be justified or badly misplaced. Those who are trusted may find that living up to it proves too burdensome. Those who trust may find themselves vulnerable to disappointment or betrayal. The fragility of trust has encouraged the development of the secondary strategies of caution and insurance against loss or damage. Trust, however, is subject to different kinds of risk: It is susceptible to unexpected changes in circumstance, or exposed to the intentions and actions of others. In *The Merchant of Venice,* for example, there are important contrasts between external risks – that the weather might not hold long enough for the ships to reach port safely – and risks that are internal to an individual's distinctive character or project. Failure may result from accident or from a defect inherent in choice or policy. It may have been bad luck that Antonio's ships were delayed by a storm; Bassanio's agreement with Shylock, however, was ill-judged, not simply because he was unfortunate to have met that particular moneylender or that Shylock was untrustworthy, but because Shylock could be trusted to fulfill the contract precisely to the letter.

A predictable hazard of politics is the occurrence of conflicts of value from which it is difficult to emerge morally unscathed. Such conflicts place great and often unbearable strain on character. Creon in Sophocles' *Antigone* changes from a publicly respected and trusted ruler to a destroyed being, barely human – "I am nothing. I have no life."[19] What fascinates is not just the moral dynamic that controls the logic of this tragic transformation, but the way in which the qualities of kingship that once constituted a basis for trust disintegrate in the face of Creon's near obsessive concern to preserve them. Here the risks of trusting increase under the impact of events and with Creon's slow and painful recognition that his failure is connected necessarily with the preoccupation with his capacity to rule.

Kierkegaard's suggestive remark that in modern states the political self is characterized by becoming rather than being ensures that the classical Greek curiosity about the qualities needed for rule is not completely lost to us. He encourages us to understand statecraft not as an instrumental activity involving manipulation, persuasion, or the calculation of power and advantage, but as the community's search for the deepest political good. In this way, the choice of morally undesirable means to achieve legitimate ends appears not as a utilitarian calculation but as a moral dilemma. Tragedy presents itself not only as a choice between the lesser of two evils but as the recognition that private virtues like kinship and friendship can be threatened by precisely those qualities that seemed genuinely to offer political hope. As Burke remarked, even the morally sensitive may be "confounded with the dreadful exigence in which morality submits to the suspension of its own rules in favour of its own principles."[20]

One of the most serious risks involved in trusting those with dirty hands is the chance that "criminal means once tolerated are soon preferred."[21] Consider Michael Walzer's well-known example of a political candidate who "wants to do good only by doing good."[22] His moral certainties are tested when "in order to win the election the candidate must make a deal with a dishonest ward boss involving the granting of contracts for school construction over the next four years. Should he make the deal?"[23] It is the candidate's goodness that creates the problem and determines his response. He is reluctant either straightforwardly to accept the deal or to reject it. He knows that the deal is dishonest and that it will guarantee his election. Although he might be tempted, he is not motivated by expediency; his future career is not more important to him than the methods he is prepared to use to further it. He is aware, too, that some support him precisely because they believe he is genuinely concerned with the public welfare; he is someone who can be relied upon not to make such deals. Rightly, Walzer stresses the way the candidate regards himself. By contrast, the Machiavellian hero has no "inwardness";[24] the candidate's reservations about making the deal are signs of moral self-awareness. Here, it is the inner life that provides the source of self-reproach: "If he is the good man I am imagining him to be, he will feel guilty, that is he will believe himself to be guilty. That is what it means to have dirty hands."[25]

In this way we know something of how a candidate might think of himself if he accepts the deal, but what might be the response of those who once believed in his goodness? He is not necessarily compromised in their eyes. They may blame the circumstances of a corrupt political world. Further, they may appreciate that he acted with great reluctance and that, in any case, if the deal has to be made at all they do not "want just *anyone* to make the deal; [they] want *him* to make it, precisely because he has scruples about it."[26] That he sees himself as morally flawed does not mean that he is so from the standpoint of those who supported him. They may interpret his dirty hands as a willingness to sacrifice his integrity on their behalf. But Walzer's emphasis on *"him"* is a significant individuation. At one point his integrity was the definitive mark of his trustworthiness. Does the fact that he now has dirty hands mean that he cannot be trusted again?

Two recent accounts of trust help us to see how it might enter this relationship. Annette Baier offers what she calls a "first approximation" of the meaning of trust:

> Where one depends on another's goodwill, one is necessarily vulnerable to the limits of that goodwill. One leaves others an opportunity to harm one when one trusts, and also shows one's confidence that they will not take it. Reasonable trust will require good grounds for such confidence in another's goodwill, or at least the absence of good grounds for expecting their ill will or indifference.[27]

Richard Swinburne places more emphasis on the nature of the harm potentially involved in trust. It is the coexistence of confidence and possible harm that gives rise to the inescapable presence of risk. For Swinburne:

> To trust a man is to act on the assumption that he will do for you what he knows that you want or need, when the evidence gives some reason for supposing that he may not and where there will be bad consequences if the assumption is false.[28]

Swinburne's example brings out the connection between trust as a means to an end and possible harm if that trust is misplaced:

An escaping British prisoner of war may have trusted some German by telling him of his identity and asking for help . . . he acts on the assumption that the German will do for him what he knows that he wants (viz provide help), when many Germans are ill-disposed towards escaping British prisoners and liable to surrender them to the police.[29]

A significant point of contrast emerges between this example and the case of dirty hands discussed by Walzer. Unlike Swinburne's prisoner of war, those who trusted Walzer's candidate did so precisely because of his moral character. They believed him to be a good man who would not dirty his hands making shady deals, even for desirable ends. However, to trust the candidate requires the possibility of harm. In Swinburne's example this arises from the fact that many Germans were ill-disposed toward British prisoners of war. How might harm arise in Walzer's case? Notice that in getting his hands dirty the candidate has not betrayed his supporters by acting tyrannically or arbitrarily toward them. He has not let them down through selfishness or simple material greed. He has given them what they want, namely a good man to represent them, but only by acting badly. In this respect, he can be trusted; he knows what it means to act instrumentally, but in doing so he has sacrificed his integrity; his hands are no longer clean, and insofar as this was the original reason for supporting him, it means that he is also no longer trustworthy. Harm arises, therefore, from the risks involved in trusting those who are prepared to dirty their hands. Once they have exchanged principle for benefit, they may become increasingly preoccupied with politics as a consequentialist activity and may no longer see the choice of morally suspect means as a specific reason for guilt. Indeed, they may come to think of themselves as exempt from moral criticism regarding means as long as the ends of political action have been achieved; to trust those who think of themselves as morally immune is to risk enslavement to the desperate or the despotic. Aristotle stresses the importance of maintaining the rule of law in near just societies and he speaks of a transgression that "creeps in unperceived and at last ruins a state."[30] Moral transgression is an essential feature of dirty hands. However, those in politics who "purge vice with vice" and "corrode the bad with bad, a spider with a toad,"[31] risk more intractable entanglements if they find their hands too closely tied to the evil or the base. Trading with the corrupt to protect the good may involve increasingly serious demands on the moral resources of those who do so on behalf of others; a premium is placed on self-awareness and experience; it is guile rather than goodness that provides the grounds for trust. Here there are risks to both truster and trusted. Those who give trust may find themselves deceived; those who receive it may find themselves committed to serial treasons once they have recognized, as Hoederer does in *Les mains sales*, that it is impossible to "govern and keep your spirit white."[32]

The moral ambivalence of trust is introduced in this context. Trust may be misplaced or betrayed. We may trust too much or too little, both in ourselves and in others. We may risk beyond reason or try to contain risk within the boundaries of prudence and caution. As Brian Vickers points out, trust is an ethical value "more demonstrated in the breach than in the observance";[33] direct repugnance and loathing are our predominant responses to "violations of trust: bribe-taking, treachery, perjury."[34] It is the risk involved in such breaches of trust that has led John Dunn to argue that "human beings need, as afar as they can, to economise on trust in persons and confide instead in well-designed political, social and economic institutions."[35]

This shift from persons to institutions is essential to liberal democratic accounts of trust as a basis for social cooperation. As the main intellectual architects of these "well-designed" institutions, utilitarianism and contractarianism assume individuals to be autonomous, moderately self-interested, and capable of rational choice. But what is lost in such self-consciously abstract conceptions of agency is our sense of the richness, depth, and moral density of human character – its qualities, virtues, and vices. Utilitarianism thinks of trust as a

17

strategy available in thinly defined psychological circumstances. It fails to understand how those who have acted
badly for the achievement of morally desirable ends may still
feel guilt even though the ends have been brought about.
Trust does not arise as a function of unrelated units perform-
ing the calculations of utilitarian rational choosers; it emerges
in an inherited context of relations and ideas whose contours
need to be mapped if the substantive content of risk is to be
appreciated. Contract theory, too, is preoccupied with nonaltruistic trust between theoretically independent agents as
the foundation of a stable, well-structured political authority.
However, as a system of precommitment "it can also be
costly, and a cause of bitter regret: when one decides to wear
a chastity belt and throw the key into the river."[36] Within its
own terms contract theory is a rational strategy for restricting
our concern with the trustworthiness of others, but, as
Gambetta remarks correctly, "Contract shifts the focus of
trust on to the efficacy of sanctions, and either our or a third
party's ability to enforce them if a contract is broken."[37]

The emphasis on the "efficacy of sanctions" is deliberate; it
is part of the attempt to develop a notion of trust appropriate
to the complexity of modern liberal democratic politics. It
expresses a proper concern with the nature of the rights and
duties of officeholders, with what they may permissibly do
on our behalf. This means, however, that trust is directed
toward the rules governing political agents rather than toward their character and actions. Our attention moves to the
safeguards that are supposed to protect us when we trust
others – the constitutional procedures of accountability and
the rule of law or, in the case of the furtherance of interests,
the rules governing rights of compensation and redress of
grievance when those who act on our behalf fail in their
public responsibilities. According to this view of politics "we
should not ask about a politician whether we would buy a
second-hand car from him but whether we would be adequately protected by a Sale of Goods Act if he sold us a bad
one."[38]

This understanding of politics takes self-interest as its psychological starting point and addresses the problem of developing political structures that will encourage rational cooperation and will be reliable in cases of default. It does not involve a substantive conception of moral character, but concentrates

> on the manipulation of constraints and interests as those conditions of cooperation on which we can intentionally and most effectively operate. We can aim to promote as much cooperation as possible by deploying some reasonable degree of coercion through self-interest, thereby making small demands on trust.[39]

The attempt to "economise on trust"[40] neglects the conditions that make the dirty hands problem both possible and serious. The conditions include a moral concern separable from an acquisitive psychology, a preparedness to act badly to achieve legitimate ends, and a recognition that others are not objects to be manipulated but individuals who exist in complex relation to one another as moral critics and as independent sources of praise or blame. The dirty hands problem requires us to see politics not as a Glauconian device for linking justice to advantage, but as an arena of republican virtue in which moral sacrifices may sometimes have to be made. Trust arises as a feature of a moral vocabulary used by those who know that rule may become arbitrary and corrupt and that moral and political concerns are not always reciprocal.

The broad tradition of republican political thought expresses a central concern with government as a qualified activity and with trust as a conditional disposition, more often refused than given, something to be held in reserve. It involves a fundamental awareness that in

> every political institution, a power to advance the public happiness, involves a discretion which may be misapplied and abused . . . in all cases where power is to be conferred, the point first to be decided is, whether such a power be necessary to the public good; [and] to guard as effectually as possible against a perversion of the power to the public detriment.[41]

In the eighteenth-century republican context political virtue meant

> a jealous, vigilant commitment to the public life: continued participation in a politics that trusted only limited responsibilities to national officials and demanded, even so, that these officials be continuously watched for any signs of an appearance of a separate set of interests.[42]

Thus, the rules constructed for the control of public offices and officeholders were designed primarily to ensure that the public good was not replaced by private interest. In point of fact, such rules are not necessarily relevant to the scrutiny of what is done on our behalf in dirty hands cases. What is at issue here is not the "appearance of a separate set of interests," but the disposition involved in putting morality aside for the public good. Similarly, contract theories derive government from agreed principles of justice, thus attempting to eliminate arbitrariness and any serious conflict between moral and political concerns. This move from personal trust to trust in fair institutional structures is a characteristically modern phenomenon. Rawls, for example, specifically excludes the noble lie from the just republic – if the rules of fairness have been correctly formulated and derived, there can be no need for it.[43] As we shall see, the Lockean shift from trusting rulers to ruling as a trust complicates public accountability without aiding our understanding of political morality and the way moral character plays a significant part in it. Locke's conception of constitutional government is dominated by trust in its various forms, so it is hardly surprising that, as Judith Shklar has argued, "where there is so much reliance on trust, there must also be frequent betrayals."[44]

For citizens placing trust in those with dirty hands, the fear of betrayal and subversion is paramount. To try to dispel such fear by replacing personal trust with rules of conduct based on deep structures of rationality has been the predominant aim of liberalism, particularly in its Kantian form. But the rule-governed constraints of universality, impartiality, and accountability are marginal to the problems of political morality, which focus on agency and disposition. In the case of moral character it is the spirit that animates and enlivens; the letter kills.

Of course, reflection on political morality in the Christian and liberal traditions has seen morality as foundational: the problem is to so transform the political world that it is fit for the occupation of moral beings. Although this transformation is incomplete, morality serves the significant purpose of providing principles against which political proposals may be checked and scrutinized. The problems of political morality, however, are not so tractable. Politics is not the sole domain of the ambitious, the ruthless, and the evil – sometimes the good have to perform morally undesirable actions if legitimate political ends are to be achieved. Moral conflict in politics takes a variety of forms. It may appear as a collision of loyalties, a clash between the obligations arising from friendship, and the impersonal requirements of state. For Judith Shklar: "It is not a choice of policies, but of personal or impersonal loyalties, one of which must be betrayed."[45]

What kind of character is involved in such a dilemma? As Shklar observes, in politics we find "excellent statesmen and awful men"; but it is also true that we find the honorable and the fair, and sometimes they are more dangerous and less worthy of trust. Alan Ryan, for example, refers to Hobbes's "hostility to the excesses of the aristocratic concern for honour; men who seize on the slightest excuse to pick a quarrel are menaces to the peace."[46]

One might add, especially so if they are recipients of a public or a private trust. Conflict may appear, too, in the form of dilemmas in which the demands of office change the basis of moral decision and impose legitimate claims on the moral integrity of the officeholder. We are familiar with the conflicts that develop between roles and the contrasting duties they require us to fulfill. From another standpoint, the dirty hands problem is one of means and ends, a calculation of benefit, a negotiation between choices or options. Conflicting moral demands – of friendship against public duty, of personal regard against public benefit – prompt reflection on the diverse attributes of character; a quality seems to match one attachment but not another; kindness may be perfectly in place in the context of friendship, but fit badly with the impartial, public requirements of justice and fairness. Does integrity involve the ordering of these different commitments or the discovering of a just balance between them? Trust seems to need some firm anchoring in character if it is to be sustained – inconstancy, fickleness, or making decisions at random is clearly insufficient. The diversity involved in human association is an essential condition of the problems of political morality. We need to explore the possibility that the conception of trust at work in such relations and commitments is not singular but plural, one appropriate to the multiple attachments that human beings form in politics and morality, and that occasionally they may be forced to break.

A stress on moral character in political morality reveals the importance of self-understanding in the relation between agents and their actions. It draws our attention to disposition and imagination; to the contrasting ways moral agents perceive their own goodness – with pride, as an admirable achievement that requires a public stage, with spontaneous indifference, or with unreflective innocence. This means that goodness can be an obstacle to political judgment in ways not fully grasped by the Kantian stress on principle or by the utilitarian concern with consequences. It is not the breach of the moral rule but the expression of a self-regarded goodness that damages the polity. This revision in our understanding of political morality has implications for our view of trust. It asks us to reconsider personal trust as a feature of relations between political agents. Does this raise the risks of trust? Judith Shklar refers to "face-to-face societies like the medieval monarchies" in which "betrayal was both personal and endemic";[47] but if the risk is raised, is not the moral value too? Moral insight by the trusting into the character and motives of the trusted may reduce the risks of trust, but notice that it is not simply a matter of replacing personal trust with trust in well-founded institutions and rules. Bernard Harrison refers to the example of Mr. Casaubon in George Eliot's *Middlemarch:*

> Mr Casaubon, we may be sure, can be relied upon to discharge in a straightforward and honourable way any moral claim whose neglect, if discovered, would expose him to public censure, because in his intense and fastidious egoism he could not endure the thought that anyone might be in a position to bring a charge of dereliction of duty against him. George Eliot wants us to see among other things, I think, that there is nothing in this kind of rectitude capable of counteracting the effects of Casaubon's egoism in isolating him from relationships of genuine trust and openness with others, because there is nothing in it capable of preventing him from acting in a mean and unjust way when the possibility of public censure is absent.[48]

What guarantees Casaubon's public trustworthiness are his vanity and fear of public rebuke. Discovery of his true character allows us to trust his behavior, but then only conditionally and with a strong sense of moral reserve. Harrison comments:

> What has to be noticed about this example is that anyone astute enough to grasp the connection between Casaubon's rectitude and his personal vanity has (i) good reason to repose a mechanically inferred trust in Casaubon's performance of any public duty, and (ii) equally good reason for not extending that trust beyond certain well-defined limits.[49]

There is, therefore, no straightforward or morally compelling shift from personal to institutional trust. Public rules may conceal hypocrisy as effectively as they allow us to appeal against breaches of trust. Rule by Casaubon? Would we not prefer the traitor who can be openly impeached? Here our reasonable preoccupation is with how trust can be secured. Trust between friends requires no such guarantees. A natural and spontaneous outlook trusts what it discovers in ourselves or in others, "although unclear where it will lead."[50] To impose tests for trust is clearly inappropriate here, but as we shall see, such trials are not strategies exclusive to the indecisive, the often disappointed, or the frequently betrayed. In private relationships marked by psychological intensity or sexual obsession, they can have a powerful public resonance. Even in circumstances where trust and the risks it involves are mediated by formal rules, by an ethic of officeholding, it is significant that the experience of dirty hands cannot be completely dispelled. In the 1979 film *Kramer versus Kramer*, the lawyer representing a father who is suing for custody of his child knows that he may have to discredit the man's ex-wife when she takes the witness stand; he knows that he is going to provoke her deliberately into behaving badly or into revealing an indiscretion or an instability detrimental to her case. He knows that he is going to treat her harshly. Nevertheless, even though the client is aware that such behavior is common in law courts and that refraining from it may lose him the case he has clear reservations; his lawyer responds: "Do you want the kid or don't you?"

Some sense of the limits on a lawyer's conduct in such cases is necessary, but how can this be established? Can the client stipulate in advance what may or may not be done in his name? Should he assess the lawyer's actions by reference to their outcomes – if he wins the case, how much has it cost him? Are limits established by the moral character of those involved? Is this the way a community's legal rectitude is maintained? Recent philosophical discussion of such examples has been concerned with the disanalogies between law and politics, stressing that power, concealment, and allegiance in political life are not easily expressed in the language of impartiality or in codes of conduct.[51] Machiavelli's "I love my native city more than my own soul"[52] is transformed by Hannah Arendt to mean "the crucial decision for all who devote their lives to politics," namely, "whether one is capable of loving the world more than one's own self."[53] The relation between the public and private realms is one of Arendt's basic concerns; as we shall discover, it is pivotal in understanding the nature of trust and betrayal. Mill's general claim that "the trustworthiness of human assertion is . . . the principal support of all present social well-being"[54] can mislead. The priority of the public realm is not so straightforward. In certain circumstances the exercise of specific virtues may threaten the values on which a political community depends. It is not necessarily a sign of failure if a private virtue is dissociated from the public sphere. Indeed, Creon's claim to authoritative rule in both state and household is challenged by Antigone precisely on the grounds that it destroys the moral regard due to kinship: It breaches a compelling private trust.

Disanalogies between the public and private realms draw our attention to trust in "relationships of shifting and varying power asymmetry and shifting and varying intimacy."[55] Dirty hands relationships have this character. They lack moral definition. In some cases motivation can appear ambiguous; in others, where interests are not at stake, incompleteness can make them vulnerable to tragic misunderstanding. Are they practices that inescapably "squander trust"?[56] Describing Robert E. Lee's decision to remain loyal to the South, Judith Shklar remarks that "it is not creed but character that raises treachery out of its usual depth."[57] Here the relation between trust and moral character in politics receives due emphasis. To trust rule by the good but ineffectual is to invite obvious political dangers from the scheming and the ill-intentioned; to rely on the practical and the pragmatic is to risk their evading the most basic human decencies if an achievable policy should present itself. But political morality reveals more complex antinomies. What is it to trust the noble who draw the moral limits to politics in terms of self-sacrifice' who may not demand as much of others as they do of themselves? By contrast, what is it to put our faith in "the delusive plausibilities of moral politicians,"[58] to trust those who are prepared to sacrifice the lives of others for the public good, who are prepared to dirty their hands? For Martin Hollis: "Politics is for foxes and we cannot really complain if those we appoint to be dishonest then do what is asked of them. Complaints must wait until the fox

25

loses his integrity. In the nature of the case, there is no public measure of that moment."[59] The identity of this "public measure" will be a recurrent theme. Political agents who experience moral guilt for actions performed on our behalf have to regain a public world if they and we are to recognize their remorse. Exploration of moral character reveals the perspectives of those faced with conflicting loyalties, with choosing which is the lesser of two evils or which moral value outweighs another. How trust begins, how it is sustained, and how its breach might be survived are discovered not by reference to an abstract starting point but in the narrative of a human life. The origins of trust, the tests to which it is subject, and our responses to betrayal are the logical stages of this book. Machiavelli was well aware of the elusiveness of trust in the changing circumstances of politics: "Rulers (especially new rulers) have often found that men whom they had regarded with suspicion in the early stages of their rule prove more reliable and useful than those whom they had trusted at first. . . . But it is very difficult to generalise about this, since men and circumstances vary."[60]

To try to dispel such difficulties we must turn our attention to dirty hands and moral character.

Chapter 2

Dirty hands and moral character

The heaviest penalty for declining to rule is to be ruled by someone inferior to yourself. That is the fear, I believe, that makes decent people accept power . . . it is forced upon them because they can find no one better than themselves or even as good, to be entrusted with power.

Plato, *Republic*

Confusion of the language of good and evil; I offer you this sign as the sign of the state.

Friedrich Nietzsche, *Thus Spake Zarathustra*

In the following discussion I want to look at the area of moral character, how individuals come to trust others and the way they identify specific moral dispositions in those others as grounds for their trust. A clear line of thought here would link the most securely grounded trust with the *best* moral dispositions, those whose aim in life is the maintenance of moral excellence. And we want to ask how the experience of politics affects the morally excellent.

How does moral character enter the discussion of dirty hands? A political agent who acknowledges moral guilt while carrying out political policies believed to be desirable does so from a standpoint of character: Our attention is drawn to moral identity and self-understanding. Character provides a location for both action and moral self-awareness, so that for Hegel only "by resolving can a man step into actuality, however bitter to him his resolve may be";[1] decision is grounded in and expressive of character – "a characterless man never reaches a decision" is Hegel's formulation.[2] Moral character and self-reproach are essential to this way of thinking about the problem of dirty hands. The dispositions and actions that constitute a human life are recognized as possessing a distinctive shape, a moral form that is a source of identity and identification. We think of features of character as permanent, as enduring in the face of often severe strain or challenge. Sometimes traits of character persist when we would rather they did not; so while they are not immune from change, as "permanent states, these will explain not merely why someone acted this way *now,* but why someone can be *counted on* to act in certain ways."[3] This stress on counting on someone links moral character to public estimation and judgment. It introduces the notion of reputation – what an agent's character is generally believed to be – and it suggests a close relationship between character and what gives us grounds for reliance and trust. Of course, reputation may or may not be justified, but the connection between public expectation and individual character is nevertheless strong. We are not always deceived by appearances, not always disappointed by public report. Kurt Baier describes the shared practice of judging character in a way that brings out these points: "The function of judgements of character is to acquaint members of the moral community with how well given individuals have, in the opinion of their peers, performed as moral agents. Such information is important for the formation of trust and distrust, without which morality could not work."[4]

As moral character displays identity and not simply an unwelded collection of attributes and actions, it can be publicly recognized and judged, thus providing a basis for trust and distrust. For Baier, "A good reputation is obviously an important asset, a bad reputation a liability. At the same time, a deservedly bad reputation serves to protect others against unwarranted trust."[5] For the morally good individual whose character is distinctive and dependable, the decision to act politically is often associated with the sense of what Hegel termed bitterness of resolve. In the forum of politics, the qualities of nobility that would normally warrant trust divide character against itself, so rendering trust suspect and unsure. If the task is to examine excellence of character and to ask how it can provide a basis for trust, then we might want to look at an example like Brutus in Shakespeare's *Julius Caesar*. His nobility was essential to his character; his motive was an honest concern for the public good. Mark Antony's final judgment of Brutus is neither accidental nor ironic; "his life was gentle, and the elements so / so mixed in him that Nature might stand up, / And say to all the world, 'This was a man!' "[6] What Antony sees is not just a moral quality leading to political error, but a man who has struggled with who he inescapably and morally is. Political commitment for Brutus is a commitment of character. What is brought to politics is not a useful ability or skill, not a specific familiarity with power or a capacity to achieve ends efficiently, but the individual force of a stainless reputation, one that is disinterested, honorable, and without ambition. From this standpoint political engagement is not a neutral, impersonal activity untouched by self-estimation and attachment to others. When Brutus reflects on the path of conspiracy and betrayal, it is immediately apparent that political commitment and loyalties of character will not survive undivided.

> It must be by his death: and, for my part,
> I know no personal cause to spurn at him,
> But for the general. He would be crowned:
> How that might change his nature, there's the question:
> It is the bright day that brings forth the adder;
> And that craves wary walking.[7]

Politics for Brutus is not as it is for Cassius, his co-conspirator, a realm of utilitarian calculation. He is not envious of Caesar; he fears not what Caesar may do to him but what he can do to Rome if he is corrupted by the power his office confers: "The abuse of greatness is when it disjoins remorse from power."[8] The reference to remorse is significant. Brutus knows Caesar well and loves him, but he reasons that "tis a common proof"[9] that great power risks great abuse, "that what he is, augmented, / Would run to these and these extremities."[10] Brutus's conclusion is decisive:

> And therefore think him as a serpent's egg
> Which, hatched, would, as his kind, grow mischievous,
> And kill him in the shell.[11]

Once committed to assassination, the conspirators need to protect themselves against discovery and disclosure, but Brutus rejects an oath of loyalty as either unnecessary or irrelevant to such protection. If the conspirators trust each other, a mutual promise is superfluous, at best a reinforcement of a deeper tie; if they do not, no simple promise will sustain their undertaking:

> But do not stain
> The even virtue of our enterprise,
> Nor the insuppressive mettle of our spirits,
> To think that or our cause or our performance
> Did need an oath; when every drop of blood
> That every Roman bears, and nobly bears,
> Is guilty of a several bastardy,
> If he do break the smallest particle
> Of any promise that hath passed from him.[12]

Brutus's refusal to swear an oath fits uneasily with his consenting to wear the mask of friendship toward Caesar. Nobility of character cannot coexist with such indignity; Brutus is a man divided against himself. The conflict between character and political commitment is illustrated further in Brutus's disastrous misjudgment in allowing Antony to speak at Caesar's funeral. He is true to his character in doing this but, as Cassius realizes, it is a risky permission. It reveals Brutus's lack of insight into the motives of those less disinterested than himself, his attenuated political sense, and his patrician assumption that an open, rational account of his conduct is sufficient to guarantee political success. Brutus's language here is the opposite of dissemblance. He makes no attempt at concealment: "We will deliver you the cause, / Why I, that did love Caesar when I struck him, / Have thus proceeded";[13] "our reasons are so full of good regard / that were you, Antony, the son of Caesar, / you should be satisfied."[14] This is the confidence of an honorable man, convinced by the rightness of his motives and actions, who believes that it is impossible for others, including Antony, to disagree with him. "I will myself into the pulpit first, And show the reason for our Caesar's death: What Antony shall speak, I will protest he speaks by leave and by permission."[15] Crucially, at the close of Brutus's speech the citizens give their approval, but they fail to understand his argument – "Let him be Caesar" cries one.[16] The ambiguities of politics have escaped Brutus. It is a necessary preface to Antony's triumphant manipulation of the crowd.

In *Julius Caesar* moral character finds itself vulnerable to subterfuge. Cassius schemes from the start to involve Brutus in the assassination plot in order to make political capital from his unsullied reputation. Of course, Brutus is too honest to see Cassius's letters as a trick and is easily deceived; his nobility thereafter provides a risky ground for trust. It is significant that Brutus is not prepared to will the political good only by doing good. He is prepared to dirty his hands, and, once committed, his character requires that he play the assassin's role to the full. Throughout, it is his moral character that distinguishes him from his fellow conspirators, and Antony's judgment of him after the battle at Philippi acts as a confirmation – Brutus is honored among foxes.

From examples like this, we learn about the peculiar nature of the relationship between moral character and trust: What causes problems here is how politics engages with moral perfectibility. And if we can explore the reasons why the morally excellent wish to enter politics at all, then we will certainly deepen our understanding of trust in the public context.

In Plato's view – and it is in Plato that we see the debate first set out – the good enter politics unwillingly to minimize the consequences of rule by the evil and the base. Once politi-

cally involved, however, they are unavoidably confronted by
the dilemmas of political morality. This emphasis on the qualified nature of a moral concern with politics is echoed by
Bernard Williams, who finds in it a powerful reason for restricting the incidence of dirty hands: "The point . . . is that
only those who are reluctant or disinclined to do the morally
disagreeable when it is really necessary have much chance of
not doing it when it is not necessary."[17] Moral reluctance may
originate from character or from the ideals that give a human
life sense and worth. Both contribute to the aims and purposes of an individual life and both rule out specific courses
of action as inconsistent with character or contrary to ideals.
Delicacy of feeling, the morality appropriate to "the beautiful
soul," in Hegel's phrase, cannot by itself explain the reservations of those who face acting badly in politics when it is
necessary. These individuals must certainly have a sense of
their own moral worth, but they must also appreciate the
value of the public world, which the acceptance of dirty
hands is intended to protect or defend. Desperate measures
are not always taken by desperate men; but if the problems
of political morality are to have any force, they must be addressed by those who at least recognize the existence of a
public realm independent of their private moral sensibilities.
In this respect, a great deal depends on the extent of moral
reluctance, on the strength of moral reservation. On what
terms is reluctance dispelled or reservation put aside? Brutus
is neither a sensitive soul nor a political realist; he is a noble
man who enters politics to protect the republic from the very
real danger of tyranny. For him the terms of political engagement are severe – assassination ("it must be by his death")
and betrayal.

   Plato's analogy between soul and city implies a close relationship of trust between ruler and ruled. The just are trustworthy not simply because of the benefits of cooperating
with them, but because of their inherent nature. Plato's conception of philosophical rule by reference to the interests of
the whole city is intended to place rule on a rational basis and
in so doing establish a well-grounded trust between Guard-

ians and governed. However, a rigid typology of human nature and an insistent rationalism restrict Plato's perception of the way politics involves moral character, the terms of engagement it sets, and how they may be reluctantly accepted.

One powerful Platonic legacy is the search for a moral perfectibility in which to place our trust. However, by contrast with Plato's reconstructed political world, ideals in unreformed politics play a part that is neither compellingly rational nor based on an uncontested understanding of human nature. In a less determinate political vocabulary, we may be more familiar with ideals as masks of cruelty than as secure guarantees of moral rectitude. Indeed, once ideals are separated from nature, the character of political rulers is open to question. In the context of deep skepticism regarding the claims of metaphysics, such a separation acquires dramatic political sense. For Richard Rorty, "What our future rulers will be like will not be determined by any large necessary truths about human nature and its relation to truth and justice, but by a lot of small contingent facts."[18] We are asking then what these "small contingent facts" might look like.

So, in relation to political morality, there may be moral reluctance to make the decisions actually taken, "I was reluctant to do x but it was the only thing to do in the circumstances," or with a disinclination to face up to the demands of office, possibly an attempt to avoid them. A further "contingent fact" is the relief felt by some political agents at not having to take the hard decisions that office sometimes involves. During World War II, for example, in early November 1940, the choice had to be faced whether to take the necessary measures to defend Coventry against an impending German air raid or to protect the intelligence source that enabled the government to know about it. One participant in the discussions of the so-called Ultra secrets comments:

> It was decided only to alert all the services, the fire, the ambulance, the police, the wardens, and to get everything ready to light the decoy fires. This is the sort of terrible decision that sometimes has to be made on the highest levels in war. It was

unquestionably the right one, but I am glad it was not I who had to take it.[19]

Similarly, in the absence of a polity consisting of philosophically defined natures determined by the preponderance of reason or desire – in Plato's metaphor, natures of gold, silver, and bronze – trust is often given in full awareness that those who receive it are actually dealing in precisely those "crooked propositions"[20] that Plato rejects. Unsupported by the knowledge that gives the noble lie its sense, the relationship between trust and political morality now takes on a less secure and more easily misrepresentable shape. This is Sir Henry Channon describing certain political attitudes expressed at the time of the Munich crisis and the coming of war:

> I came to the conclusion that there would be no war, no matter what people said. Rab, too, has implicit faith in Halifax and Chamberlain and agreed with me that both were linked together by an understanding. Either would do an even dishonest deed to reach a high goal. The ultimate object was all that counted.[21]

Here a great moral purpose – the avoidance of war – is seen to justify the outweighing of another moral value. A morally desirable end may be achieved more efficiently by an intelligent, morally controlled deviousness than by strict adherence to principle. Here the good intentions of the agent now constitute the object of trust. Risk is thereby increased for both the self-esteem of the truster and the wider political community if trust is misplaced. By contrast, Plato in the *Republic* defines the Guardians by their concern for the common good, for the well-being of the polis. This is their essential moral and political motivation and character. Outside the scope of Plato's rationalism, however, ideals can prove illusory and fallible, so placing a strain on trust. When ideals are breached, either we view the idealist as a fallen idol or we seem compelled to shift trust to precise motive and intention, so providing the opaqueness necessary for both the risk and the moral value of trust.

There is an intriguing modern example, expressed dramatically, in Oscar Wilde's *An Ideal Husband*. Sir Robert Chiltern – "his manner is that of perfect distinction, with a slight touch of pride"[22] – is regarded by his wife as both ideal husband and ideal statesman. She discovers that an attempt has been made to blackmail him into betraying a public trust by threatening to reveal his earlier involvement in a dubious financial arrangement. His high character and moral tone are now viewed by her with suspicion; his integrity is now open to question. Neither the form of the good nor good form can provide her with a basis for recovering trust. The exchange between Sir Robert and his wife toward the end of the first act of Wilde's play establishes the distance between them. For him, "politics is a very complex business. There are wheels within wheels. One may be under certain obligations to people that one must pay. Sooner or later in political life one has to compromise. Everyone does."[23] For her, however, "it can never be necessary to do what is not honourable. Or if it be necessary, then what is it that I have loved!"[24] The moral logic of this statement marks a significant fact. This is not a disagreement between strangers, between political agents unaffected by feelings of attachment. When Lady Chiltern discovers that the blackmailer actually does have a hold over her husband, that he began his political life with fraud, her disgust at his betrayal is joined by self-loathing: "You were to me something apart from common life, a thing pure, noble, honest, without stain. The world seemed to me finer because you were in it, and goodness more real because you lived. And now – oh, when I think that I made a man like you my ideal! the ideal of my life!"[25]

What Lady Chiltern is looking for in her husband's conduct is evidence of sincerity. She no longer sees him as an ideal and must look to his motives if she is to trust him at all. His motives, however, may be mixed; his self-awareness may be incomplete; his deepest need at one point in time may later be a reason for regret. In the play, rather staged manipulations of plot ensure that trust is redeemed. Nevertheless, Lady Chiltern is made to realize that what she can count on is not an unsustainable idealism, but moral character struggling to preserve itself in the predicaments of an imperfect world; as her sister comments, "An ideal husband! Oh, I don't think I should like that. It sounds like something in the next world."[26] The ordinary human fallibilities on display in the Wilde play stress the exercise of virtue in particular circumstances and draw our attention away from high-mindedness, from a loftiness of moral tone.

In philosophical terms, we find Aristotle shows an acute awareness of the political dangers set by "someone who is pre-eminent in virtue";[27] indeed, his major concern is precisely with the avoidance of the different kinds of moral and political excess. Aristotle concentrates on the natural integration of moral character and political community. By so doing he hopes to exhibit the institutional values that diminish the incidence of moral conflict and the moral character that displays a reasonable sensitivity to moral cost. This involves stressing constitutional values, such as justice, which provide a rule-governed embargo on wrongdoing, and the redemptive values, such as shame, pardon, and forgiveness, which restore a community's sense of moral balance once it has been politically disturbed.

Aristotle is vital to any discussion of trust because his understanding of an integrated polity implies a close, formative interaction between city and individual character. Equally, he asserts that rulers possess distinctive attributes: "The ruler ought to have moral virtue in perfection";[28] "practical wisdom only is the characteristic of the ruler: it would seem that all other virtues must equally belong to ruler and subject."[29] And it is in his discussion of magnanimity and where it is going to lead us that we find an essential clue to a deeper view of trust.

The virtuous ruler, then, acts moderately and justly for the well-being of the city. Officeholders are described as custodians of reason and fairness; Aristotle writes: "We do not allow a *man* to rule, but *rational principle*";[30] rewards come to those who hold office in the form of honor – actions performed for their own sake elicit the respect and good opinion of the governed. On Aristotle's view, therefore, the attributes of ruling are not valuable because they are means to the achievement of goods external to themselves. They have a noninstrumental or intrinsic worth, as Nussbaum writes:

> All true excellence of character has a relational nature: without making political and other-related concerns ends in themselves, one will lack not only justice, but also the courage, true moderation, true generosity, greatness of soul, conviviality, and so forth. . . . In each case, one cannot choose these excellent activities as ends in themselves (as the definition of excellence requires), without also choosing the good of others as an end. Deprived of this end, then, we lack not a part of our good, we lack the whole.[31]

Aristotle considers that if such personal qualities are essential to ruling, then they must be understood in this way. Magnanimity is the first virtue of rulers as far as honor is concerned. The magnanimous ruler understands that honor is related necessarily to desert. It is acquired only in connection with the search for the public good. Such a ruler "does not regard honour as the supreme good, and so he will not sacrifice virtue for honour; for he cares about the common good, not primarily about being honoured for seeming to advance it."[32]

Excess is excluded, too, when it appears in dispositional form. An unreflective innocence is no basis for rule. A godlike superiority of virtue does not reflect the circumstances of life or actual moral psychology – "most people," Aristotle remarks, "wish to get benefits, but avoid doing them, as a thing unprofitable."[33] Aristotle's account of the moral qualities of ruling is designed for the world as it is and not as an excess of morality would like it to be.

Aristotle understands politics as the crucial integrative activity. Although he does not devalue the part played by risk, contingency, and uncertainty, his overwhelming concern is with politics as a natural feature of life; it is a shared, noninstrumentally defined good, organic to the human soul. Vulnerable to disorder, however, politics expresses its nature through education, so contributing to the evolution of a balanced and fair society governed in accordance with practical reason. In this way, the development of decent institutions encourages the cooperative virtues and diminishes conflict, so reducing the incidence of those problems that give rise to dirty hands. Although Aristotle acknowledges that in politics – as in any other area of life – different virtues are conducive to different purposes, they cannot be used for political gain; indeed, in the main he excludes "constitutional tricks,"[34] as he also does harsh measures adopted for political advantage.

The complexity of an Aristotelian practice resides in differentiation not only of function but also of virtue. Aristotle's sensitivity to the gradations involved in moral conduct does not preclude an awareness of conflict that is sharper-edged for the individual who has to face it and more perplexing for the political community to contain. He acknowledges the existence of tragic moral dilemmas in which one human loyalty crosses another and cannot therefore be fulfilled without loss. The agony of Agamemnon's dilemma at Aulis is not unique to the ancient institution of kingship. Those charged with protecting the Ultra secrets in 1940 faced a choice that was as bitter and unenviable. All those who govern with moral self-awareness fear its appearance.

Aristotle asks us to consider how political agents respond to the hard moral choices they have to make – with regret, shame, or remorse; such moral responses have a significant public place. Hard moral choices have their primary effect on those who are their victims – those who are treated as a means to the well-being of others, asked to bear burdens others do not share, or sacrificed for a singular moral good. To survive such tests, Aristotle argues that a political community must avoid too wide a gap between a public and private moral vocabulary. A strong sense of legality and justice provides a basis for this, not simply through an obedience to law but also through a commitment to just institutions and practices that

38

reduce uncertainty and anxiety when hard decisions are made. Reaction to one's own dirty hands can often be extreme, ranging from the evasion of responsibility through self-deception or attaching blame to others, to the self-disgust involved in a clear recognition of what has been done. Those who are the unwitting victims may feel anger and resentment. For them the public realm is no longer a focus for trust. On the Aristotelian view, public law and moral character together establish grounds for rational deliberation in these cases; they provide an enclosure of moderation that secures the polity against such harmful disturbances.

Aristotle sees virtue and intelligence as inseparable. His moral psychology enables him to identify the various forms of moral failing, weakness, and vice, but not the ideal familiar to us that intelligent rule can be exercised for evil purposes; for Aristotle, tyranny must be a form of political ignorance. Of course, neither Aristotle's magnanimous ruler nor Walzer's "moral politician" lacks self-restraint. We cannot say of them as Cobbett said of the drunkard, "sometimes he is one man, at other times another."[35] On the contrary, magnanimous rulers are confident of their identity, inspiring both respect and trust. Can "moral politicians" share this certainty? They do not disdain the indignities of rule. For them dirty hands do not necessarily signify failure. They may have to endanger or transgress the values on which the community depends in order to protect it. Aristotle conceives violation of moral and civil law to be the most serious injury a society can undergo. How can such a violation simultaneously sustain it? Dirty hands can cease to be seen as an intrinsic feature of character and come to be regarded as an extendable instrument of policy. Attributes of character such as shame and forgiveness, which seem essential if dirty hands are to be publicly and privately redeemed, can be replaced by a utilitarian emphasis on consequences as a method of political choice. Politics is therefore seen as a technical activity in which trust is placed in the scientific administration of ends rather than in moral character and resource. Reclaiming the double Aristotelian emphasis on well-grounded institutions and moral character is, therefore, one of the central concerns of contemporary political philosophy.

It is significant that in the *Nicomachean Ethics* itself the difficulties of matching moral choice and cost, of giving a rational account of the relation between intention, risk, and outcome, are acknowledged.

> It is difficult sometimes to determine what should be chosen at what cost, and what should be endured in return for what gain, and yet more difficult to abide by our decisions; for as a rule what is expected is painful, and what we are forced to do is base, whence praise and blame are bestowed on those who have been compelled or have not.[36]

This is a region of bewilderment. The connection between choice and outcome has been lost. The ground for fresh decision seems insecure and the route that led to such a position appears now to be inexplicable. These features of conduct are not unique to dirty hands, but they seem to find a presence there that gives ambiguity and lack of finitude a formidable role. Meinecke's classic account asks us to reflect on trusting and holding trust, in conditions of political insecurity.

> If a statesman feels himself obliged by "necessity of state" to violate law and ethics, he can still feel himself morally justified at the bar of his own conscience, if in doing so he has . . . thought first of the good of the State entrusted to his care. Thus the realm of values is capable of shedding an ennobling light far into the inmost recesses of problematical conduct. But nevertheless such conduct still remains problematical and dualistic, because the conscious infringement of morality and law must in any circumstances (whatever motives may have prompted it) be a moral stain, a defect of Ethos in its partnership with Kratos. Thus all conduct prompted by raison d'état fluctuates continuously back and forth between light and dark.[37]

For Meinecke, one of the major risks involved in *raison d'état* is that it "is continually in danger of becoming a merely utilitarian instrument without ethical application, in danger of sinking back again from wisdom to mere cunning. . . . It can become a mere technique of statecraft,"[38] but the range of moral oscillation here is not just between goodness and expediency. So magnanimity, which at first sight seems so promising for our purposes because it appears to offer a secure basis for trust and reliable barrier against dirty hands, in fact often seems trapped by precisely those dependencies it urgently seeks to avoid. Is this really the case, and if so what are the political implications?

Magnanimity, the quality of being justly proud of one's virtue, does seem to contain the attributes we find politically valuable. Magnanimous characters avoid trifling dangers but are willing to risk their own lives for the sake of others when the threat to them is great. They disdain receiving reward or benefit, but welcome the opportunity to confer honor on others who deserve it. They love openness and truthfulness. They avoid dependence on others, except those who are their friends. Neither humble nor vain, they possess virtue in due proportion. They do not bear grudges or ask for favors unnecessarily, and they are contemptuous of mere ambition, material benefit, or advantage.[39] These dispositions are not in themselves problematic. As John Casey tellingly points out, the essential difficulty "lies precisely at that point where certain morally good qualities – such as goodness of will – pass over into something else."[40]

In politics that point can be traced in the different ways magnanimity as a foundational virtue is transformed into a substantial hazard. Machiavelli, so concerned, as we saw in the previous chapter, with the inadequacies of the virtues in politics, often refers to the political ineffectiveness of magnanimity in situations of acute risk. Those whose pride in moral character requires openness in dealing with others can be blind to conspiracies against them, as Soderini was when he tried to deal with the factional conspiracy against the republic with "patience and goodness."[41] Scipio, too, Machiavelli describes as having been in his humanity too tolerant, so risking rebellion from the restless who belied "the love which

41

their ruler may have evoked by his decency."[42] What enables
the tribunes to plot so effectively against Shakespeare's Coriolanus is his nature, which is "vengeance proud."[43] "Marked
you his lips and eyes?"[44] – the tribune's question to his fellow conspirator – is also a perceptive political observation.
Coriolanus is incapable of dissimulation. From a Machiavellian standpoint his "sovereignty of nature"[45] is a sign of in-
tractability, itself a guarantee of political failure. If pride in
virtue offers an identifiable nature to conspirators so allowing them to economize on risk, it can also block effective
subversive action. Brutus in *Julius Caesar* is capable of assassination for the public good, but not of dealing decisively with
Mark Antony to protect it. Machiavelli cites the conspiracy
against Nero as one made possible by Piso's trustworthiness
and public reputation, and equally obstructed by these qualities.[46] Extraordinary action, for Machiavelli a constant awareness of the strategies required by public necessity, is unavailable to those whose martial attributes are sustained by a high
opinion of their virtue.

Although magnanimity exists in contrast to mere aloofness,
to ambition, to a haughty quarrelsomeness,[47] in the public
perception it can nevertheless represent a reason for fear and
uncertainty. For Hobbes, characteristically and acutely aware
of the dangers of personal dispositions in public places, the
magnanimous man displays a "glory well grounded upon certain experience of a power sufficient to attain his end in an
open manner."[48] It implies an ease of action not shown by
anger, which "argueth difficulty of proceeding,"[49] and as such
expresses a "pre-eminent virtue,"[50] a megalopsychia that can
only be regarded with disbelief by others who are more prone
to human imperfections. A sensitivity to the dangers of honor
in excess recognizes how private virtue can pass into public
vice. Such nuances of political morality are Machiavelli's subject in his examination of the banishment of Camillus from
Rome.

Camillus was admired because of his magnanimity, his care
for those in his command, his prudence, good order, and

greatness of soul, but these very qualities led to public fear and hatred. Camillus gave to the public funds the money raised from sale of goods taken from the Veientes rather than distributing it with the booty of war. In so doing, he deprived private individuals of what they saw as rightfully their own, so guaranteeing their dislike. He desired further, in his pride in his civic virtue, to be seen as equal to the sun by having his triumphal chariot pulled by four white horses, and he took the rewards of war from his soldiers to placate Apollo. Machiavelli describes Camillus as appearing to a free people as "proud and puffed up,"[51] but by itself this would not be sufficient to establish magnanimity as a political threat if the people gained by it. "When men share in the prince's swollen pride, they do not notice his deprivations," as Mansfield comments.[52] Machiavelli's conclusion here is entirely consistent with his view of politics as a realm of appearance. Camillus may have considered his virtue to be godlike, but he should not have appeared in public as a man intent on "acting as a god."[53] Virtues must be matched to political necessity, to be maintained or suspended temporarily as the case requires. Magnanimity is not a virtue appropriate in all circumstances, but a mode of conduct to be displayed when the occasion demands. Unlike the Aristotelian ruler, the Machiavellian political hero is defined by the capacity to achieve this effect. As he writes of Francesco Sforza, later duke of Milan, in *The Prince*:

> Anyone who considers it necessary in his new principality to deal effectively with his enemies, to gain allies, to conquer (whether by force or by cunning), to inspire both devotion and respectful fear in the people, to be obeyed and respectfully feared by troops, to neutralise or destroy those who can or must be expected to injure you, to replace old institutions with new ones, to be both severe and kind, both magnanimous and open-handed, to disband disloyal troops and form a new army, to maintain alliances with kings and other rulers in such a way that they will either be glad to benefit you or be slow to injure you: for all these, no better examples can be cited than the actions of this man.[54]

Coriolanus, on the contrary, regards his virtues as closed to negotiation with political imperatives. He is openly contemptuous of those he considers to be his inferiors, regarding them as unworthy of trust, not to be depended on. In Shakespeare's play the public response to this is made apparent early in the first act. Coriolanus is feared not simply because he is a member of the patrician class, but because his pride in his attributes and abilities is genuine; he is, for this reason, called by the citizens "a very dog to the commonalty."[55]

Machiavelli further stresses the importance of impeachment as a public institution for protecting the republic and taming the ambitious, but there is little in his discussion of Coriolanus to explain why his character and circumstance combine to such tragic effect. As Mansfield comments, for Machiavelli "a republic needs an order through which the 'universality' – all things or nature – has its revenge on men, or else some men will be too much encouraged in their desire to master others."[56] The tragic element – a conflict of right with right existing half-independently of character – is absent in this account. Similarly, Machiavelli describes Coriolanus as having all the qualities of a good military leader;[57] in this respect, therefore, and within narrow limits, he is to be trusted, but we are told little about the deeper aspects of his character, which are intrinsic to the dilemma he faces and the problems faced by any state wishing to contain him. At issue is the relation between fear, trust, and virtue. Here again the public legacy of pride in virtue is flawed and suspect.

For Coriolanus magnanimity is the morality appropriate to those whose virtue is self-willed. Such beings are self-legislating, but not in the Kantian sense of confirming rational autonomy and respect in concert with others. On the contrary, Coriolanus desires to "Stand, / As if a man were author of himself, / And knew no other kin."[58] In the attempt he discovers that such a self-conception is unendurable, a psychological impossibility. Torn between his nature and his country, he decides to betray Rome and join the forces of its enemy, Aufidius, a decision born not of treachery but nobility. A magnanimity that is not of this world but requires "a world elsewhere"[59] for its confirmation is a terrifying assault on public trust. Coriolanus is feared, too, because, in Judith Shklar's phrase, "he scorns elections."[60] His tragedy does not arise, however, simply from "his political incompetence";[61] when his mother, Volumnia, pleads for mercy for herself and the city, she addresses her son's nobility, a disposition she has herself nurtured and encouraged. This subtle shading of private and public emotion was not missed by Hobbes, who suggests that for Coriolanus gratification is found in the knowledge that he is seen and glorified through his mother's eyes – "all the delight Marcus Coriolanus had in his warlike actions, was, to see his praises so well pleasing to his Mother."[62] In consenting Coriolanus acts in character, but in so doing he reveals why he can never be held in public trust. His motivation here is entirely personal; it is to his mother's plea that he finally accedes; as Machiavelli describes it, "he set out for Rome, but turned back rather out of devotion to his mother than to the Roman forces."[63] But outside the filial domain, as Mansfield perceptively remarks, "those who fear a captain of dubious loyalty like Coriolanus or Caesar, are caught between their fear and their need of a captain they can trust."[64]

A consistent theme throughout this discussion is the insufficiency of even the very best of personal dispositions and the corresponding need for a focus for political trust. Magnanimity as Hobbes understands it is "a sign of power,"[65] a "contempt of unjust, or dishonest helps."[66] What prevents the magnanimous from acting wrongly is not an intrinsic love of the good but pride in virtue. Such a disposition places stress on self-estimation and self-mastery, a control over the passions and indisciplines of the soul. We have seen how the desire to be independent of human feelings can end in being trapped by them. Magnanimity does not sustain a political community but stimulates in it conflicts of loyalty, division, and distrust, leading to a final determination to betray it. Hobbes in his analysis of the politics of magnanimity does not examine this tragic outcome. Independence is, of course, a crucial Hobbesian political value, but it is, he thinks, more adequately sustained by *fear* than magnanimity. How can this be so?

Tracing the logic of Hobbes's skeptical account of human nature gives us the major part of the answer to this question, in terms derived from his model of human character as egocentric, acquisitive, and afraid. But, as has been pointed out,[67] it is significant that Hobbes allows for a different mode of conduct and, with it, a different moral persona. Hobbes's notion of gallantry, like Aristotle's idea of magnanimity, stresses honor before life, places action before passivity, and is founded in self-assurance and self-sufficiency. It is difficult to see how the complex moral psychology of this disposition squares with Hobbes's normal view of human motivation as self-interested. Magnanimity is neither a convenient or pleasing mask nor a means to an end. Although Hobbes denies any "inconsistence of human nature, with civil duties,"[68] there is no doubt that his priority is a secure civil order in which the natural virtues and decencies can be expressed free from assault. Magnanimity, as found in the character of a Sidney Godolphin, "slain by an undiscerned and undiscerning hand,"[69] is not enough. There is a further crucial point to be considered. In order for Hobbes's derivation of political authority to be sound, the promise to obey it must be anchored in something more reliable than simply giving one's word. Hobbes explains what in his view are the alternatives:

> Either a fear of the consequence of breaking their word; or a glory, or pride, in appearing not to need to break it. This latter is a generosity too rarely found to be presumed upon, especially in the pursuers of wealth, command, or sensual pleasure; which are the greatest part of mankind. The passion to be reckoned upon is fear.[70]

For Hobbes, then, pride in the sense of attempting to become godlike is in Oakeshott's words, "a delusive insolence," a "destroying nemesis."[71] As the endeavor by the well-intentioned and spirited to obtain peace only through just conduct, it does merit genuine praise and admiration. It is noticeable, however, that in the final argument it concerns Hobbes less than

> the minimum conditions in which the endeavour for peace could be the pattern of conduct for even the least well-disposed man. These minimum conditions are that there shall be one *law* for the liar and the ox and that both should have known and adequate motives for obeying it.[72]

Here the prime motivation is fear. The tension between pride and fear is perhaps never completely erased in the political thought either of Aristotle or Hobbes. From different philosophical starting points they stress the significance of law as a ground for justice and freedom, both seeing, as Aristotle does, "that for men of pre-eminent virtue there is no law – they are themselves a law."[73] Hume, too, emphasizes the civic disutility of the moral hero. Although Hume finds pride to be generally agreeable and beneficial, courage in excess – as heroism or military glory – can produce "the subversion of empires, the devastation of provinces, the sack of cities";[74] Hume, like Burke, whose contempt for "the secular applause of dashing Machiavelian politicians"[75] is similarly based, argues that we can be so dazzled by the character of heroes, such as Alexander the Great, that we are prone to lose sight of the havoc they can wreak.

Hobbes and Hume respond in different ways to the rarity of magnanimity, establishing a polity appropriate to individuals construed as autonomous and sovereign by reference to the ideas of artifice and utility and, ipso facto, subjecting trust to the tests derived from such ideas. Hobbes, indeed, as Quentin Skinner points out, "speaks systematically and unapologetically, in the abstract and unmodulated tones of the modern theorist of the state."[76] This philosophical language of politics has dramatic implications. For Hobbes sovereignty resides in conceptual artifice; here the substantive densities of moral character are out of place. The vocabularies of public and private life, therefore, have a distinct logical reference. Allegiance is owed not to an individual, but to a political structure, namely, the state whose authority is severed from the contingent characteristics of its agents. Office is sharply distinguished from officeholder. The noninstrumental nature of civil law is distinguished from the instrumentalities of those who are subject to it. The focus of this vocabulary is the development of the modern state. It is theorized by Hobbes as an abstraction removed from the concrete attributes of individuality. Trust in the language of political modernity is construed as policy rather than passion. It is no longer a frail if often admirable moral resource, but a strategy for anticipating the decisions and actions of others, possibly officeholders, whose personal characteristics are seen as incidental to their authority and power.

But, contra Hobbes, the ambiguities of trust do not arise merely from a failed ruse or tactic, an unpredicted development or outcome. They are embedded in a rich and varied moral life, which tolerates such ambiguities and has the residual strength to survive them. A significant moral equivocation in the context of friendship is that it is possible to trust too much and too little. Juliet Du Boulay refers to the experience of regretting trust after it seemed to be well grounded. Giving confidence to friends is dangerous because if the friendship ends, "the secrets entrusted to either party when the relationship was good are all revealed";[77] such a possibility is not fully captured by trust as policy. The mutuality intrinsic to friendship is not open to tactical definition, and neither, therefore, is the associated risk of betrayal. Trusting too little can involve similar feelings, as Elizabeth Bennet discovers in Jane Austen's *Pride and Prejudice*:

> "How despicably have I acted!" she cried; "I, who have prided myself on my discernment! I, who have valued myself on my abilities! who have often disdained the generous candour of my sister, and gratified my vanity in useless or blamable distrust. How humiliating is this discovery! yet, how just a humiliation!"[78]

Here, distrust is blamable not simply for its uselessness, but because it springs from vanity. The desire that the agent's own estimation of her qualities should be the sole basis for public admiration has blocked the capacity for trust. In fact, there is no strategic objection to trust. What prevents it is the desire to appear to others in a way that confirms a favorable self-portrait. Both trusting too much and too little express trust as passion, not policy.

It should not be assumed that trust as passion has an insignificant role in public life where relations are not necessarily mediated by close friendship. As Bernard Harrison rightly points out, a trust that is not conditional on interest or desire is presupposed by many familiar social relationships:

> If we cannot full-bloodedly trust one another not to cheat at cards, then we are not related to one another as fellow-players, but as card-sharp and sucker, though for a time it may not become clear which of us is which. If we cannot full-bloodedly trust one another not to wrong each other in pursuit of some personal advantage, then we are not related as friends, but as people who happen for the moment to have a use for one another. If we cannot full-bloodedly trust one another not to sell out a common cause or the national interest, then we are not related to one another as fellow citizens or as co-workers for the same cause, but as opportunists or climbers on the same bandwaggon.[79]

Perhaps nowhere in politics is such trust more problematic than in the area of political morality. Contractarian and utilitarian accounts of political agency attempt to control the incidence and extent of dirty hands by constructing well-grounded institutions and by restricting the range of morally justifiable objectives. A uniform moral psychology provides the basis for a framework of just institutions and a defensible strategic trust. In my view, in relation to political morality this way of thinking neglects the sense in which the problems of dirty hands find a location at different points in a political narrative. Such problems do not occur in a vacuum. They are not generated exclusively by theories of the state and political obligation, but emerge as stages in a course of action. They have their origins, their present concerns and outcomes. An abstract moral psychology cannot capture the origins of that tension between trust and civic virtue which gives political morality its moral edge. The conception of trust appropriate to agents of rational and moderate self-regard is sustainable only by diluting the most solid attributes and qualities of moral character.

A contractualist derivation of a just legal order aims at the removal of serious conflict between moral and political considerations, though conflict, in point of fact, however, would appear to be at the center of problems in political morality. Action does not stem from a hypothetical starting point, from an original position populated by agents of a standard psychology. Commitment to political rule is not defined through covenant or agreement, but expressed in the context of the contingencies of character and circumstance. Action in political morality is flawed; it is marked by a recognition that others have to be treated as victims if a justifiable political end is to be achieved. The consciousness of this dilemma is essential to the idea of dirty hands. It cannot be displaced by consigning it to a realm of ignorance, to be removed progressively as enlightenment dawns.

Of course, the stress in Hobbes on law as a system of agreed, public, and authoritative rules is intended to exclude precisely those political crimes which accompany dirty hands. Public law is superior to personal rule because laws and their sanctions act as a deterrence to disobedience. In particular, they deter political crimes. Assassination, treason, betrayal, bribery, perjury, and counterfeiting are all crimes against the public realm, offenses against the state, and they are on utilitarian grounds more serious than private crime, a threat to the existence of the state and more damaging to public trust.[80] Hobbes's thought at this point contains an ambiguity that is significant for my argument. He is uncertain about the status of spies, classifying them as "private ministers";[81] although their authorization and concerns are public, they pretend otherwise. How then can they sustain a public trust? Just as important, perhaps, Hobbes does not regard torture as an intrinsic wrong but as an unreliable method of obtaining information; what is confessed "tendeth to the ease of him that is tortured; not to the informing of the torturers."[82]

Equivocation between the right of self-preservation and utility is partly a function of Hobbes's method, which in its stress on fear as the crucial political motivation neglects the substantive character of human loyalties and capacities for self-sacrifice.[83] Furthermore, the link in contract theory between a "thin" view of agency and the human virtues is noticeably insecure. A just political order is not simply the best bargain available to moderately self-interested rational agents. Political morality involves the dark possibility that not only interest but also goodness may have to be put aside if justice is to be protected. How political agents who adopt the measures necessary for such protection consider themselves, how they might think of their own moral worth as diminished even though their actions have been successful is, therefore, a major problem. The maintenance of self-respect is a vital human good. What are its boundaries? At what point in the incurring of dirty hands is it replaced by shame, and the request for forgiveness?

Dirty hands may be controlled by self-criticism internal to moral character. The magnanimous disdain the dishonorable and, therefore, consider that they have no need for forgiveness; if they have done nothing wrong, there can be no occasion to forgive. In so doing, however, they have to accept that their disdain is not devoid of consequence. They are willing to give up their lives to save the city, but they will not lie for it. This moral scrupulousness is surely too self-directed to sustain a political morality that merits public trust, because the claims of virtue and the polity are required to remain in unresolved tension. As we suspected, therefore, magnanimity, however promising as a starting point for this discussion, fails as a sufficient focus for public trust. We need, therefore, to stress the attributes of character in a way that separates action from self-directedness and absorption and keeps its gaze clearly on a public world. This shift to public perceptions cannot be achieved on the basis of a minimalist contractarian psychology, but it *is* necessary if the logic of political morality is to be adequately located. Arendt provides us with significant clues in this respect, which will later be examined more closely. Courage, the determination to leave the security of a private domain to act on behalf of others in the public world, the honoring of the commitments undertaken, the place and range of public forgiveness when they are broken, and the simple recognition of the rarity of magnanimity, are construed by her as fundamental political values, which necessarily leave magnanimity behind. Once outside the Aristotelian synthesis of virtue, practical wisdom, and politics, we seem to be closer to Nietzsche's designation of the political as the realm of conflict and confusion. One way of confronting this is by examining the claim that in politics dirty hands are better checked not by moral character alone but by the external structures of a just and trusted civil order.

Chapter 3

Trust and political morality

The power of Kings and Magistrates is nothing else, but what is only derivative, transferred and committed to them in trust from the People, to the Common Good of them all.

John Milton, *The Tenure of Kings and Magistrates*

Lawfulness sets limitations to actions, but does not inspire them.

Hannah Arendt, *The Origins of Totalitarianism*

We have discovered that moral character alone appears insufficient as a basis for trust in politics. Historically those political philosophers who have addressed this problem have seen a solution in the liberal idea of the state as a structure of rights and duties protecting citizens against potential harm at the hands of rulers who make hard decisions on their behalf. In other words, the focus shifts from the moral character of the officeholder to the nature of the office: We need to address then the question of how such a shift affects our understanding of trust and its moral basis.

The problem of trust arises explicitly in politics in connection with the need for action. Political conduct takes place in a context of rules that are incomplete and against a background of traditions that are open to reassessment. In this respect, it is a creative activity, calling on imagination and judgment for exploration and renewal. Machiavelli identifies its richest expression with the achievement of glory; mere wealth and power are disdained in the determination to assert republican virtues in the face of circumstance and his-

53

tory. Here character and community bear instructively upon each other. Machiavelli's political hero subjects trust to the requirements of political realism; it is given or withheld as the occasion demands. Equally, a community paralyzed by distrust finds that its politics can be displaced by passivity, brutishness, or tyranny. Between credulousness and unsustainable disbelief, a community finds a political voice in vigorous and skeptical debate. In a notable passage in *The Discourses*, however, Machiavelli remembers that a people may be misled by "the false appearance of good";[1] a state then necessarily suffers decline and ruin "when by ill chance the populace has no confidence in anyone at all, as sometimes happens owing to its having been deceived in the past either by events or by men."[2] Machiavelli's thought at this point exhibits a significant and productive tension. The idea that trust is both a condition of political agency and a strategy available to it invites us to ask how these different senses are related. If political morality is left unrestrained it becomes political crime and so abolishes trust. How then can trust as a precondition of political action generate limits on political morality? How can it establish the justifiable extent of dirty hands?

In its philosophical form liberalism attempts to answer these questions by replacing trust as a human passion with trust as considered policy, thus tracing the logic of the modern conception of the state. Personal trust as "the confident expectation of benign intentions in another free agent"[3] is too risky, too closely associated with the dangers of betrayal, to provide adequate grounds for political allegiance. Modern political societies are better constituted by trust conceived as a strategically defined reliance on well-designed procedures and institutions agreed to by agents who are notionally rational and free. That this change of focus should have accompanied an increase rather than a reduction in the hazards of political trust is not simply an accident of modern political circumstances but a significant irony whose origins lie deep within the liberal project. "The great modern crimes are public crimes," as Thomas Nagel forcibly remarks,[4] a point of

54

minor moral import if its reference is confined to tyrants and dictators, tyrannies, and dictatorships. Either the state in its modern form has not been made subject to enough moral scrutiny or the shift to institutional trust needs to be reassessed. The move from agency to state makes it very much less clear just how in modern politics responsibility, praise, and blame are to be located. Officeholders may be as much insulated by their office as identified through it. Trust in the veracity of collective institutions may be achieved only at the high cost of moral abstraction.

The tension between trust as passion and trust as policy reflects broader strains between the recognition of political necessities and the need to preserve a morally sensitive polity. Such antimonies have presented themselves historically in a variety of philosophical and political contexts. Indeed, as John Dunn has pointed out,[5] the relation between political morality and economizing on trust has itself a traceable history: "In the feudal monarchies of medieval Europe the impress of Roman public law had prompted a strong theory of the priority of claims of public utility over those of private rights, in determining the context of the rationes status."[6]

Raison d'état as the doctrine appropriate to the "claims of public utility" has moral significance only if the moral exemptions that it grants to the state are highly conditional. This does not mean, however, that determination of a morally acceptable policy is unproblematic. Aquinas, for example, is representative of Christian moral and political philosophers attempting to deal with the problem of trust and political morality in arguing that departures from moral principle are justified only in circumstances of severe emergency where outweighing arguments such as those provided by the premises of just war theory may be brought into play. For Aquinas the role of authority in the resolution of hard cases in political morality is not only of practical convenience. It also secures trust by giving both the decision and its justification a public location. The need for a common measure of agreement on the limits of political morality is sustained in Aquinas's writings through the idea of a political community governed in accordance with the authority of God and the fundamental laws of nature. These provide the ultimate grounds for the cogency of arguments within political morality and the explanation for its necessity. Imperfection and sinfulness arise from human will; the dilemmas of political morality are tragic only in the sense that they mark human incompleteness and error. Politics here finds a qualified autonomy within the boundaries drawn for it by religion. Trust is supplemented by faith.

Reinterpreted in a secular context, Aquinas's doctrine of necessity, no longer on the edge of moral permissibility, is taken to refer to the political logic that ensures the state's survival. As William Church writes: "If it is admitted that political affairs in this world may neither be entirely consonant with the highest Christian principles nor allowed to sink to the level of purely mundane expediency in which anything goes, the problem becomes the exact relevance of policy to each extreme."[7] Necessity loses its moral specificity and is merely another word for utility. In *The Reason of State*, Giovanni Botero, "recognisably an inhabitant of Machiavelli's moral universe,"[8] spells out the implications of political realism for the understanding of trust: "It should be taken for certain that in the decisions made by princes interest will always override every other argument; and therefore he who treats with princes should put no trust in friendship, kinship, treaty nor any other tie which has no basis in interest."[9] According to this view, the necessities of state are remote from political morality and trust. Politics as the calculation of interest and advantage fits uneasily with the state construed as an authoritative system of public law. Distrust as a basic political strategy threatens trust as a condition of rule. Is it possible to set limits on political morality so that trust is secured? To what extent must the necessities of state be controlled?

Trust in the human world is a necessary but fragile resource, standing in contrast to knowledge and the vice of untrustworthiness. In political morality the dangers of being too trusting are apparent for both trusters and those affected by their trust. Locke, for example, wishes to reduce such dangers by education and the growth of mutual respect; in other words, by the inculcation of the conduct and virtues appropriate to a gentleman.[10] One might ask if the discerning exercise of sound common sense is sufficient to prevent political morality running to excess. Can decency alone keep the moral costs of desirable political ends within socially manageable bounds? Locke's stress on a civic constitution whose trustworthiness is linked to its sanctions – rule of law, separation of powers, and right of resistance – suggests a less sanguine view of the frequency of betrayal. Lockean individuals whose rational motivation in accordance with divine law is the preservation of property, liberty, and self-respect require a constitution that reflects and upholds this consensus. As Brian Barry decisively argues, however, the concept of trusteeship at work here is at odds with its democratic aspirations.[11] Political trusteeship permits a degree of executive discretion incompatible with democratic control. It assumes a level of moral consensus regarding the terms of its trust which may not be justified, and it ignores the paramount political fact that governments are required to act when the aims of truster and trusted clash just as much as when they coincide.

So the attempt to tie political obligation to the purposes of government seems to pay insufficient attention to the problematic nature of what Machiavelli terms "the false appearance of the good." Here a straightforward shift from social to political trust is surely unpersuasive. Dirty hands are not incurred through arbitrariness, partiality, or avarice, but because of a conscious recognition that the public good cannot be furthered in any other way. In politics it is not true that only tyrants behave immorally. The good, too, act badly for the achievement of politically desirable ends, although this possibility receives only minimal incorporation in Locke's structure of political trust. His trust conditions require that an ethic of officeholding is open and specific, so increasing the moral demands on officeholders, but to judge Brutus and Cassius equally unworthy of trust is to ignore the moral and political differences between them. If breach of trust includes illicit private gain *and* suspension of moral requirements for the public good, it is unsurprising that in a Lockean political world the fear of subversion should be so great. Trust in the context of political morality must surely take this moral disanalogy into account. Scorn for the deepest political values is certainly involved in many betrayals, but we misconstrue both the motivation and the circumstances of governors if we construct conditions of trust solely on the basis of this bleak fact. Locke's view of trust as a precondition of any social life gives trust a value distinct from its utility and *is* a crucial insight. As William James remarks, there are "cases where a fact cannot come at all unless a preliminary faith exists in its coming."[12] Trust, as Geraint Parry rightly comments, "must play some ultimate, independent role."[13] In Locke, however, the origins of such a role are firmly located in descriptions of individual moral psychology overlaid by theological argument. His general aim is to restrict legitimate governmental action to the terms of the trust conditions. If the good that claims a prerogative justification for wrongdoing actually does come about, is trust therefore confirmed? How much consequentialist policy making can a decent polity allow before trust is unsustainable?

It is in Kantian liberalism that we can trace possible answers to these questions, in its attempt to erect an intellectual framework for politics from moral principles themselves derived from reason. For Kant trust must be grounded in an ethic based on reason, not utility; trust in a political society will not survive if its basic principles of political right are continually breached for consequential benefit or advantage. The important question then is how does Kantian liberalism construe political morality in relation to trust?

Here the basic Kantian strategy is to attach conditions to political morality, so reducing the incidence of betrayal and conserving trust. Moral reference points serve to limit political conduct and provide a certain focus for trust. As Luhmann comments: "The pillars of trust must be built on solid ground . . . the supports of trust are mainly found in opportunities for effective communication . . . in the possibility of activating the means of coercion which belong to the state on the basis of set rules."[14] The fact that rules have to be applied in practice does not in itself diminish trust, but rather directs attention to the construction of such rules and the criteria employed in their application. For Luhmann system trust encourages trust in particular cases: "Only because the security of the system is structurally guaranteed is it possible to do away with the safety precautions for particular actions in specific situations. Readiness to trust is an important instance of the general rule that the absorption of complexity through structures can relieve the burden of action."[15] So it is noteworthy that Kant's structuralism itself provides a substantial limit on political conduct.

Our focus throughout this chapter has been on office-holding as part of a structure of rights and duties, and the Kantian concern with the concept of lying will be central to our discussion here clearly because it raises fundamental questions about the relationship of trust between ruler and ruled. Kant's condemnation of lying shows how far the *arcana imperii* have been dispelled. His prohibition of it is unconditional. For him the evil of lying arises from its nature rather than from any consequences that might be contingently associated with it. Lying involves treating the person who is lied to as a means, and "even though a statement does not contravene any particular human right it is nevertheless a lie if it is contrary to the general right of mankind."[16] The spreading of disinformation and rumor, both commonplace political strategies, is, for Kant, wrong "because if such a practice were universal man's desire for knowledge would be frustrated."[17] In his famous reply to Constant he argues that lying is wrong even when aimed at the protection of an innocent person from criminal attack.[18] It is impossible both to will that lies should be told and that they should be believed. According to Kant's view, a political society governed by a law that makes truth telling conditional on the right to be told the truth when this does not violate a duty of benevolence would soon cease to be just. As Roger Sullivan puts it: "No one could believe anything any government officials might say, for they may have decided that they legally must lie, either because benevolence requires it or because the citizens have no right to the truth."[19]

Of course, Kant does not say that the moral embargo on lying requires that truth always be volunteered; indeed, there is a considerable moral leeway between discretion and deceit, which Kant acknowledges. Such a margin is politically significant. He accepts, too, that, although being honest is a feature of being trustworthy, not all cases of keeping faith are cases of honesty. Where there has been a change of heart, mind, or disposition it is often possible to hold to a trust only by being dishonest to oneself. However, Kant is more concerned to refute claims that the absolute prohibition on lying can be made conditional in instances where a lie seems to be justified by necessity: "For if necessity is urged as an excuse it might be urged to justify stealing, cheating and killing, and the whole basis of morality goes by the board."[20]

Similar arguments are deployed by Kant against the notion of a lying promise – a promise made in full awareness of the intention to break it. Giving even a conditional permission to lying, species of lying, and promise breaking diminishes veracity and removes the grounds for trust. Trusting the word of others is a precondition of trusting them to be fair in their treatment or to refrain from harm. In this respect, as Alf Ross remarks, "lies exist only as parasites on truth; they are conceivable only as exceptions which depend on the norm they violate."[21] A norm of trustworthiness does not imply that we should always be trusting. Indeed, there is nothing in Kant's rejection of lying that prohibits him from allowing that a prudent distrust is often a sensible policy. Lies, however, are different. They are parasites that colonize the host. One objection to Kant here is that a refusal to lie may leave us defenseless against evil, though attempts to square these conflicting requirements by qualifying Kant are not always successful. Sissela Bok argues that "some lies – notably minor white lies and emergency lies rapidly acknowledged – may be more *excusable* than others, but only those deceptive practices which can be openly debated and consented to in advance are justifiable in a democracy."[22]

Bok's argument is that lies by those in government destroy public trust and should be heavily constrained even in circumstances of national danger: "In principle, then, both deception and violence find a narrow justification in self-defense against enemies. In practice, however, neither can be contained within these narrow boundaries; they end up growing, perpetuating themselves, multiplying and feeding on one another to produce the very opposite of increased safety."[23] There is a difficulty here, however, insofar as the concern to preserve public trust seems to fit uneasily with Bok's defense of whistleblowing: "The fact that one has promised silence is no excuse for complicity in covering up a crime or a violation of the public's trust."[24] From Kant's perspective both lying and the lying promise – promising to abide by conditions of employment, for example, in full awareness of the intention to break them – cannot be morally justified. In its modern form the understandable wish to preserve trust by holding governments accountable is diluted by a conception of duty as little more than subjective preference. As Minogue comments: "Reason of state has thus been turned on its head. It is those who challenge states, not those who act for them, who now in practice enjoy moral immunities."[25]

If Kant's prohibition on lying appears to raise awkward questions about the possibilities of controlling political morality, the same can be said of his idea of publicity. Kant refers to this as "a transcendental concept of public right," by which he means that it is an entailment of rationality that any political principle that cannot be made public is incompatible with justice.[26] Kant's object here is to establish publicity as a formal condition of law. The difficulty, however, seems to be that, although this constitutes a prescription against secrecy, it does not apparently exclude confidentiality and neither does it stipulate the degree of openness that would appear to be morally required. Nevertheless, Kant does explicitly connect publicity with the furtherance of trust:

It must accordingly be prohibited for a state to use its own subjects as spies, and to use them, or indeed foreigners, as poisoners or assassins (to which class the so-called sharp-shooters who wait in ambush on individual victims also be-long), or even just to spread false reports. In short, a state must not use such treacherous methods as would destroy that confidence which is required for the future establishment of a lasting peace.[27]

It is important to note that Kant's arguments regarding pub-licity arise from his attempt to establish the formal conditions of political right. Clearly the fact that political morality in-volves treating some individuals as means is for Kant simply a further proof of its moral chicanery. Trust for Kant is sus-tained when the rules of justice are administered in accor-dance with the principles of right. Trust is diminished when such rules are suspended or modified for the achievement of some utilitarian good.

It is not the case, however, that Kant excludes pragmatism totally from political conduct so long as it is within the law and is consistent with the development of a just society; he does recognize that politics is a realm in which expediency, prudence, and fortune can play a major part. As a result he has to give some account of the relation between politics and moral obligation that does not leave the morally sound de-fenseless against evil. His distinction in *Perpetual Peace* be-tween the moral politician and the political moralist is central to his line of thought and hence to our discussion here. The moral politician is aware of the need to keep a distance be-tween himself and the selfishness that politics sometimes involves. Unlike the political moralist, the moral politician who experiences the failure of his policies has the assurance that his moral vision is fundamentally correct, immune from luck. Failure is not a complete disaster. It does not deflect him as it does the pragmatist. As Susan Mendus rightly says: "Failure to attain a particular end serves to unjustify the po-litical moralist, but does not unjustify the moral politician, who still has the assurance that his aim was the right one."[28]

In this way the moral politician constitutes an object of trust. He represents the enduring claims of morality, and even if the moral politician forms alliances with the base or negotiates with wrongdoers, his actions are sustained by the principles of right, which establish that there is a moral limit beyond which he cannot go: He must not lie. Does this leave him vulnerable to evil? Kant's answer is that evil will not endure.

But is there a fatal tension in Kant's project between an ethics of reason and a morality appropriate to the world? "If Kant is wrong in his conclusion about lying to the murderer at the door, it is for the interesting and important reason that morality itself sometimes allows or even requires us to do something that from an ideal perspective is wrong."[29]

It is essential to recognize that for Kant political morality is the focal point of attention between the aspirations of a well-founded republic, open and responsive to the claims of its citizens, and its paramount need to protect itself against malignity – that is to say, his aim is to unite the political precept "be ye therefore wise as serpents" with the moral injunction to be "as harmless as doves."[30] Nevertheless, as Susan Mendus remarks, for Kant "duty does not go away because of the world's contingent interventions"[31] – even the interventions of evil.

We have arrived at a point where we can see postulated a tight relationship between trust and principles of political right. Nevertheless, however attractive this claim appears to be for the purposes of our discussion, it does need to be treated with some caution. The point is that if such principles are constitutive of human conduct, then trust in them loses its element of contingency. It no longer seems expressive of risk, but seems rather unconditionally connected to reason and in this way removed from desire: How can there be any danger in trusting if it is based securely in rational principle? When trust is given against the truster's better judgment, it is surely not always involuntary or unwise. Is it not the case that human trust is conditional in the sense that it is often accompanied by an unfulfilled desire to know how its purposes are to be achieved and with what motives? So this conditionality seems to link trust to character and outcome and it is thereby divorced from politics as an activity monitored by moral principle, and placed in a realm in which political and moral considerations often collide. There trust is less securely grounded in reason and appears to conform more closely to its nature.

Further, on Kant's view the categoric moral rules on which such legal principles depend are productive of a deep social and political trust. They provide an Archimedean point against which principles and their applications can be judged, so providing a foundation for trust and an unbroken route for its renewal. For Kant, politics and trust are connected juridically. Sovereignty is expressive of "the united will of the people"[32] and "since all right is supposed to emanate from this power, the laws it gives must be absolutely *incapable* of doing anyone an injustice."[33]

The difficulty here is that problems of political morality seem to evade legal and moral certitude, and their persistence suggests a region of political choice in which right clashes not with inclination but with *right*. A morality that takes law as its model may exclude actions, but it surely cannot inspire them. In Kant, politics is secondary to morality understood as a framework of rules. Such a system of moral legislation is dependent on the idea that morality can issue from rational choice alone. It is, however, notoriously difficult to identify an impartial standpoint that is notionally separate from contingent sensibilities and yet sufficiently close to them to distinguish the just from the unjust, the fair from the unfair. Indeed, it may be that one of the deepest fallacies in the Kantian project lies in the belief that impartiality is recoverable only by postulating a world free of the particularity of psychology and circumstance. If this is true the liberal premise that such a belief provides a logically secure mode of political assessment and allegiance must be lost. For Kant moral character as an empirically defined collection of attributes and dispositions is subsidiary to autonomy as rational detachment from contingent personality. The rational point of view is a basis for moral consensus. The philosophical subtext here is the claim that political morality is problematic because it represents a failure of rationality and that it arises from an autonomy only half-reached, in a community whose rational grounding is incomplete. Clearly, such a claim is open to question in a variety of ways. Doubts may be raised about its postulates – rational agency conceived as neutral, devoid of social attribution; its mode of derivation; and whether a moral identity engineered through dualism and division is actually sustainable. Such criticism does not entail the abandonment of Kant's critique of utilitarianism, but it raises the possibility that in specific moral and political dilemmas the unwelcome necessity of balancing gain against loss is the only criterion available.

At this stage it might be argued that this bleak conclusion can be avoided by diluting the moral requirements of a strict Kantianism to leave an ethic of officeholding that is both practicable and a check on dirty hands. Such an ethic might be understood "as one in which the agent has some special relationship to parties involved, which will give him an honourable motive for overruling his objections to such acts."[34] For example, in an adversarial legal system one's effectiveness as a lawyer often requires conduct that is unacceptable from a moral standpoint. Now, clearly, in such a case some limit on behavior other than the interests of the client is desirable – the simple fact of acting on behalf of another does not itself constitute a moral blank check. Where the line is drawn, however, is complicated by the presence of differing perspectives on the part of those involved, and even by the possibility that manipulation, evasion, and cunning will have a corrupting effect on the moral character of lawyers who use them.[35] Whereas maintaining a distinction between harassing a witness for the personal satisfaction of the lawyer and rigorous questioning in the course of a proper legal scrutiny of testimony is obviously an elementary requirement, determining the difference between discrediting and humiliating a witness is less clear-cut a judgment and one that is necessarily problematic.

The need for limits on such conduct also directs our attention to the moral characteristics required of officeholders, in this case, judges. Hobbes, for example, describes what makes a good judge as *"a right understanding* of that principle law of nature called *equity,"*[36] something that for Hobbes is derived from natural reason; "contempt of unnecessary riches, and preferments";[37] the ability in making judgments to put aside "all fear, anger, hatred, love, and compassion";[38] and the patience to listen, diligence to attend to what is said, and the memory to apply what has been reflected upon. In his sermon on Unjust Judges,[39] Cobbett further explores a significant aspect of Hobbes's theme, pointing out that the moral character expected of judges is related internally to their legal function, and the place of law in a community requires that it is administered impartially, without arbitrariness and preference. The fear that the execution of justice may be obstructed by the character of the judge is expressed by Cobbett through a quotation from Micah: "That they may do evil with both hands earnestly, the prince asketh, and the judge asketh for a reward; and the great man, he uttereth his mischievous desire: so they wrap it up."[40]

Wrongdoing by those in authority excludes public utterance, and it must therefore be disguised, injustice done in the name of justice. For Cobbett, this "deprives the sources of power of all confidence."[41] He describes this *"wrapping up* as . . . the great secret of judicial iniquity."[42] It increases crime and stimulates social resentment and anger, encouraging the displacement of due punishment by revenge. In this way, it is seen as a massive breach of public trust.

Cobbett's fear is that law is a disguise for corruption and partiality, not that it is on occasion practiced in a morally unacceptable way for the achievement of a good end. This points to disanalogies between political and legal conduct; as Bernard Williams remarks, concealment in politics is less specific than in the law.[43] We see political agents as having allegiances and commitments that resist assessment by a strict ideal of impartiality. Their determination to stay in power suggests an ambivalence between ambition and public concern, which surely renders trust in their motivation and judgment less secure. And moral flexibility may not be allowed or trust given so generously to officeholders if we are the victims rather than the beneficiaries of their decisions. Equally, officeholders who regard a degree of moral license as a guarantee of their moral self-esteem are not likely to inspire trust. It is hard to see moral adaptability, therefore, as a solution to the problem of trusting those who act badly on our behalf, or more than an acknowledgment of the tension between utility and right, which still remains.

Furthermore, there are clear difficulties in the Kantian attempt to render moral principle immune from luck. Political agents, as Susan Mendus points out, are condemned thereby to taking "a step in the dark,"[44] comforted only by the ex post facto illumination shed by Kant's teleological conception of history. The objection, however, is that moral choices in politics risk failure not simply from external misfortune but more significantly from the internal nature of the project and the part played by the agent's character and dispositions in carrying it out.[45] The idea that officeholders may be victims of circumstance and character surely challenges the association of freedom and rationality: It places political agency in a context of radical insecurity; it draws our attention to the temporal dimensions of character, to how dispositions may be at odds with their times as well as in tune with them; to how outcomes may not match even the best of intentions; and to how conceptions of the value of a particular enterprise alter over time with the changing vantage points of character.[46] Bringing trust into a relation with history cannot but give political morality a sharper focus. No longer a function of abstract rationality, political morality will then find what certainty it can in the hope that its moral costs will actually issue in a future benefit. So trust in this context will be related to uncertainty not in the strategic sense of choice but in relation to the possible disjunction between moral aims and their outcomes. The diverse ways moral agents perceive their own virtue has to have a crucial bearing on political morality and trust. My argument is that contrasting dispositions such as pride in virtue or unreflective goodness mean that morality is an obstacle to political judgment in different ways and not simply a framework of moral principle through which some political proposals cannot pass. Moral perplexity may then mark not a failure of rationality but rather a loss of innocence. Trust does not take its shape from a uniform instrumental rationality in which the dominant fear is that of being a dupe, but rather arises as a response to the moral character of those who face a political test. Political morality is a species of moral dilemma. That trust involves considerable risk here is undeniable. However, the claim that trust is necessarily ill-advised, that it is credulousness or naïveté, expresses a determination not to be taken in which is surely inconsistent not only with any substantial sense of political allegiance or loyalty but also with the way we respond to those confronted by conflicting moral choices.

To put it another way, and this is the vital point I wish to make here, we need to focus on the idea of testing trust, the risks of trust, and the dilemmas of trust in specific narrative situations – in which case utility cannot be the central constitutive feature of dirty hands. What is at issue is not the neutral calculation of means for the achievement of ends, but the standpoint of moral character against which morally difficult choices are made. Political morality is not to be understood as a kind of moral accountancy. The utilitarian assessment of an outcome as the lesser evil may soon see it as not evil at all, and the claim that wrongdoing is done only when it is necessary can quickly translate into the probability that it will be done when it is not. As Martha Nussbaum recognizes, it is not the presence of moral dilemmas alone that diminishes trust. What matters is how officeholders take decisions and how they respond morally. Using the decision to bomb Hiroshima as an example, she says that even supposing this to have been the best available decision in the unwelcome dilemma facing those charged with making judgments on our behalf, it still matters deeply whether the bombing is to be treated simply as the winning alternative, or, in addition, as a course of action that overrides a genuine moral value. It matters whether Truman takes this course with unswerving confidence in his own powers of reason, or with reluctance, remorse, and the belief that he is obligated to make whatever reparations can be made.[47]

This way of calling attention to the political significance of remorse and guilt establishes a distance between political morality so understood and utilitarianism. Indeed, Nussbaum regards a sensitivity to the values involved in a moral quandary as an essential antidote to social choice theory understood as an impersonal, technical method of conflict resolution. Officeholders who recognize moral perplexity are aware of limits on what they can acceptably do, thus preserving a recognizable sense of trustworthiness. By contrast, the claim that human attachments are merely second best to the independent, rational evaluation of preferences destroys trust by transferring what constitutes a limit from the human to the technical realm. A further important reason for reducing the hold of utilitarianism on political morality is that it neglects what Martin Hollis calls "the crucial interplay between private and public office."[48] There are, of course, occasions where the utilitarian balance is unclear, but what Hollis rightly wants to bring out here is that utilitarianism obscures the difference between public and private life. For a private individual behaving in the same way as the state's agents, "there could be no excuse."[49] The problem of dirty hands arises then as a specific feature of the duties of office.

The actual dilemma Hollis examines is that of Colonel John Hill who authorized but did not instigate the massacre at Glencoe. For Hollis the dilemma that Hill faced arose from a conflict of roles. He was torn between his duty as a civilian governor to pacify the clans by diplomacy and gain their confidence, his military duty to obey the order to kill the Macdonalds at Glencoe as an example to discourage others from unrest and open rebellion, and the expectations of normal decent human behavior applying to him irrespective of his public roles. Obedience to the military order involved the sanctioning of murder under trust, for the Argylls under Hill's command had been peaceably billeted at Glencoe for some time; yet Hill had made use of Highland codes of honor in gaining the Macdonalds' confidence. For Hollis,

> that [Colonel Hill] was a good man I presume from his conscientious effort to act in a Christian manner. That the best may not be attainable is shown by the moral dilemma which he tried to resolve. He was caught in a chain of command which had the People at one end and the victims at the other. His dilemma was that of inescapable responsibility under partial constraint and his hands were dirty before he even began to resolve it. For that, I maintain, is the nature of the game.[50]

Hollis doubts whether Hill "saved his honour in saving his authority. But that is being exact about murder under trust."[51] Indeed, trust figures in this example in a variety of ways. Hill appears as a reliable officer, appreciative of his military duty both to give orders and to obey them. His diplomacy and efforts to bring about trust imply that he was conscious, too, of the clans' mistrust and circumspection regarding government policy. The serious breach of trust that challenged his integrity was a requirement of his military role. As Hollis puts it: "There was no place for him to stand prior to that of a Christian governor."[52] This means that Hill did not stand to the clans in any other relation. Dirty hands in Hollis's view derive from the duties of office. This certainly brings out the political aspect of Hill's dilemma, but in doing so the full depth of moral character is left undisclosed. We see that Hill's delay in giving the order is not moral evasion; there is no attempt to limit his responsibility by merely hinting at his orders, or disguising them, wrapping them up. Hill had no directly personal interest in the events (the lives of his family were not at stake), though there might be an argument for saying that his decision to allow his military duty to outweigh his civil duty *will* affect our view of him as a decent human being.

For a contrasting example there is Shakespeare's *Macbeth*, which shows murder under trust more substantially exposed. Here political relationships are mediated by a personal trust absent in Hill's case. Macbeth consciously exploits trust for political gain. In plotting the murder of Duncan he says of him:

> He's here in double trust:
> First, as I am his kinsman and his subject,
> Strong both against the deed; then, as his host,
> Who should against his murderer shut the door,
> Not bear the knife myself.[53]

In this world there is no trust in trust. Political ambition displaces human fidelities. Of course, utility does not always dictate to faithfulness as we can clearly see, for instance, in Cicero's discussion of the example of Regulus, a Roman soldier taken prisoner during the Carthaginian wars. He was sent back to Rome "on parole, sworn to return to Carthage himself, if certain noble prisoners of war were not restored to the Carthaginians."[54] To Regulus as a moral agent with a healthy respect for his own well-being, interest exhorts that he stay at home with his family; his capture was a misfortune of war, his promise obtained by constraint. Nobility and courage, however, point another way. As Cicero makes clear, one feature of Regulus's bravery is his belief that the decision is not one for him as a moral individual, but for the community as a political entity. He refuses to vote, therefore, in the deliberations of the senate on the grounds that his oath has bound him to his country's enemies. He insists that it is not politically expedient that the prisoners be returned; they are young and of military value to the state's enemies, whereas he is "bowed with age."[55] Regulus is aware, too, that his return means death by torture, "by enforced wakefulness."[56] Here, what is expedient for the state is coincidental with the moral conviction that trust ought not to be broken. What Cicero finds additionally valuable about Regulus's conduct is that "it was he who offered the motion that the prisoners of war be retained."[57] For Regulus, it had to be a political

decision – "he was not content to stand upon his own judgement but took up the case in order that the judgement might
be that of the senate."[58]

So we have three cases in which political imperatives,
moral character, and trust bear upon each other in complex
ways. Trust may be breached for reasons of political policy or
for ambition, or adhered to as an article of moral and political
faith. It may be an instrument of policy or an expression of
moral commitment. What conception of trust is appropriate
to political morality? We might look at some modern philosophical ideas about trust insofar as they have a bearing on
this question. Dirty hands cases involve both insecurity and
uncertainty. For Luhmann trust is an indispensable response
to modernity. It is an essential means of reducing social complexity; in Alan Silver's phrase, through trust "one treats as
certain those aspects of the modern world which modernity
makes uncertain."[59] But this is only possible in Luhmann's
view by jettisoning personal trust in favor of trust in systems.
In relation to political morality the deficiencies of this position are clear. Insofar as dirty hands involve the consciousness of wrongdoing by an agent who possesses distinctive
moral characteristics and attributes, personal trust cannot be
so easily eliminated. To do so is to make the reductive move
of treating human agency as if it were uniform, human character as if it were a unit in a prearranged game. If dirty hands
are not constituted only by the duties arising from office or
the utility of a particular policy, then neither is trust when it
is expressed in this context. In political modernity the meaning of political morality can be retained only by recovering
the sense of what it is to trust another, in other words, by
reclaiming that which modernity sees as archaic. Trust in
those who act badly on our behalf to avoid harm or to advance a political good is not simply a reduction of complexity.
Trust may increase complexity by imposing a moral burden
on the officeholder and by creating additional dangers for the
truster. As Annette Baier comments: "The special vulnerability which trust involves is vulnerability to not yet noticed
harm, or to disguised ill will."[60]

The element of risk here is essential to the moral significance of trust as well as to any imprudent exercise of trust.
Theorizing trust on a contractualist model emphasizes the
voluntary choices of agents whose moral psychology is assumed to be uniform and not fully altruistic.[61] However, it is
difficult to see how this argument can proceed without assuming the truth of what it is intended to prove. The expression of
trust changes the circumstances of both truster and trusted; as
Baier points out "trust alters power positions."[62] What is of
most significance here is the subtle shading of private and
public concerns. Political morality clearly involves asymmetries of power. Trust in this context is as much an admission of
vulnerability as it is in private human feeling. Indeed, if we
had no awareness of the degree of self-surrender involved in
compassion, love, or sexual need, could public trust ever be
anything more than slavery or subservience? For trust in relation to political morality, Baier's well-aimed criticisms of contract as a paradigm of human trusting are apposite:

> Contracts distribute and redistribute risk so as to minimise it
> for both parties, but trusting those more powerful persons
> who purport to love one increases one's risks while increasing
> the good one can hope to secure. Trust in fellow contractors is
> a limit case of trust, in which fewer risks are taken, for the
> sake of lesser goods.[63]

The idea that trust involves exposure to not yet noticed harm
introduces a moral subtlety missed in nonaltruistic accounts
of trust, which is surely significant for an understanding of
political morality. Michael Slote refers to the possibility of
someone being harmed by deceptions and betrayals about
which they know nothing: "Someone ignorant of his wife's
infidelities is worse off simply in virtue of those infidelities,
and quite independently of how his marriage seems to him."[64]
Slote then complicates this conventional picture by imagining
that while both wife and husband are successfully deceiving
one another, "each has an attitude of trust towards the other
despite his or her own deceitfulness."[65] For Slote, mutual trust

here is anachronistic – it is "neither valuable nor praise-worthy, except when underlaid by basic fidelity, or trust-worthiness."[66] So an unjust society that is nevertheless char-acterized by civility appears odd in much the same way as a marriage in which mutual trust is accompanied by mutual infidelity. One might extend the argument by pointing out that citizens can be ignorant of the dirty hands incurred on their behalf, but, in contrast with a husband or wife who dis-covers that he or she is being deceived, it is not so straightfor-ward a matter to decide if they have been harmed. That is to say, trust is not intrinsic to politics in the same way as it is to friendship. For D. O. Thomas this leaves political life awk-wardly poised between Hobbesian skepticism and the Ser-mon on the Mount. He argues rightly, however, that whether to trust "is not a question of deciding in general whether we ought to prefer trusting to relying upon sanctions, but rather a question as to whether we can distinguish certain situations in which the duty to trust is always paramount."[67]

Linking trust to moral ties and perceptions is certainly necessary if the problematic force of trusting in the circum-stances of political morality is to be revealed. Trust must be conceived in such a way as to bring out its full moral sense – that is, officeholders who incur dirty hands are not simply relied upon, but trusted. As Thomas points out, reli-ance carries the risk of any sanctions invoked proving in-effective, but trusting means not employing sanctions at all and thus risking "losing what a sanction would secure."[68] In this respect, Bernard Harrison's understanding of uncondi-tional moral trust is relevant.[69] Such trust involves a belief in the integrity of another's will, which is logically separate from that person's commitments and interests. In this way, the continuation of trust is independent of questions con-cerning its pragmatic value. Thus, as Baier writes: "Where the trustor relies on his threat advantage to keep the trust relation going, or where the trusted relies on concealment, something is morally rotten in the trust relationship."[70]

The search for a noncontractual account of the origins of trust fits with a concern to explore the inspirations of political action. For Hannah Arendt politics is a realm of action in which the human aspiration for immortality can express itself. Courage is needed to leave the enclosed private realm and assert and defend political beliefs in public. Arendt's view of political morality derives from the logic of this account of the public world. She rejects the understanding of politics which requires morality to give way to advantage, but she resists the absolute morality on which such a rejection conventionally depends. This gives political morality the tragic quality essential if the moral place of trust in it is to be understood. The notion of an origin, a starting point, is seen by Arendt in relation to natality, beginning afresh. It is action rather than labor or work that in Arendt's view of the human condition is closest to natality. The sense of founding, of starting anew, of initiative, is the key element of the political. It is an existential moment. The contractualist dependence on artifice is brushed aside in this conception of politics. Our attention is drawn to the way in which trust like action "has an inherent tendency to force open all limitation and cut across all boundaries."[71] In my view, to stress trust as a feature of human development involves considerable departure from trust construed as an attribute of a static framework of rules and regulations. In this way the capacity of a human community to survive breaches of both public and private trust, whether it is vulnerable or resilient in the face of betrayals, is not examined through the calculation of gain against loss or the scrutiny of conduct against a set of abstract principles purporting to be foundational. A sense of the past enables the discernment of the ancestry of trust. A sense of the human goods that are highly prized, including political and private attachments, enables us to discern its fragility.

Chapter 4

Origins and agents

All persons possessing any portion of power ought to be strongly and awefully impressed with an idea that they act in trust.

Edmund Burke, *Reflections on the Revolution in France*

The intrusion of the contractual relation, and relationships concerning private property generally, into the relation between the individual and the state has been productive of the greatest confusion in both constitutional law and public life.

G. W. F. Hegel, *Philosophy of Right*

A significant feature of trust is its logical complexity. It is a disposition of character and a valuable public good, a policy available in competitive circumstances and a condition of human exchange. Credulity and deceit are predictable hazards that derive from character. Trust may be misplaced or abused. Personal disposition is not, however, the only component in a relationship of trust. What is entrusted must be of value to the truster. Trust is a hazardous undertaking precisely because what is entrusted may be exposed to injury, harm, or loss. Private information may be given in confidence to an unreliable acquaintance. A family heirloom may be entrusted to the charge of a careless friend, or, as in Euripides' *Hecuba*, a beloved child may be entrusted to the safekeeping of a treacherous king for the duration of a war. Human attachments may be protected by trust or act as a spur to its betrayal. Trust reveals that what is entrusted to another matters significantly to the truster. The consequent risks of dependence and the fear that others may prove untrustworthy prompt reflection on how trust may be secured. The basic Hobbesian solution to the problem of trust in circumstances of minimal altruism is extended by Rawls to include the effects of "relations of friendship."[1] The sanctions applied by the Hobbesian sovereign to deter rule breaking and to restore the political fabric if it is damaged are paralleled by potential feelings of guilt. Punishment and guilt are artificial mechanisms that buttress cooperation and social stability. The fact that one is a political and the other a psychological sanction makes only a marginal difference. In Rawls' view, "the effect . . . of relations of friendship and mutual trust is analogous to the role of the sovereign."[2] On this account trust is secured by showing how it derives from agreements made by rational, moderately self-interested individuals in the original position. The principles of justice establish a basis for trust by creating a sense of mutual well-being and fair treatment. The weaknesses of contractualism, however, are apparent in its deliberately "thin" conception of human agency and its explanation of the origin of trust. Given the moral psychology of individuals in the original position, it is unsurprising that they should fear promise breaking or that trust should be so heavily circumscribed by constraints. Trusting others does not always lead to weakness and insecurity. It is not because the trusted always place their advantage first that trust is vulnerable to loss and disappointment. On the contrary, showing confidence can inspire confidence in return. Openness may move others to reciprocal faithfulness; deceit often breeds deceit. The claim that the risks of trust derive from a general human untrustworthiness seems unwarranted. A decision to face the risks of trust is not always a sign of imprudence: It may indicate a willingness to sacrifice oneself for others. We need to ask, therefore, how the fear of betrayal is connected with the value of what has been entrusted. This involves giving an account of how such value originates and how it is served by trust.

It is a necessary feature of contractualist method that individuals are seen as rational constructs whose attributes are determined by the requirements of theory. The original position, too, is not original in any historical sense. It is an abstract, logical device whose function is to provide contract argument with its theoretical starting point. Individual human attachments, however, cannot be brought to life from such a static and empty beginning. They are rooted in inherited circumstance, in a historical context that provides a ground for identity, for a sense of the self. Trust needs this sense as much as it needs a language for its expression to others. In learning a language, as Oakeshott remarks, "we do not begin by learning words, but words in use"[3] – words, that is, whose diverse meanings can be discerned in use. Trust originates not from a neutral point, devoid of social attribute and ethical meaning, but from concrete historical circumstances in which goods have a substantial, but not uncontestable worth.

Analysis of the readiness to trust – of how trust originates as a feature of an agent's commitments and loyalties – involves circumstances, character, and motivation. A community in which mutual fidelity is well established possesses a confidence in its values that enables it to withstand social and political scrutiny and challenge, so encouraging what Hegel calls a "readiness for extraordinary exertions."[4] Here Hegel is in fact giving an account of the connection between trust as a condition of political well-being and trust as a strategy, the one sustaining and limiting the prudential deployment of the other. Indeed, in the absence of a basic political fidelity, it would be impossible to construe political morality as anything other than a betrayal. The wrongdoing involved in dirty hands expresses an engagement with politics that a mature and morally sensitive society should be capable of enduring. Desperate measures do not always denote a treacherous character. The moral asymmetry between action and intention suggests another way of exploring trust in relation to political morality. Wrongdoing for a desirable political purpose may be viewed from a perspective of character that is not ideal, not Archimedean. It is expressive of political attachments and values, of what an agent sees as possessing political worth. Thus, Sophocles portrays the wily Odysseus using an innocent and trust-inspiring Neoptolemus to trick Philoctetes. For Odysseus trust originates as a means to an end; it is brought about by the requirements of policy. For Philoctetes trust cautiously finds its object in goodness; it comes from his belief that Neoptolemus cannot lie, cannot be a deceiver. For the trusting Neoptolemus, it is an initially shocking idea that trust is nothing more than an additional instrument of policy; a trusting nature is brought into contact with worldliness, innocence with the cunning of Odysseus. The sources of trust are discovered in the values and attachments that bring about its need. Significantly, this calls our attention to the interstices of conduct in which human beings are unclear about what they should believe or do, unsure about their own motives or plans, and uncertain of the intentions of others. By contrast, a trust actually thought to be well founded can be betrayed, as Medea's trust was by Jason, and the consequences may be violent.

On other occasions the willingness to trust may be less clearly drawn. Agents may be impelled to trust others by the strength of their feelings toward them – passion concealing from judgment the possibility that love does not guarantee fidelity. Trust can arise almost without the truster realizing it and may be close to passivity, only finely distinct from taking the other for granted. Indeed, a trust that is unreflective of another's independent needs is hardly worth the name – its culpability arising from the confusion of trustworthiness with quiescence. Those in receipt of such a trust risk finding that their natural wish to make their acts and thoughts their own is termed disloyalty. In Zola's *Thérèse Raquin* is this the trust that Madame Raquin puts on offer to Thérèse? Does sexual repression cause treachery and murder? Here the relation between trust, betrayal, and human needs takes on a more distorted shape. To speak, then, of the origins of trust is to describe the variety of ways in which agents become conscious of the freedom of others. Thus, Philoctetes, as a man personally familiar with faithlessness, is first warily cognizant of the goodness of Neoptolemus; Philoctetes' trust is born from hesitation and inquiry.

Giving political and sexual engagements a prominent place enables us to explore how trust comes into being and why it might be betrayed. It allows us to see its inspiration and its collision with desires and modes of characters, with other separate human goods and values. For Hegel, "The serious-ness and importance of the situation in its special character can only begin when its definiteness comes into prominence as an essential difference and, by being in opposition to some-thing else, is the basis of a collision."[5] The problem here is not how to calculate the benefits of trust or the utility of deceit. From the perspective of the agent it is how to recognize a deception, how to identify a liar. Trust is often more difficult to start than to maintain, a complexity that in the *Philoctetes* is examined through a linkage with knowledge and experience, with memory and aspiration. The collisions explored by Sophocles involve rival conceptions of honorable conduct, conflicting views of the moral limits of politics. In this world political morality is not a matter of utilitarian calculation. Its inhabitants do not look to saintliness or an unalloyed ruthless-ness for the attributes of rule. From this standpoint political morality is a conflict "in which different virtues appear as making rival and incompatible claims on us . . . our situation is tragic in that we have to recognise the authority of both claims."[6] In the *Philoctetes* political morality is of significance to individuals who see the precise force of separate moral and political claims. The conditions external to action – time, place, and occasion – constrain human choice, allowing Phi-loctetes himself only a bare and minimal existence. Against this background trust not only starts as a narrative or story, the origin of a continuous, though not unchanging sequence. It has a more primitive, basic role. What then are the circum-stances of trust? How can its identity be captured?

In his discussion of Shakespeare and Greek tragedy, Adrian Poole relates tragedy to trust: "It is characteristic of tragedy to test the value and virtue of words, especially those words in which men and women try to put most trust."[7] A human inheritance is morally complex; it comprises earlier legacies and transgressions. In the *Philoctetes* the need to trust finds its

broadest origin in war. As evidence of the fragility of public
and private trust, the Trojan war serves as a paradigm. The
seduction by Paris of Menelaus's wife, Helen, is a breach of
guest trust that provokes slaughter on a historic scale. It represents an "archetypal transgression,"[8] and will lead eventually
to the destruction of Troy and the near ruin of the Greeks. In
the uncertain course of a long and painful war, Odysseus is
sent on a mission with Neoptolemus to Lemnos to obtain the
bow of Philoctetes, for, according to the oracle, Troy will be
defeated only when this is in the hands of the Greeks who
beseige it. Philoctetes is resentful at the wrongs inflicted on
him by his Greek comrades who have banished him to a life
alone, and he refuses to give up the bow, a refusal that means
unavoidable conflict with Odysseus's purpose in coming to
Lemnos. Throughout the play Sophocles constantly emphasizes Philoctetes' noxious and incurable wound. This "fester-
ing ulcer" causes great suffering to Philoctetes who refers to
himself as a "poisonous infected wretch." He is a man in
agony, enduring the incessant spasms of pain of a deadly
affliction. In his distress and incapacity Philoctetes is a man set
apart, but his terrible state might be thought to represent a
powerful moral demand on his fellows and a reproof to those
who would resist it. Philoctetes' possession of the all-power-
ful bow makes an ironic contrast with his own physical weakness. Later when Neoptolemus responds to Philoctetes' cries
of pain he finds that his political intentions have come up
against a moral limit. Political necessity is outweighed by the
alleviation of another's suffering.

This is the immediate background to the different expressions of trust explored in the play, and, as Hegel remarks, it
provides the initial focus of ethical attention: "Now this refusal, like the wrong of being marooned in which it origi-
nated, could have been brought about in all sorts of other
ways, and the real interest lies not in the illness and its physical distress but in the conflict which arises as a result of
Philoctetes' decision not to give up the arrows."[9] Philoctetes'
resentment is for treatment he received in his distant past.
After years of exile, a half-life of isolation and solitude, he

now finds that his possession of the bow has made him important, has given him political value. Why should he help those who so cruelly disregarded him? Why should he trust them?

Circumstances are important to Philoctetes primarily because he considers himself a victim of them. An accidental misdemeanor, an injury incurred by chance, made him a burden to his fellows, an object of disgust and loathing. The decision to dismiss him utterly may have been justifiable on utilitarian grounds,[10] but it leaves Philoctetes indignant and bitter. His circumstances have been changed beyond all recognition; his abandonment is a terrible eviction from human habitation. Left devoid of human companionship, he is an object to be pitied. Unhoused, Philoctetes has, "no-one to help him bear his pains / . . . lost and alone / . . . Tortured with want and the pain / He can never cure; / And none to answer his cries / But the echo in far off hills."[11] His desolation is in effect a return to nature. Philoctetes' banishment is an enforced reversal of the step from nature to society, almost a requirement to shed himself of human attribute. But on his barren island Philoctetes cannot be a noble savage, at one with nature, unaware of socially defined emotions, wants, and needs. His regression must be incomplete; past identity and memory ensure that he is always conscious of his wretchedness and of the compelling urge to return. Although Philoctetes cannot be a primitive, his state does involve "primitive associations."[12] In Arendt's language the terms of his existence are set by labor, the minimum physical effort required to keep alive; and work, the creation of the elementary artifacts of subsistence; but not action, the search for glory in concert with others. This deprivation costs him the distinguishing mark of the human, which lives now only in recollection. Philoctetes' solitude prevents him from exercising trust. Nature is solely an object of expectation and prediction. There is no one in whom trust need be placed, no one to uphold or betray it. This is a significant emptiness. Trust is absent not simply as a useful tool, but as a constitutive feature of the human. In this respect, Poole's remark is entirely apposite, Philoctetes' "life is the embodiment of handicap."[13]

Yet Philoctetes has survived both the sufferings of his near untreatable wound and his isolation. The reason is his possession of the bow. Ownership is perhaps the most basic of the bow's multiple meanings. Its status as a gift given to Philoctetes by Heracles is marginal to disputes over the entitlement to use it. As Poole comments: "The moral and political dilemmas surrounding the bow are all concerned with the ways in which the bow may pass from one hand to another, whether it is freely given, seized by force or trickery, with what motives or ends in view."[14] Without the bow Philoctetes cannot hunt and so cannot live; it is his lifeline, a necessary artifact. It is also a means of his rejoining society, the reason for other human beings traveling to his island at all. But the bow is a weapon of war and therefore its control is subject to political argument. The disagreement over it signifies the clash between moral and political claims. In this way Philoctetes' recovery of the public world is brought about through conflict, through a complex struggle in political morality, which has the bow as its focus. It is Philoctetes' fate to have his unbearable solitude broken by Odysseus and Neoptolemus, by the man he hates most and trusts least and by the boy he does not know.

The ending of Philoctetes' involuntary isolation marks the need for trust. To leave his solitary state he is faced with the prospect of trusting Odysseus, perhaps the original model of craftiness and cunning. Philoctetes' rediscovery of the human world is characterized by a collision of motives and virtues. To reenter it he must experience deceit and risk. His social rebirth is almost as painful as his exile. Initially, Philoctetes is unaware that it is Odysseus who has ended his seclusion. By contrast, Odysseus has the advantage of foresight and surprise. He knows that Philoctetes will be resentful, anxious to redress his grievance, suspicious, and reluctant to contribute to the common Greek cause of defeating Troy. As an agent of this common political purpose Odysseus is willing to lie to achieve it. He is a pragmatist willing to trade virtues for political advantage. But his ethical standpoint is utilitarian rather than merely opportunistic. As Nussbaum comments: "He gives his approval to any action which he believes will best promote the general welfare, and resists the argument that there are certain actions which should not be done by an agent because of his character and principles, decrying this view as a form of squeamishness."[15]

The initial dilemma is clear. Odysseus cannot obtain the bow by force. The owner of such a weapon has complete security. Indeed, what gives the bow its value to the Greeks is precisely what makes it difficult to capture. Equally, Philoctetes seems not open to rational persuasion. He is unlikely to surrender the bow voluntarily. This is not yet a problem of political morality. From a utilitarian point of view, it remains a choice of the most efficient means to bring about a desirable end. Obtaining possession of the bow by treachery may involve leaving Philoctetes to his solitary fate, but this is secondary to the bow being regained. Utility takes priority over the end of exile. Odysseus requires a ruse to deceive Philoctetes. He finds one in the person of Neoptolemus; in so doing, his utilitarian conception of his enterprise is unavoidably displaced, so allowing the full moral conflict involved in political morality to become apparent.

Neoptolemus is confronted by conflicting demands. He is poised between Philoctetes' moving need for human companionship and the urgency of Odysseus's political purpose. Political morality is not to be understood in terms of agents of uniform psychology and motivation who would argue from a standpoint of self-interest, and so readiness to trust does not arise "because the security of the system is structurally guaranteed."[16] It originates in a context of deeply opposed desires and perspectives, and in Odysseus's eyes Neoptolemus seems the perfect vehicle for his plot to obtain the bow by deception, through the exploitation of friendship. Neoptolemus shares Odysseus's motives – the bow will bring victory to the Greeks and glory for those responsible for its return – but not his character. Hegel links trust with growth in understanding: "Faith and trust emerge along with reflection; they presuppose the power of forming ideas and making distinctions."[17] What Neoptolemus must reflect on is the proposal that he act dishonorably to achieve desirable political ends. Character is faced by conflict between two irreconcilable ethical positions regarding the place of trust in politics. Is its breach a fundamental moral stain or a pragmatic means whose justification lies in the end it serves? Odysseus brings powerful arguments to bear against Neoptolemus's initial reluctance. The prize of victory will bring benefits to all Greeks, and particularly to those who are instrumental in bringing it about; Philoctetes is a man not to be trusted, not to be approached incautiously, without fear. Neoptolemus is not bound by any promise to Philoctetes, not having taken part in the original expedition. It is noble to act in ways that help friends and further the progress of the war. Neoptolemus is simply acting under orders; the authority and responsibility belong to Odysseus. In any case, how can one small act of slyness possibly outweigh the many acts of goodness to be performed in the future. Odysseus exhorts him:

> I know it goes against the grain with you
> To lie, or act deceitfully; but then,
> Success is worth an effort, make it now.
> We shall be justified in the end; for the present
> Let honesty go hang, only for a day,
> I beg you; and then you can live for ever after
> A paragon of virtue. Will you do it?[18]

In the ensuing discussion it transpires that Neoptolemus does value public reputation. At this point he becomes vulnerable to Odysseus's arguments. He agrees to the strategy because it will lead to glory. He will be thought of as courageous and wise.

Neoptolemus is not a moral innocent.[19] He is not completely ignorant of vice. But his character is in passage; it contains inconsistent commitments and certainties. He is unaware of the need to trim ideals to fit circumstances. As Odysseus points out to him:

When I was your age,
My hand was readier than my tongue; but now
I've learnt by much and bitter experience
Words count for more than deeds in the world of men.[20]

In agreeing to Odysseus's plan Neoptolemus loses his innocent belief that it is possible to achieve good only by doing it.
The moment Neoptolemus expresses his concern that his
face might "betray" him, he reveals himself a prey to wrongdoing, though not necessarily to evil. His innocence shields
not courage but cunning. But unlike Odysseus, for whom
the problem of regaining the bow is largely technical, Neoptolemus is forced to reflect on his conduct. What he comes
to see is, in Kierkegaard's phrase, "that he himself has
brought guilt into the world, has himself lost innocence by
guilt."[21] How this comes about is crucial to the interplay of
trust and political morality.

In the meeting between Neoptolemus and Philoctetes, the
origins of trust in character and motive find an initial fulfillment in action. The man Neoptolemus meets is a figure to be
pitied rather than feared. As Poole describes him, Philoctetes
"is almost intoxicated by the sensuous pleasure of hearing
another human voice, let alone a voice that speaks the same
language, let alone a voice that brings news of his friends, let
alone the son of his greatest comrade, the mighty Achilles."[22]
Philoctetes has experienced a partial regression; in his case,
human development has been arrested, turned back on itself.
Trust as a social virtue is stunted. It is a tragic irony, therefore,
that trust must find the source of its renewal in Neoptolemus,
who is open, youthful, and candid, but also an agent of Odysseus. In this first meeting Neoptolemus achieves his aim of
gaining Philoctetes' trust. He pretends that he does not know
him, not even offering him sympathy and help. He protests
that he is no friend of Odysseus, complaining to Philoctetes
about – actually Odysseus's own invention – the Greeks' decision not to return to him the arms of Achilles, his own father.

In this meeting between a natural delight in rediscovering
human society and a trust-inspiring nature, Philoctetes and

Neoptolemus develop a mutual understanding. They share a common ancestry whose authentic voices speak as kin to kin. They talk in a shared moral vocabulary in which praise and blame are attached to the same objects. They agree that it is shameful to refuse aid to someone at the mercy of another. It is a language that provides a home for trust; it gives Philoctetes the confidence that his appeal will not remain unheard. But these values are sharply contradicted by Neoptolemus's commitment to the Odyssean project. He cannot treat Philoctetes as a friend and yet return his trust with deceit, his urgent need for human sustenance with lies. He cannot desire two incompatible reputations, be esteemed as loyal and as the means of achieving a great military victory. At this stage, the inconsistencies in Neoptolemus's position are not apparent to him. He agrees to take Philoctetes home, in speaking to the chorus his hypocrisy is clear: "Well then, it shan't be said that I was less ready / Than you to help a friend in need. / Come on, then. / We sail."[23] But for the time being, as Blundell remarks, "this shunning of disgrace remains a lie."[24]

Trust and political morality are suspended at this point in unreal balance. Philoctetes believes that his enforced banishment is about to end. Neoptolemus is not yet aware of the impossibility of sustaining a treachery that is against his nature. Odysseus assumes that his manipulation of the human inclination to trust and the capacity to inspire it actually is working to his advantage. In reality, however, Neoptolemus is now morally blemished, his hands stained. He has become like Philoctetes in that both need to recover in some way that which they have lost. But is purity recoverable? Can Neoptolemus's innocence be restored? Odysseus's assumption that trust can be exploited instrumentally is crucial here. Its limits chart the boundary of a utilitarian conception of trust. Odysseus understands human identities and attachments as significant only insofar as they are relevant to the production of consequences. But in his concentration on outcomes, in his lack of straightforwardness and obsession with secrecy, Odysseus ignores the possibility that between Philoctetes and

Neoptolemus, between the diseased and the vigorous, there will grow a relation of genuine regard. The false tale that Neoptolemus tells creates a superficial bond of trust between himself and Philoctetes that furthers Odysseus's purposes, but significantly it also contributes to an authentic trust that later obstructs them. As Poole comments: "This false story anticipates a truth, in that Neoptolemus will be moved to trust the fellow feeling which his story creates, and make the false story come true."[25]

When in his deceitfulness Neoptolemus deliberately puts aside compassion for the sufferings of Philoctetes, we observe a series of significant refinements. It is not hands experienced in disloyalty that are stained further, but the clean hands of a boy innocent of betrayal. An ethic of helping friends and harming enemies is unsettled when the pursuit of an agreed and uncontested aim requires that it is a friend who must be harmed. Odysseus believes that he is exactly the kind of man the community can trust to unravel political morality to its advantage; but its confidence founders precisely on his inability to identify a genuine human feeling. Neoptolemus's involvement in deception derives from values he shares with Odysseus. He must also trust that Odysseus knows what he is doing, that the plan will lead to the expected outcome. Philoctetes' need to return to human society and the trust he must exercise to regain it are based on his belief that the world is actually worth reclaiming.

Protagonists in Shakespeare's *Troilus and Cressida* do not face the problem of rediscovering a world that is lost to them. Their anxieties stem from the difficulty of attaching value to objects that exist in the world they already have. Why are certain goods prized and others not? Human desires and political allegiances bear some relation to the worth of their objects. But in the absence of certain knowledge why trust either? What is it that gives Helen her value? What is it that makes a war worth fighting? In Shakespeare's treatment of the Trojan War, reason of state finds a tense conjunction with human emotion, public necessity with private passion. Achilles is both warrior and friend; Troilus both soldier and lover. To Philoctetes trust comes from a standpoint of deprivation and exile, neither deriving from abstract reasoning about half-articulate constructs in an original position, nor emerging dialectically as the expression of a fully reflective consciousness. In *Troilus and Cressida*, too, the instigation of trust escapes the confines of theory, but here it issues from love, its frailties arising from attachments that seem fated. How do human desires and commitments originate trust and its betrayal?

Public and private expressions of trust establish themselves in broad and specific locations. *Troilus and Cressida* presents love and war as massively disrupting experiences. As John Bayley remarks: "Cleverness is gently and amusedly revealed, in the context of war and the context of love, as usually neither gentle nor amusing."[26] Shakespeare portrays the problematic nature of human existence lived for its own sake and on its own terms. *Troilus and Cressida* explores conduct and identities that involve contradictions and inconsistencies, examining sexual infidelity and military conflict not from a single moral standpoint but in terms of imperfection and incompleteness. John Bayley distills the realistic, recognizably modern tone of the play: "A good man (but he is not so good perhaps) is butchered in a hole-and-corner way by some thugs, themselves manipulated by cynical men who enjoy power. Meanwhile a girl has betrayed her lover, but perhaps in any case his love did not deserve her faith?"[27]

The complexities of trust and political morality appear first in the two great council scenes. These are interludes in the prosecution of the war that allow reflection on past transgressions and reconsideration of future policies. Throughout the course of their debate (I iii) the Greeks never once doubt the justice of their cause, although they argue over means and they have become disorderly, prone to factionalism. In fact, preoccupation with competition among themselves seems to have blunted their military effectiveness. Ulysses' degree speech is not simply a piece of political rhetoric aimed at provoking the becalmed Achilles into action. It constitutes an attempt to restore to the Greeks a trust in themselves and in their enterprise. Ulysses (the Romans, and Shakespeare's Odysseus) is still a manipulator, cunning, devious, and duplicitous. But these features of character do not wreck the moral imperatives of order; instead, they serve to bring them into close contact, and potential conflict, with urgent practical needs. It is appropriate, therefore, that Ulysses should adopt the trick of the rigged lottery to try to rekindle Achilles' interest in the war and to counter his preoccupation with Patroclus. Through a "device let blockish Ajax draw / The sort to fight with Hector: among ourselves / Give him allowance as the worthier man, For that will physic the great Myrmidon / Who broils in loud applause."[28] Pride and envy, which are disintegrative and factious, can be turned to political advantage. Ulysses is, of course, completely unconscious of irony; the restoration of trust through a deceit holds no fears for him. This ruse is not simply Machiavellian. It is a significant comment as much on Ulysses' utilitarian conception of political morality as on his cunning that what eventually prompts Achilles to fight is not trickery but the death of Patroclus.

The connection between trust and worth receives more explicit attention in the Trojan Council. Here the question raised is quite specific: Is Helen worth the cost? Its range, however, is universal: What are the grounds for the attribution of value? Trust assumes the value of what is entrusted – value has to be present in the transaction between truster and trusted or it is difficult to see how trust is involved here at all, although any difference in perceived value does not have to entail thereby a lessening of trust on one or the other side. The question here is, In Shakespeare's play are we to understand value as intrinsic or manufactured by desire? A contrast between an absolute and a relative conception of value is at work here. Indeed, Hector's arguments somewhat inconsistently deploy both conceptions. Helen has inherent worth, but this should not perpetuate the war. Both Trojan expediency and natural justice require her return:

> If we have lost so many tenths of ours,
> To guard a thing not ours nor worth to us,
> Had it our name, the value of one ten,
> What merit's in that reason which denies
> The yielding of her up?[29]

> Nature craves
> All dues to be rendered to their owners: now,
> What nearer debt in all humanity
> Than wife is to the husband?[30]

To Hector "'Tis mad idolatry / To make the service greater than the god,"[31] so love requires a sense of the independent worth of its object and, by contrast, infatuation imputes value without evidence. To be overtrusting is to see security where none exists. Jealousy, trust, and betrayal can be established by objective proof; *this* is the conduct that has provoked jealousy, *here* is the evidence of betrayal. In direct opposition to Hector's view, Troilus's response – "What is aught but as 'tis valued?"[32] – sets loose the relativist hounds to dangerous effect. This explains in part Hector's shift from a pragmatic to a moral stance, but, more important, it breaks the link between trust and its object. Helen's value is not now intrinsic but is dependent on the contingencies of political negotiation and bargaining. She is a means to an end and her continued retention merely a possible quid pro quo. Troilus's question is, therefore, an appropriate way of furthering his argument: "Why keep we her? The Grecians keep our aunt: / Is she worth keeping?"[33] In politics conflict frequently takes place over territory whose intrinsic value is minimal. For Troilus what transforms this from a trivial to a serious issue is the achievement of glory. "She is a theme of honour and renown, / A spur to valiant and magnanimous deeds, / Whose present courage may bear down our foes, / And fame in time to come canonize us."[34] Hector draws explicitly on Aristotle to rebuke Troilus for being too hasty and quick in judgment. Significantly, the wish to be remembered as a victor places trust in a wider intellectual context. The relation between action and temporality is now at stake. Does time render human goods prey to fortune or is it an indispensable nexus, a source of nourishment and strength?[35] At the close of the Trojan Council, Hector is persuaded; he has once again shifted his ground – "I am yours, / You valiant offspring of great Priamus."[36] Troilus's argument that value is determined solely by the valuer changes the locus of trust, rendering it vulnerable to the predispositions of the inner life. Trust becomes the plaything of the will, so making any Iago's work easy. It is a considerable irony that Cressida's faithlessness later shows Troilus the consequences of this belief.

Is trust merely a political counter to be used as the occasion demands? Ulysses certainly thinks so. As a view of politics, however, this seems inconsistent on its own terms. Political morality can be so strangled by deviousness and deceit that even deceivers fail. A relativistic conception of value contributes to this crisis of trust so that present worth is uncertain, contestable, and impossible to establish, and political agents must look to their future reputations. Troilus's love for Cressida shifts the focus from public to private attachments, but the skeptical strain remains. Trust whose prelude is love displays crucial ambiguities. Love expresses the need for both transparency and concealment, a desire for a truth not open to manipulation and a fear of betrayal. Later private and public themes will have a significant mutual bearing: Cressida's infidelity will prove a powerful political catalyst. In their initial declarations of feeling, both lovers link trust to nature and to the limits of human expectation. As John Bayley comments, these first exchanges of confidence "make visible the true levels of such an emotional relation – the hidden level of privacy, calculation and the will, and the open assertions of faith and trust, of innocency, of undying love."[37] Constancy is so placed in conjunction with distrust that the natural association of love with trust is not completely lost. Uncertainty about another's feelings prompts caution but does not outweigh the commitments that passion dictates. Cressida is experienced to a degree, teasing and flirtatious, knowing about the likely course of Troilus's love:

"They say all lovers swear more performance than they are able, and yet reserve an ability that they never perform."[38]

As Kenneth Palmer says, in this sexual reference "she is a true niece to Pandarus, in lowering the tone of a conversation."[39] Her shrewdness determines her trust. The future is uncertain, the self is a hazard of conflicting emotions and needs, and all is of the moment. For Troilus, however, love *precludes* expression in the language of negotiation. It is not a consequence of strategies or bargains, its attributes open to reckoning. In clear contrast to his earlier belief that value arises solely from the valuer, Troilus now wishes to be loved for what he is, "Praise us as we are tasted, allow us as we prove, our head shall go bare, till merit crown it."[40] Who Troilus is establishes why Troilus can be trusted. The revaluing of value has lifted love above the transient and distinguished its language from rhetoric, because if sexual desire is not the simple expression of impulse, if satisfaction is not just an immediate gain, then there can be nothing for rhetoric to conceal. There can be a place for the genuine, for the discovery of a truth open to the scrutiny of another. The pledge "As true as Troilus"[41] is, however, made by him in the awareness that constancy is an ideal vulnerable to the effect of time on character and commitment. Cressida's expression of fidelity is less conditional in this respect; if she should prove faithless, it will be remembered even when "blind oblivion swallowed cities up, / And mighty states characterless are grated to dusty nothing."[42] The betrothal performed by Pandarus has the appearance of a legal ceremony, a bargain sealed, an agreement freely entered. But the shadowy nature of these hurried proceedings – being married by Pandarus, the fixer! – shows how peripheral the idea of contract is to the status of trust. Faith and faithlessness derive from character and the problematic nature of valuing and trust is given in close proximity to doubt. Transgression is not simply a challenge to the public practice of promise keeping but to moral identity. Cressida's trustworthiness matters to Troilus because it is related necessarily to his sense of moral worth.

Cressida's earlier "wished myself a man"[43] suggests an ambivalence that is not a query about sexual identity. It reveals an "uncertainty of being,"[44] an overriding equivocation. It expresses the fear that love may be just lechery, that trust may be no more than the need of the moment. For Troilus, too, attachment begins in uncertainty – whether to trust wholeheartedly or to reserve commitment, whether to confess completely or to hold back. As John Bayley comments: "Her starts and hesitations are the equivalent of Troilus' love-speeches: in one sense not to be believed, in another sense wholly true to the immediacy of the feelings."[45] How the insistent negativity of "not to be believed" is resisted is a rebuttal of nihilism. Both Troilus and Cressida experience shifts of feeling that act as obstacles to mutual recognition, but this does not make them liars. They are not engaged in deceiving either themselves or each other when they declare their love. Lies may be justified for many reasons, but not those told by habitual liars. There are many kinds of liars, too. One such is Calchas, a traitor, a man without qualities or attributes whose maneuverings necessitate the testing of faithfulness, and increase the risks and the rewards of trust.

The Sophoclean theme of estrangement is raised in the modern consciousness to an obsessive concern. Shakespeare's delicate tracing of the ambiguities of motive becomes a preoccupation with division and divisiveness. Cressida's "I have a kind of self resides with you, / But an unkind self, that itself will leave / To be another's fool"[46] refers to her desire for Troilus and her wish to keep tactical control. In the context of modern reflexivity, these apparently ordinary remarks signify a more disturbing dualism – between intention and desire, thought and action – which challenges identity and agency, giving social origin a crucial presence. Character certainly involves ways of setting moral limits on itself that distance it from social role. Nevertheless, a tension remains between moral character and social self, between the human being and the priest, the teacher or the judge. In both private and public contexts, this division plays a part in shaping our conception of trust when individuals transgress.

Contract as a social artifice does not therefore completely capture what is at stake in such transgressions. Hegel, for example, at a number of points in the *Philosophy of Right*, attacks contractualism as a basis for marriage – it is "thus degraded to the level of a contract for reciprocal use."[47] At one extreme is "the marriage . . . arranged by the contrivance of benevolent parents; the appointed end of the parties is a union of mutual love, and their inclination to marry arises from the fact that each grows acquainted with the other from the first as a destined partner."[48] But Hegel states "marriage is not to be dissolved because of passion."[49] How are these statements related? Hegel is concerned with the philosophical significance of marriage. He sees it as an ethical institution whose meaning escapes definition by legal contract and romantic love, and yet the contiguity with passion of marriage as social arrangement is suggestive of artifice and repression. The question is, How is trust formed in such a context? No doubt a refined relation between contrivance and natural development appealed to eighteenth-century sensibilities, but for a more enlightened age freedom requires a more visible presence. How then does freedom relate to trust here? Zola's *Thérèse Raquin* explores the fragility of trust through a portrayal of its origins.

The relation between character and circumstance was, of course, a major nineteenth-century concern. Mill's feeling that he was "the helpless slave of antecedent circumstances . . . as if my character and that of all others had been formed for us by agencies beyond our control, and was wholly out of our power"[50] draws our attention to potential and growth being stunted by an adverse environment. In *Thérèse Raquin* city and family are part of the conditions of life influencing individual conduct. Both are deeply embedded in economic and social relations that underlie agency. Circumstances are claustrophobic, suffocating, and diseased, and trust and betrayal are shaped by the conditions of their emer-

gence. The moral and physical architecture is that of the side
street, the passage or corridor oblique to a main, public thor-
oughfare. Streets are "narrow, dark," pavements "greasy,"
"black with grime," populated by "shops . . . in which weird
shapes move and have their being."[51] Action is confined exter-
nally by the commercial relations of the small bourgeoisie. It is
shaped, too, by family relations. Madame Raquin's way of
life – that of a retired shopkeeper whose small investment
provides for her needs – is unexceptional, a model of moral
ordinariness. She lives surrounded by the shabby and faded
icons of bourgeois life. Trust arises first in this household, in a
realm of "secretive privacy,"[52] introverted and closed in on
itself. Camille, Madame Raquin's son, is physically retarded,
emotionally ignorant, as Zola describes the formative relation
between mother and son: "For fifteen years Madame Raquin
had waged war against this succession of terrible ills trying to
snatch her boy from her. And she beat them all by patience,
loving care, and adoration."[53] Camille is an egotist manufactured out of love and his affection for the expression of compassion is directed only toward the self. Weakness and sickli-
ness, the vulnerability of the sick to the special attention of
those who care for them, are contrasted by Zola with the
natural strength and vigor of Camille's cousin, Thérèse, who
had been raised with him since their early childhood. She is
the child of a colonial intermarriage, her mother "a native
woman of great beauty,"[54] whose upbringing alongside her
cousin has ensured an "enforced invalidism,"[55] causing intro-
spection and cloistering physical and emotional needs. Having only an impoverished public existence Thérèse inhabits an
intense dreamlike inner life. Private fantasy has displaced public nourishment.

What Thérèse Raquin experiences in her early years is an
involuntary uprootedness. No less than Philoctetes, she is an
innocent victim, an exile from her birthplace, but in her case
deracination is both more complex and complete. Her unnatural home is not a realm devoid of human habitation, a
place of banishment like Lemnos, but a society in which

natural needs are heavily and intricately masked and distorted by social mediation. Philoctetes has experienced an
enforced regression from which he can learn, from which he
can hope through trust to regain the world he has lost.
Thérèse can neither return nor progress. She is a being divided. Her world lacks conversation, but her desire to make
genuine contact with others, to seek, to feel, and to trust is
held in artificial suspension. Philoctetes *is* diseased. Thérèse is treated as if she were diseased. Unlike Philoctetes, therefore, her exile is a double estrangement from her
nature.

Marriage between Thérèse and Camille is suggested with
the best of intentions. It is arranged with "serene goodwill";[56] Thérèse not seen as a being with sexual needs but
simply as a nurse to Camille. In a relationship completely
lacking in sexual tension – to Camille his cousin might "just
have well been a boy"[57] – distrust simply does not arise. Unconscious of any other consideration but a comfortable, benevolent concern, Madame Raquin regards the marriage as
natural and inevitable. In reality it is akin to a child marriage
and for Thérèse it constitutes an imprisonment, a confine-
ment of nature that leads to multiple crime. The bourgeois
life that follows the marriage is for a time conventional.
Thérèse is passively obedient, unconsulted. Madame Raquin
returns to the language of commerce – profit and loss, buy-
ing and selling, interest and rent. The domestic entertain-
ment is regular, moderate, and safe. Undemanding of its
participants, its habitual comments, coded and predictable
remarks, leave Thérèse half-deranged:

> Sometimes she was seized with hallucinations and thought
> she was buried in some vault together with a lot of puppet-
> like corpses which nodded their heads and moved their legs
> and arms when you pulled the strings. The heavy air in the
> dining room stifled her, and the eerie silence, the yellow glim-
> mer of the lamp, filled her with vague terror and inexpressible
> anguish.[58]

Hegel describes the ethical origin of marriage as "the free surrender by both sexes of their personality."[59] The notion of a "free surrender" captures the tension between choice and desire. But for Thérèse marriage fulfills neither freedom nor desire. It embodies a complex asymmetry between male and female, weakness and strength, disease and vigor, social order and individual incompleteness. Her subordination continues unrecognized. She is a stranger in the house; Madame Raquin is blind to her inner life, to the dangers of an unnoticed frustration, to an unseen hate. Tony Tanner remarks that "contracts . . . *create* transgressions";[60] although marriage as a convenient arrangement falls short of an explicit contract, from Thérèse Raquin it still requires docility and dislocation. Then her adultery marks the end of her quiescence. She becomes "a wife who is not a wife, a prostitute who is not a prostitute, the keeper and breaker of the insecure security of the contract of marriage."[61] Now her life means deceit, concealment, secrecy. Trustworthiness ends not through the discovery of her betrayal – she continues to be regarded as obedient, inert – but through her own realization that she enjoys deceit: "Ah, how she was deceiving these worthy souls, and how happy she was to deceive them with such triumphant impudence."[62] Here, treachery arises not as a means to an end, not as a moral weakness, as a reluctant choice, a lesser of two evils, but willingly, a revenge for repression, for the imprisonment of her spirit and body. In *Thérèse Raquin,* Zola delineates one pattern of sexual restraint, charts one nexus of trust and frustration.

The existence of a disjunction between trust and morality has not escaped philosophical attention. Annette Baier, for example, remarks that only "if we had any reason to believe that most familiar types of trust relationship were morally sound would breaking trust be any more prima facie wrong than breaking silence."[63] For Baier, those who are subject to injustice in the context of trust should attend to "the virtues of a watchful distrust, and of judicious untrustworthiness."[64] Thérèse, like Tolstoy's Anna Karenina, finds her natural vitality curbed by artifice and coldness but, unlike Anna, she is not

faced by moral conflict between two deep and seemingly incompatible attachments. In Zola the absence in Thérèse's life
of any rich or complex set of social relationships gives greater
prominence to the primitive nature of her violation of a social
code. Her conflict is indeed between an impulse and a duty.
Hers is a singular betrayal, a transgression that remains concealed. Only her lover, Laurent, and Thérèse herself know of
the deceit. Adultery originates deception; infidelity examines
trust, tests it, probes the willingness to lie, to breach another's
faith. Laurent's motives, too, are less complicated by love
than a near hedonistic self-regard; he "only decided to embark
on the enterprise when he had satisfied himself that it was
really in his interests to do so."[65] Later, the Benthamite calculation of pleasures and pains proves a treacherous and destructive guide. Public ignorance of wrongdoing coexists out-
wardly with the need to keep feelings secret. Hegel's sharp
distinction between the emotional and the public realms requires qualification because the state inspires commitments
and loyalties that cannot be formulated only juridically, and
law sets limits on the expression of feelings: "It is because
marriage depends entirely on feeling, something subjective
and contingent, that it may be dissolved. The state, on the
other hand, is not subject to partition, because it rests on
law."[66] A relationship in which continued trust conceals an
unrecognized infidelity involves a public *and* a private dislocation. The moral limits on trust in this context can be explored
by seeing how it is tested.

Annette Baier's argument about the moral decency of trust
suggests a starting point. Given that trust may be exercised
in circumstances of considerable injustice, how can its moral
decency be tested? Baier first outlines the nature of rational
or sensible trust. Rational trust exists if trusters have no reason to suspect that those they trust have motives that seriously conflict with their own aims. It may, however, continue
to be a sensible course even when motives actually do conflict, but only if trusters possess sanctions sufficient to deter
possible harm or those they trust skills at concealment sufficient to maintain the truster's ignorance. Excessive use of

threats by the truster and disguise by the trusted both contribute to making their relation less stable. While these conditions are rational, possibly sensible, Baier thinks that they cannot make trust moral. She writes: "The trustor who in part relies on his whip or his control of the purse is sensible but not necessarily within his moral rights in continuing to expect trustworthiness; and the trusted who sensibly relies on concealment to escape the penalty for untrustworthiness, may or may not be within her moral rights."[67] Thus, the test for a trust to be morally decent is that "its continuation need not rely on successful threats held over the trusted, or on her successful cover up of breaches of trust."[68] Baier argues that this can be extended to test trust by seeing whether it survives its own complete expression. So if those who bestow trust come to see that it is being exploited by the skill at concealment of those who receive it or if those who receive trust come to see that it depends on nothing more than the capacity of the truster to inspire their fear, then "trust is morally corrupt."[69] For Baier, "A trust relationship is morally bad to the extent that either party relies on qualities in the other which would be weakened by the knowledge that the other relies on them."[70] As Baier rightly emphasizes, much depends at this stage of the argument on the nature of the qualities involved. She claims that whereas love, concern for a common good, and professional responsibility are more likely to encourage mutual trust, stupidity, fear, and blindness do not. Other features of character, such as "good nature, detachment, inattention, generosity, forgiveness, sexual bondage to the other party in the trust,"[71] are less clear as far as the expressibility test is concerned. Quite clearly, as Baier says, trust is undermined by the knowledge that others are simply counting on one's good nature, but then the question becomes one of establishing what it means for someone to be counted on in that way. It is noteworthy that Baier assumes that while it is generally true that individuals do not regard reliance on fear, ignorance, or cowardice as morally acceptable grounds for trust there are some specific situations in which fear or ignorance may be appropriate. Ignorance plays a legitimate part in some cases "such as trust in national intelligence and security officers to look after national security, [where] some ignorance in the trusting is proper, and awareness that such persons may be relying on one's not knowing what they know will not destabilize any trust one has in them to do what they are entrusted to do."[72]

For Baier, then, the moral test of trust asks how trust *would* survive mutual knowledge of motivation and whether it *does;* in this way Baier preserves the element of risk that is at the heart of trust. If "mutual reliance can be accompanied by mutual knowledge of the conditions for that reliance, trust is above suspicion, and trustworthiness a nonsuspect virtue."[73] The idea of putting trust to the test is instructive. The morality of trust is rightly located in its contact with others, in the way it responds to challenge from their varying temperaments, characters, and needs. For Baier, it involves a qualified Kantian claim that the limits on moral trust are found in mutual knowledge. Trust in its moral aspect is required to pass the expressibility test in a way that is close to the Kantian requirement that the principles of right submit to the formal criterion of publicity. Baier is not unaware of the different senses of testing trust and of the complexities involved in establishing which qualities or mental states are capable of inspiring it. Indeed, it is here that her argument needs to be pressed further because precisely those features of character "whose sensitivity to exposure . . . seems more variable"[74] are the most difficult to assess in relation to the moral decency of trust.

In both public and private life individuals may find that different virtues make incompatible claims. They may be faced by decisions in which one moral requirement outweighs another. The achievement of a public good may mean the breach of a private trust, or, by contrast, self-realization may endanger a significant public responsibility. In such circumstances individuals often feel that they cannot escape without loss, without a strong sense of self-reproach. In relation to political morality such dilemmas together with an associated sense of remorse are central. In private attachments, too, a sense of guilt, of moral stain, is often found when moral duty is reluctantly put aside in favor of individual fulfillment – when, as in *Anna Karenina*, it is precisely the impulses that seemed to promise the best hope of freedom that "launched their victim on a path which led to self-destruction."[75] Trust does seem to relate closely to qualities like openness and forgiveness that are considered admirable, but in these public and private contexts – the stress on both is not accidental – such human qualities are ambiguous, their moral significance as a locus of trust more equivocal.

Consider the idea of testing the moral decency of trust where the quality at issue is trust itself. Henry James takes this as the subject of his short story, "The Great Condition."[76] During a sea voyage Mrs. Damerel receives proposals from two gentlemen who are both equally fascinated by her. The one feels that she must have a questionable past and refuses to take her word on trust. Ignorant of her past, he cannot bring himself to marry her, and he refuses to meet her "great condition" that she will reveal her "secret" only after six months of marriage. He leaves to discover Mrs. Damerel's past for himself. On his return, he learns that she has in fact married his rival who was prepared to put aside his suspicions and take her on trust and has still not questioned her even though fifteen months of marriage have passed. He learns further that there never had been a secret. He failed her test as soon as she became aware of his lack of trust in her. Her husband's happiness by contrast is inextricably bound up with his sense of trust; this she protects by insisting that he remain ignorant of the fact that there was no secret to reveal. His trust is its own reward. These "high- and dirty-minded gentlemen,"[77] as Gorley Putt describes them, respond in different ways to the testing of their trust: The one by giving it instantly, seeing in it a moral virtue whose value is intrinsic, sufficient in itself; the other by withholding it, regarding it only as a conditional value, highly dependent on the grounds or evidence that can be discovered for its support. To Mrs. Damerel a man who trusts only when it is safe to do so is not a man worthy of trust.

Trust may be complicated, too, by the recognition that not all betrayals are by traitors, not all lies told by liars. Concealment can be undertaken from motives that do not necessarily threaten trust. As Judith Shklar points out, there are some who "would have to betray themselves if they did not betray others."[78] She cites Joseph Conrad's short story, "The Secret Sharer," in which a young sea captain protects a murderer who on another ship had killed a disobedient crew member who was endangering its safety during a storm. The sea captain realizes that the man might easily have been himself. Indeed, he treats him almost as his double, a "secret sharer" in the moral stain of killing one so that all might be saved. A nicely ironic twist in the plot means that, in allowing the man time to escape, he thereby risks the lives of his crew and the safety of his ship – although he is fortunate and no disaster in fact ensues. His courage in remaining true to himself outweighs his responsibility to his crew. But would a captain who was less morally aware prove more worthy of trust? Baier's test leaves the answer unclear.

It is difficult, then, to isolate exactly what makes a quality sensitive to the risks of exposure. This is noticeably the case in political morality. Initially, Philoctetes trusts Neoptolemus because he is a fellow Greek, a young man of open disposition who offers a substantial hope of ending Philoctetes' banishment. But Neoptolemus has a concealed motive, knowledge of which would of course make clear to Philoctetes that this is not a relationship of genuine trust. Neoptolemus's trustworthiness fails because it cannot be expressed without contradiction, without revealing his true motives. But Neoptolemus is not a habitual liar. He is a morally decent individual who agrees to act as Odysseus's agent for what he considers a worthy political cause. Both his motivation and his conduct are mixed. Unlike many liars, he has moral qualms about deceiving Philoctetes. He does not lie to him in order, for example, to instill jealousy, or to keep him ignorant of his own good or to harm him.[79] Deception is not undertaken to transform good into evil or to make trust impossible. Neoptolemus considers that he can tell this one lie and remain morally un-

scathed. When he realizes the full extent of Philoctetes' dependence on him, this ceases to be true; his goodness enables his
trust to reassert itself and be reexamined. In *Troilus and
Cressida*, too, what is perceived is cloaked by the desires of the
percipient. Like Philoctetes, whose trust in Neoptolemus is
consonant with his wish to escape exile, Troilus's love for
Cressida gives him a powerful but not unambiguous motive
for trusting her. Does his trust in Cressida stand or fall by
reference to what he knows about her? Or is his trust internal
to his love? There are many problems in the idea that individuals can detach their willingness to trust from their character
and feelings for others in order to arrive at a neutral or impartial judgment of trustworthiness. Similar difficulties are present when the question of the moral decency of trust is raised in
Thérèse Raquin. Asked like Neoptolemus to show compassion
for someone whose disease has made him loathsome, Thérèse
is further required unnaturally to sacrifice her emotional life.
Why shouldn't she cultivate a "judicious untrustworthiness"?
Why should morality be sustainable only through the repression of the inner life? Is it possible for Thérèse to stand apart
from her self and calculate the consequences should she be
identified as an object of distrust?

A concentration on the origin of trust and the agency involved in it enables us to clarify both the value of what is
entrusted and the standpoints from which trusting takes
place. Both emphases are necessary if the depth of dirty
hands problems is to be fully appreciated. These qualities
arise from character, from the human capacity to make commitments and to live up to them when they conflict with
other moral values or virtues. Neoptolemus's decision to deceive takes its moral sense from his belief that the successful
achievement of a political aim will release him from guilt.
Philoctetes' strategic willingness to trust Neoptolemus derives from his overwhelming need to regain a world that, in
spite of its infidelities, does provide a common human habitation. Troilus in allowing his love to dictate his trust risks his
moral identity, risks the defeat of his sense of moral worth.
Thérèse betrays trust through emotional deprivation. Love

unsatisfied is displaced by lust, sexual indulgence traded on as a means of revenge, a mockery of respectability. The attachments and mental states in which trust is given, suspended, or breached extend the idea of a test for trust into difficult areas. If ignorance of another's motives and purposes is not a morally acceptable basis for private trust, then why should it be so in politics? Making it a definitional feature of what it means to entrust government agents with secrecy is not persuasive. We have deepened our sense of the relation between knowledge, ignorance, and trust by giving greater prominence to circumstance, character, and motivation, to the opening moves in specific political and moral narratives in which trust plays a significant part. Once agents have committed themselves to others, or to a course of action or the pursuit of particular goods that involves breaches of trust, then the danger of trust in both public and private contexts becomes more apparent. It is now time to explore the risks and rewards of trust.

Chapter 5

Risks and rewards

> We do not need to discuss cut-throats, poisoners, forgers of wills, thieves, and embezzlers of public moneys, who should be repressed not by lectures and discussions of philosophers, but by chains and prison walls; but let us study here the conduct of those who have the reputation of being honest men.
>
> Cicero, *De Officiis*

> No government should ever believe that it is always possible to follow safe policies. Rather, it should be realised that all courses of action involve risks: for it is in the nature of things that when one tries to avoid one danger another is always encountered.
>
> Machiavelli, *The Prince*

Trust involves a complex anticipation of benefits and hazards. It depends, as Luhmann rightly remarks, "not on inherent danger but on risk."[1] However, risks have no dependent existence, but are created through human commitments, actions, and decisions. That a course of action involves risk tells us nothing about its morality. Its presence does not determine the rightness or wrongness of an action. When, for example, Nancy in Dickens's *Oliver Twist* confides in Rose Maylie, she trusts the word of those who can save Oliver that her part in the affair will never be made public. She has to make this commitment if she is to save Oliver and protect Sikes, but in doing so the risk is greater than she thinks because she is in fact overheard. Trust is no longer an effective means of achieving a moral purpose, but a sign of vulnerability, which places Nancy in great danger. What is divulged is a plot to save a friend, but if it had been Fagin overheard talking, the subject might easily have been the disposal of stolen property or the corruption of an innocent: The risk lies in being overheard. In Nancy's case it is the truster who takes the risk. In different circumstances others may be put at risk or exposed to harm. As Nancy is well aware, without being exposed to risk her moral end cannot be achieved. To consider risk alone when reaching decisions is to subject conduct to an almost general paralysis. As Shelly Kagan comments, "there is absolutely *nothing* that I can do which does not carry *some* risk of harming others."[2] What gives Nancy's moral concern its significance is not only that she risks being harmed herself, but that she does so in the realization that her attempt to save Oliver and protect Sikes may not succeed. Risk is defined by Simone Weil as "an essential need of the soul."[3] Unlike fear, it does not destroy the capacity to act. In some contexts risk is an essential element, as in gambling where it is always possible for the dice to fall differently. In other contexts, individuals are prepared to face risk through love or a specific duty or obligation. Simone Weil's view of the connection between risk and fear bears comparison with Nietzsche – if risk is absent, courage is untested and the soul is left "without the slightest inner protection against fear."[4] This claim stands in sharp contrast to the Hobbesian idea that risk is a function of individuals who are "minimally trusting, minimally trustworthy adults who are equal in power."[5] In the sense in which Simone Weil uses it, risk does not only derive from the difficulty of matching action and consequence. It is not unique to the problem of reciprocity or of social cooperation between rational egoists, but arises in the way individuals show resolution in living up to their commitments and ideals. Moral action is performed as much in the shadow of internal weakness and irresolve as external hazard. Individuals risk morally failing themselves as well as selfishly reneging on agreements made with others.

The idea that there is an internal relation between trust, risk, and courage is remote from attempts to ground social cooperation in sanctions or mutual interests. For some this is a reason for locating trust not in moral character but in structural agreements that are self-regulating and reinforcing. Geoffrey Hawthorn writes: "I can trust my friends in so far as I trust myself. I can even be brought in principle to see the virtue in virtue. But I see no reason to believe that the reason to believe in it will, just *as* that reason, hold."[6] The belief that morality has an intrinsic value distinct from expediency may provide exactly the disguise traitors need. It is true, as Hawthorn comments, that "there can be treachery in a kiss . . . betrayal in an honourable mien,"[7] but the moral psychology of treason is more complex than the Judas model can allow. Honor in some acts of treachery is not an expedient shield, but a substantial feature of moral identity. In political morality, the good individual who acts badly for desirable political ends is not thereby a traitor. The claim that trust ad hominen is intrinsically less reliable than trust in structures of rules or the assessment of consequences needs to be treated with caution.

A medical researcher convinced of the value of a line of inquiry as a cure for cancer tells a deliberate lie in order to obtain the scarce funds needed to continue the work. Does this consequentialist justification make the researcher more or less trustworthy? Perhaps the contrast between individual character and beneficial states of affairs has been drawn too rigidly. For John Dunn, "even saints and heroes, whilst they may well be undeterred from fulfilling their duties at whatever costs to themselves, must submit to the discipline of other-regarding consequences."[8] But saints and heroes do not just pay attention to the ways others may be affected by their actions. They place others first through a degree of self-denial which is not always present when consequences are taken into account. It is, therefore, exactly *how* consequences are regarded by moral agents which determines the moral difference. Does the medical researcher see the lie as an exercise in instrumental rationality? Is it simply the most efficient means of securing support? Or is it told reluctantly, seen as a moral stain, a reason for blame? Utilitarian accounts of moral conflict have great difficulty capturing what is at issue here. A gap exists between motivation and consequence which, as Gilbert Harman comments, leaves utilitarianism remote from actual conduct: "People are not only motivated to maximise utility but also have other motives which they take to be morally respectable, in some cases even morally required, without being irrational, stupid, or uninformed."[9]

In relation to political morality, the weaknesses of what Harman calls the "critic centred"[10] nature of utilitarianism (both act and rule) are readily apparent. Hume, for example, accepts that it is necessary to "give a greater indulgence to a prince or minister, who deceives another; than to a private gentleman, who breaks his word of honour."[11] Public utility, which is the source of promise keeping in normal times, is also, according to Hume, a reason for promise breaking in times of emergency. He asks:

> Is it any crime, after a shipwreck, to seize whatever means or instrument of safety one can lay hold of, without regard to former limitations of property? Or if a city beseiged were perishing with hunger; can we imagine, that men will see any means of preservation before them, and lose their lives, from a scrupulous regard to what, in other situations, would be the rules of equity and justice?[12]

Further, in his *Essays* Hume argues explicitly that in specific political circumstances the rules of justice may be outweighed by utility:

> What governor of a town makes any scruple of burning the suburbs, when they facilitate the approaches of the enemy? Or what general abstains from plundering a neutral country, when the necessities of war require it, and he cannot otherwise subsist his army?[13]

John Stuart Mill, too, regards moral conflict as apparent rather than real. For Mill, Agamemnon's dilemma at Aulis is not one of right set against right, but "one of supposed religious duty which where it intervenes, takes away the conflict, by removing the sense of moral wrong from the sacrifice."[14] Mill's own example of moral conflict is that of "a people required by a powerful enemy under penalty of extermination to surrender some distinguished citizen, say the Carthaginians in the case of Hannibal,"[15] but this, too, turns out to be resolvable because "the morality of utility requires that the people should fight to the last rather than comply with the demand."[16] For Mill resistance to tyranny has an "indirect utility"[17] even when it fails because it makes "tyranny cost the tyrant something, and that is much better than letting him indulge it gratis."[18]

However, utilitarianism involves difficulties that significantly weaken its account of political morality in relation to trust. To the extent that it takes the production of beneficial states of affairs as its primary moral focus utilitarianism neglects those substantial moral issues that derive from agency and character and it leaves crucial aspects of trust relationships unexplained. Political agents may feel moral guilt even though the beneficial consequences of their actions have actually come about. Those who are subject to hard political decisions may remain distrustful even though they have not themselves been harmed by them. If political morality is construed solely as a technical exercise in instrumental logic, those who are subject to it risk being treated as expendable units in the calculation of the maximum good. Equally, utilitarian decision makers risk being corrupted themselves by the belief that a neutral, quasi-scientific evaluation of consequences is possible. Agents who act badly for the sake of desirable ends do so from a standpoint of character that is vital to an understanding of how they come to terms with themselves and with what they do. The claim made by Euripides' Hecuba that "numbers and cunning joined are irresistible"[19] may be challenged by locating the risks and rewards of trust in moral character, in how individuals display moral self-awareness in circumstances that demand hard political choices.

Public utility alone is not sufficient to ground public trust because it leaves the moral character of rulers dangerously unexplored and can demand from individual citizens a degree of moral sacrifice that is not defensible by reference to their individual utilities. It further leaves obscure the distinction between the just and the expedient, a distinction that suggests that in order to inspire public trust rulers require an acute sense of the moral limits on political conduct, even in cases where the gains of a given course of action are obvious. Cicero describes such a case in his discussion of the deserter. Pyrrus threatens Rome with a long and bloody war, but a deserter from his army reaches the Roman general, Fabricius, and offers to return and poison his commander. With the approval of the senate, Fabricius, however, refuses and returns the deserter to Pyrrus:

> If the mere show of expediency and the popular conception of it are all we want, this one deserter would have put an end to that wasting war and to a formidable foe of our supremacy; but it would have been a lasting shame and disgrace to us to have overcome not by valour but by crime the man with whom we had a contest for glory.[20]

Here the problem of trust is not open to solution by reference to the consequences of the proposed action because it is these which have been deliberately set aside. In Fabricius's argument consequences are not displaced by a more efficient scheme of defeating the enemy but by the moral feelings of shame and disgrace that are internal to his character. Trusting Fabricius is connected with what trusters already know of him and is not automatically weakened by his decision to keep his hands clean even though this means the continuation of the war and prolonging the risk to the lives of his fellow citizens. Thus, Fabricius's decision to put expediency aside endangers himself and others, but does not necessarily make him less worthy of trust.

The problem is compounded by the difficulty that the wrongs of political morality are not unquestionable wrongs "in the way that a surgeon who silently killed a patient in order to save the lives of four or five would be doing something unquestionably wrong."[21] Rights and wrongs, however, cannot be established by reference to consequences alone. Moral identity is relevant, too, because it is not only the sacrifice of the one patient that creates the moral difficulty but also the character of the surgeon who could commit such an act. Equally, Fabricius's decision not to authorize the poisoning of a military opponent is bound up with his character and with those values that link him to his enemy. If he had been at war with a tyrant, Fabricius might have decided differently. In this way the problem of trusting those who face hard moral and political choices is one of recognition. What is at issue is not the balance of argument between one set of consequences and another but the sensitivity of the trusted to conflicting moral imperatives.

We might consider, for example, the role of character in Thucydides' account of the Athenian debate about the launching of an expedition to Sicily.[22] Here trust, risk, and reward are related in a way that reveals character's problematic force. The rewards are clear and attractive – the Athenians will gain materially; they will extend their imperial power; a successful campaign will bring glory, in addition to employment and economic benefit; and their Spartan enemies may be discomforted. But there are great risks, too. As Nicias remarks at the start of his speech against the expedition, there are always human beings who are prepared "to risk what is theirs already for doubtful prospects in the future";[23] thinking this an unalterable feature of character, he appeals instead to prudence and rational self-interest. The Sicilian enterprise will imperil the empire: "This is no time for running risks or for grasping at a new empire before we have secured the one we have already."[24] Sicily is too remote from Athenian interests and obligations to be of any rational concern. There are no ties of kinship to inspire trust – the Egestaeans in Sicily who suggested the expedition "do not even speak our own language."[25] Even if the campaign proves successful, the Sicilians cannot be controlled. On the other hand, if it turns out a failure, it will strengthen Sparta's hand. In any case, an Athens weakened by plague and war is better advised to build up its internal defenses rather than involve itself with

> exiles who are begging for assistance and whose interest it is to tell lies and make us believe them, who have nothing to contribute themselves except speeches, who leave all the danger to others and, if they are successful, will not be properly grateful, while if they fail in any way they will involve their friends in their own ruin.[26]

Risks and rewards are finely balanced. Is it wise to mount an expensive and hazardous undertaking that is so heavily dependent on trust? Material gains are here matched against political risks; morality enters the equation only in the possibility that the Egestaeans may be lying. To this point Nicias's argument has been heavily consequentialist, but his personal attack on Alcibiades, who is in favor of the expedition, changes the tone and draws attention to the problem of trusting in character. Alcibiades is "the golden boy of Athens";[27] he is reckless and daring, whereas Nicias is cautious and moderate. Brilliant and dangerous, personally extravagant, capable of putting his own esteem before the good of the city, Alcibiades nevertheless offers the chance of success. Reward requires that he be trusted. It is noteworthy that in consequentialist terms the disagreement between Nicias and Alcibiades is difficult to resolve. Much hinges, therefore, on judgments of character. Alcibiades' rhetoric challenges the Athenians to remember how risk sharpens their political vigor and determination to succeed: "If everyone were to remain inactive . . . we should add very little to our empire and should be more likely to risk losing it altogether";[28] "the city will wear out of its own accord if it remains at rest, and its skill in everything will grow out of date; but in conflict it will constantly be gaining new experience and growing more used to defend itself not by speeches, but in action."[29]

Privately dissolute, ambitious, but possibly badly served by his enemies, Alcibiades nevertheless offers trusters a high chance of success. As Thucydides comments: "Although in a public capacity [Alcibiades'] conduct of the war was excellent, his way of life made him objectionable to everyone as a person; thus they entrusted their affairs to other hands, and before long ruined the city."[30] Public reward and political success can sometimes be put at risk by private lawlessness, although Thucydides' point is that had the Athenians continued to trust Alcibiades as a leader of the expedition the chances are it would have been successful and their trust in him rewarded; that is, the trusters changed their minds about Alcibiades' private conduct and public integrity – his trustworthiness – and thus suffered the consequences. On a later occasion Alcibiades betrays Athens to join Sparta, but his character remains the same: He appears to be incapable of changing or concealing his nature.

The antimony between reward and distrust in Thucydides' description of Alcibiades' encouragement of the Sicilian expedition derives much of its force from the fact that Alcibiades is recognized clearly as someone who is not to be privately trusted. Whereas the rewards of the project exist only as anticipation, vulnerable to misfortune of different kinds, Alcibiades' character *is* identifiable and known. His is not, however, a case of dirty hands: We must assume that for Alcibiades the dirty hands problem does not exist. Alcibiades may willingly act badly for political reasons but trusting him does not necessarily risk his continuing to act badly when good ends have been achieved. It does involve the risk that Alcibiades' character may hinder the achievement of a common political objective, and this is a hazard of dirty hands, too. The problems of recognition are most acute with regard to liars or deceivers, but they are also present in cases of active hypocrisy where virtue or goodness is simulated. Trusting others may be a hazardous undertaking where what is taken to be kindness or benevolence is actually self-interest or self-regard. Equally, individuals may be prevented by obsession, preoccupation, or weakness from trusting themselves to carry through a decision they have made. Thus,

Alcibiades' self-infatuation is open to discernment by others, while perhaps remaining opaque to himself.

Stressing trust as a problem of recognition brings out ambiguities unnoticed by utilitarianism, but at the same time the origins and nature of trust seem more socially equivocal: Does the exercise of this virtue derive from the truster or the trusted? In this respect, trust is logically but not substantively akin to the notion of prejudice. Christopher Ricks cites the *Oxford English Dictionary* definition of prejudice as a feeling that is "prior to or not based on actual experience."[31] But, as Ricks points out, difficulties arise about *whose* experience prejudice is supposed to be prior to, and there may be times, in some emergencies, for example, when individuals may not actually be in any position to make a judgment of their conduct, let alone an unprejudiced one. Ricks writes: "If I were naively strolling in Central Park at midnight, and there came towards me some tattooed and leathered people swinging baseball bats, to take to my heels would admittedly be an act of prejudice; it would be prior to and not based on actual experience since I have never seen any such people harm a fly."[32] The risks involved outweigh the possibility that some harmless event is taking place because, as Ricks comments, "it would not be much comfort to look up through one dying eye and to murmur, 'Well, at least I wasn't prejudiced.' "[33]

Recognition is a familiar and significant feature of trust. Friends are recognized as deserving a special faithfulness. Readiness to trust often depends on the discovery of a characteristic or attribute that is known to the truster, as when Philoctetes recognizes Neoptolemus as a fellow Greek. But there can be failure of perception, too. Guest trust may not see malevolence or greed, love may be blind to infidelity, loyalty to treachery, or commitment to betrayal. Trust may be disappointed through an unseen flaw in the trusted or by the reemergence of a weakness thought to have been controlled. A sudden discernment of a breach of trust, like Madame Raquin's terrible, mute recognition of Thérèse and Laurent as her son's murderers, so deracinates the spirit that we are reminded that trust is not just a useful tool of policy but expresses the deepest human feelings and needs. In this way, *what* is seen in the trusted plays a significant part in the risks and rewards of trust. Perception is not solely a matter of individual judgment: It can involve shared expectations. We do not normally expect children to be worldly or prudent, and although there are certainly social contexts in which these characteristics are forcibly encouraged, it is difficult to think of an upbringing like this as anything other than odd. Michael Slote brings this out well when he asks us to "imagine, for example, a schoolboy who takes out an insurance policy on his own life in order to protect the interests of his future wife (whoever if ever she may be) or one who saves half his allowance against the needs of his old age."[34] Additionally, the natural and unreflective candor of childhood trust, in which adults trust, too, is open to distortion and corruption, a process Orwell describes in *Nineteen Eighty-Four*. In the closed world of Oceania the political manipulation of language includes the language of childhood: "Hardly a week passed in which *The Times* did not carry a paragraph describing how some eavesdropping little sneak – 'child hero' was the phrase generally used – had overheard some compromising remark and denounced its parents to the Thought Police."[35] The "children" of Winston Smith's neighbors, the Parsons, are neither children nor adults – "all children nowadays were horrible."[36] Enthusiastic members of the spies, desperately keen to be taken to see the hanging of the Eurasian prisoners, obsessively concerned with rooting out the enemies of the state, the Parsons' "children" are portrayed as child-agents of the Party, their childhood traits manipulated and their trusting natures eroded so that they are no longer worthy of trust: "It was almost normal for people over thirty to be frightened of their own children."[37] A feature of Orwell's technique is his stress on the absence or distortion of a familiar attitude or a habitual response so as to make us more aware of the ways they ordinarily find a place in our lives. A world in which childhood trust can no longer be recognized as such is a world in which trust risks misplacement not simply by individual error, but through systematic distortion.

In *Nineteen Eighty-Four* the normal human capacity to recognize another as a stranger, a friend, a potential enemy, or a lover is absent. Winston is not willing to risk even a cautious and circumscribed trust in Julia until he receives her note, and then his perception changes completely and he begins to trust her. Both he and Julia later place themselves at O'Brien's mercy in the mistaken belief that he is leading an underground movement against the Party. The level of risk and reward depends on judgment and on the ability to identify another's character and motives. In moral situations where one value is risked for the sake of another, risk and reward depend crucially on *what* is recognized in the trusted. Isabella's dilemma in Shakespeare's *Measure for Measure* is this – Should her chastity be sacrificed for the sake of her brother's life? We notice that Isabella, so prudish about herself, is quite willing to deceive Angelo by substituting Marianna. And the situation is compounded by Isabella's distrust of Angelo, the man who forces her to confront it, so when he crudely promises her that her brother will not die "if you give me love,"[38] she responds "Ha! little honour to be much believed, And most pernicious purpose! Seeming, seeming!"[39] Vulnerability and powerlessness here create both the need for trust and the realization that her sacrifice might be in vain; trust, then, empty of reward. For Kierkegaard "the Good is one thing; the reward is another that may be present and may be absent for the time being, or until the very last."[40] Saving her brother's life does not constitute a reward for Isabella in any conventional sense because it is not a prize or a nonmoral gain. Actions may be performed *only* for their rewards, or sometimes action may be its *own* reward, but to Isabella her brother's life represents a more complex recompense. Wittgenstein argues that in its ethical sense the reward "must reside in the action itself,"[41] as distinct from any consequences that happen to flow from it. But there are significant areas of human life in which this distinction seems less clear-cut. Isabella is prepared to sacrifice her religious vows not for prudential gain but from a sisterly duty. The obligations of morality often clash with commitments inspired by politics, art, or love, which challenge the claim that morality has a necessary priority. In these predicaments individuals are faced by moral decisions that increase the risks of trust. Neoptolemus is trapped in such a dilemma: "O God, what shall I do? Deceitful twice, Twice false, whether I speak or hold my tongue."[42] Trust faces impending crisis in which it will be tested severely. Moral character is caught in a complex middle game in which reflection and the need to act set the boundaries of trust.

In the *Philoctetes* conflicts between stratagem, decency, and sincerity frame the risks and rewards that accompany human decisions. Consequentialist considerations are involved at specific points in the narrative, but they do not exhaust the issues of political morality that dominate the central concerns of the play. At first Odysseus's plan goes well and the ruse seems to offer great rewards. Philoctetes' refusal to be persuaded by the tale of the false merchant, in reality an agent sent by Odysseus to add urgency to the proceedings, simply increases his dependence on Neoptolemus by further encouraging his belief that Neoptolemus is worthy of trust. Their friendship seems to be confirmed when Philoctetes actually allows Neoptolemus to handle the bow: "And live to remember you are the only man / Thought worthy, for your goodness, so to do. It was for goodness I myself was given it."[43] This remark shows the measure of Neoptolemus's success in deceiving Philoctetes, who gives his trust and friendship almost without condition. All Neoptolemus now needs to do is to secure Philoctetes and the bow on board ship and his mission will have been accomplished. Neoptolemus has lied for political advantage; to achieve a justifiable political goal he has become a false friend. But the sight of Philoctetes in agony forces him to change his mind.

Once Neoptolemus sees the full misery of Philoctetes' illness and the horror of his abandonment, he begins to realize that deceit is no longer possible. Neoptolemus's nobility makes him increasingly sensitive to the moral obstacles that stand in the way of Odysseus's plan. He has been affected by the sincerity of Philoctetes' response to his own deceitful expressions of friendship and deeply moved by Philoctetes' regard for his own dead father, Achilles. Neoptolemus's feelings of decency are aroused, too, by Philoctetes' criticism of Odysseus's cynicism, so when Philoctetes gives him the bow, exhorting him not to hand it to his enemies, and then begs him not to leave, without extracting a formal promise from him, Neoptolemus's responses are those of a man who is starting to feel the first touch of moral reservation about his project. Neoptolemus is at this stage of his moral awareness quite able to agree not to give the bow to anyone else and not to leave Philoctetes because these fit with the requirements of both decency and policy. But the inconsistencies in this double motivation soon become apparent; Neoptolemus finds that his enterprise is at odds with his character and cannot be sustained. He has acquired the bow treacherously but his right to it derives only from his friendship with Philoctetes. Trust is not, therefore, simply a utilitarian instrument of policy because, although it has certainly enabled Neoptolemus to obtain the bow, it also prevents him from taking it. As Blundell comments: "The bow thus symbolises his relationship to Philoctetes: each needs the other, but their friendship cannot bear fruit unless it is based on authentic mutual trust and loyalty."[44]

When Philoctetes falls asleep, exhausted by the effects of his wound, Neoptolemus's dilemma is made yet more apparent. Why not take the bow and leave Philoctetes who is in any case helpless? Neoptolemus's response to the chorus who suggests this course of action shows how far his moral self-awareness has deepened. (And Neoptolemus also realizes that they need to have Philoctetes with them as well the bow.) "He does not hear us, certain; and we have got his bow; / But that's no use to us, if we sail off without him. / The victory must be his; the god said we must bring him. / How shall we look, our task half done, and that by fraud?"[45] It is a significant moment. Neoptolemus now "knows that one method of attempting his task is useless. To this knowledge his own reawakened decency has brought him."[46]

When Philoctetes wakes he finds Neoptolemus in a state of moral bewilderment. Philoctetes's persistent entreaties, his wretchedness, vulnerability, and powerlessness are now recognized by Neoptolemus as having a genuine claim on him – it is now no longer possible for him to treat Philoctetes as Odysseus wishes as simply a means to an end. The virtues that Philoctetes admires in him – nobility and piety – are now incompatible with his commitment to Odysseus. He realizes that the methods he has employed for political ends are not neutral but subject to moral scrutiny and reflection. Neoptolemus cannot disguise his inner struggle from Philoctetes who innocently believes that it is his wound that has caused Neoptolemus offense, but Neoptolemus corrects him: "The offence is here! A man betraying himself / To do such deeds as one not of his nature!"[47] Neoptolemus's concern does not now conceal a hidden motive and is therefore transparent and authentic. What remains problematic, however, is how he can act on it. He decides to tell Philoctetes the truth that they are en route to Troy. When this proves insufficient, he tries to persuade Philoctetes with an appeal to justice and expediency; he asks for forgiveness when he refuses to return the bow: "I cannot do that. I must obey my masters / For duty's sake and for my own."[48]

For C. M. Bowra "the trouble with lying is that in the end it makes the liar feel ashamed."[49] Neoptolemus's revelation that they are going to Troy comes to Philoctetes as a terrible blow, which shatters his faith in Neoptolemus and destroys his confidence in his capacity to recognize another as worthy of trust: It has ruined his world. In a long and painful speech, Philoctetes laments his betrayal and ruin; he has been twice deceived and without the bow death is his only future: "This is my reward for trusting one who seemed / Incapable of guile."[50] In his despair Philoctetes appeals to Neoptolemus's sense of the disgrace involved in what he has done – "Can you face me unashamed, your suppliant / Who crawled to you for pity?"[51] – and he asks for the return of the bow, now convinced that he is surrounded by treachery and more determined than ever not to go to Troy:

> I know there is no wickedness in you.
> The part you have come here to play was taught you,
> I think, by wicked men. Leave it to them.
> Give me my weapon, and go.[52]

Odysseus's intervention, calling Neoptolemus a traitor when he is about to return the bow, is significant and ironic because it is Odysseus's deviousness and cunning that are responsible for Philoctetes' distrust. Neoptolemus's honest attempt to avoid dishonor by not lying to Philoctetes a second time simply furthers his suspicion and makes him all the more convinced that Neoptolemus is an agent of Odysseus. Once deceit has been used, it becomes increasingly difficult to recognize a truth for what it is. Philoctetes sees that Neoptolemus is not wicked by nature, but this is not in itself sufficient to inspire trust. Odysseus's trickery has left Philoctetes more rather than less obstinate in his refusal to go to Troy. Neoptolemus's unwillingness to perpetuate the deceit has relocated the risks and rewards of trust. To keep the bow without Philoctetes will not help the Greeks take Troy and will also commit the serious crime of leaving him defenseless for no important overriding reason. On the other hand, to return it risks endangering Odysseus. At this stage in the play, then, Philoctetes is left a prisoner of Odysseus, the man he most despises, and a victim of political morality. He now sees the true relationship between Odysseus and Neoptolemus, that "it was [Odysseus's] vile mind that lurked behind the loophole and schooled [Neoptolemus's] unwilling innocence to this proficiency in guile."[53] The Greeks, he complains, were responsible for his terrible banishment. Why, then, should he help them – when "every breath of life I draw is agony and torment, my sufferings your sport"?[54]

> And now, what do you want of me? Why do you seize me and carry me away? I am nothing, long dead to you. God's

plagues upon you, am I not still the poisonous infected wretch I was? What of your sacrifices to the blessed gods, if I am of your crew? What of the pollution of your drink-offerings? Such was the pretext on which you banished me; does it not still hold good? Go to your miserable death, as surely as you will, for what you did to me, if there is any justice in heaven.[55]

The conflict between Philoctetes and Odysseus is a genuine moral conflict, each convinced of the rectitude of his own position, the one certain that justice requires that those responsible for his long exile are punished, the other sure that the general advantage outweighs a single transgression. But Philoctetes is left alone by Odysseus in a dreadful repetition of his first banishment: "You're welcome to the length and breadth of Lemnos; / And we must go. Since you refuse the honour / Your treasure should have brought you, let it be mine."[56] Further attempts at a settlement of the issue are made by the sailors whom Neoptolemus out of pity instructs to remain and who try to persuade Philoctetes that it is his choice that has determined his fate. Thus, the decision to harm his enemies is his alone; it causes harm to all Greeks and is therefore unjust. The chorus, too, appeals to Philoctetes on behalf of the gods and, as his friends, to acknowledge in goodwill his own freedom of choice and the legitimate claims of Odysseus and Neoptolemus. But Philoctetes has "excellent reasons to distrust them all."[57] His bow has "a new master, master of deceit . . . Whose shamelessness / A thousand times, O God, / Has here tormented me!"[58] Philoctetes wishes nothing more than to die, his resolution intact, leaving the Greeks unsatisfied in their quest for victory at Troy.

Neoptolemus's self-awareness has developed to the point where he must distance himself from political morality. To do this he has first to restore the bow to Philoctetes, even though this brings him into conflict with Odysseus and denies the Greeks the opportunity of glory. Shame requires the rectification of the wrong, and so when Odysseus asks why he has returned, Neoptolemus's reply is immediate – "to undo the wrong I have already done."[59] In his obedience to Odysseus's orders, Neoptolemus considers he has "used base treachery against a fellow-creature."[60] He needs to show remorse, which means that authority, loyalty, and expediency must be put aside even though legitimate political aims are lost thereby and Odysseus is put at risk. In their dispute Odysseus and Neoptolemus not only disagree about the nature of justice but also about the place of trust as a moral value. For Odysseus it is a device to be used realistically as success demands. Neoptolemus, on the other hand, sees gradually that it is an essential feature of justice and as such has priority over other considerations. Nothing of value can be gained through betrayal; the wisdom in Odysseus's view of political morality is illusory. Neoptolemus underlines this point in reminding Odysseus that neither force nor cunning equals wisdom and justice:

N.   The wise Odysseus is talking like a fool.
O.   You're not only talking but acting like a fool.
N.   Justice is sometimes better than wisdom.
O.   Justice! To throw away what I have helped you to win?[61]

When Neoptolemus returns the bow, he resolves his dilemma. Although moral character displaces political ambition, Neoptolemus's choice supports Philoctetes' values but not necessarily the man himself. As Blundell shows,[62] if his choice is understood as between Philoctetes and Odysseus considered solely as friends, Neoptolemus's dilemma would have been insoluble. Help to the one would necessarily mean harm to the other. Instead, he appeals to a standard of justice that recognizes the merits of Philoctetes' case *and* allows him to defend Odysseus against the charge of cowardice and protect him when Philoctetes tries to use his newly regained bow against him. Neoptolemus's response is a moral rebuff and shows his moral authority – "to have done it would have been unworthy of yourself or me."[63] How then is Neoptolemus to regain Philoctetes' trust?

There is courage in Neoptolemus's decisions first to refrain from lying again to Philoctetes and second to return the bow to him. Both reveal his newly discovered and hard won certainty concerning the nature of moral value. In *Troilus and Cressida* no such unconditionality exists. The recognition of value is a dangerous quicksand, impossible to chart. The development of the play's middle ground begins with the agreement to exchange Antenor and Cressida, which has been organized by Calchas, the traitor, the man devoid of "time, acquaintance, custom, and condition."[64] This bargain coexists ironically with Pandarus's "a bargain made"[65] between the two lovers in the previous scene, and it anticipates the later disastrous collapse of Troilus's faith. Calchas, who describes himself as without attribute, invites reflection on identity and temporality – the two subjects that dominate the play's central debate. Shakespeare portrays human action against a background of uncertainty first in a sustained reflection on the relation between time and action. What makes events turn out as human beings wish? Human reputation and artifact, the images of Cressida and Troy, are both vulnerable to changes brought about by time, a process portrayed by Shakespeare as mainly one of disintegration and destruction. There are, of course, saving imperatives derived from patience, the belief that too early success will bring eventual failure, and from perseverance, the certainty that the glory won through the exercise of the competitive values will be remembered and thus keep time at bay. Is chance in the play a matter of external fortune or internal character? Clearly, it is luck that Diomed acts as guardian to Cressida in the exchange with Antenor, but is it *just* a fortunate perception that enables Ulysses to see straight through Cressida when she arrives at the Greek camp? Ulysses' famous speech (III iii), like his scorn for Achilles, is a rhetorical ploy to force Achilles to recognize what he has become. Only if he can be made to see through the pride that has becalmed him will he be of any military use to the Greeks. Ulysses tries to show him that time is arbitrary, destroying fame and mediocrity alike, bestowing reputation irrespective of worth; only through constant action can he keep the world's attention – "perseverance, dear my lord, / Keeps honour bright: to have done, is to hang / Quite out of fashion, like a rusty mail / In monumental mockery."[66] Ulysses's advice to "take the instant way"[67] reflects his belief that only utilitarian strategies provide security when time allows almost anything to happen, almost any prize to be attached to any quality, and when human worth seems self-authenticating and human beings "label themselves."[68]

In *Troilus and Cressida* human action already rendered insecure by the inconstancy of time is further weakened by division between identity and attribute. What are the grounds of belief? What provides a basis for trust? Recognition goes awry in both simple and complex cases. Individuals are mistaken or deliberately refuse to recognize one another. In Achilles pride and identity are crucially connected. Pride distorts his judgment and self-knowledge, preventing him from distinguishing between what is of genuine value and what is not. Agamemnon remarks to Ajax: "Your mind is the clearer, Ajax, and your virtues the fairer. He that is proud eats up himself: pride is his own glass, his own trumpet, his own chronicle; and whatever praises itself but in the deed, devours the deed in the praise."[69] For the characters in this play trust is almost wholly a problem of recognition because its exercise depends on an alert identification of attribute and reputation. Attribute is, as Kenneth Palmer points out, "a dangerous term"[70] because it refers not only to those qualities in individuals which others observe and use as a basis for judging character, moral worth, and trustworthiness, but also to their reputations. As Achilles sees it, "And not a man, for being simply man, / Hath any honour, but honour for those honours / That are without him, as places, riches, and favour, / Prizes of accident as oft as merit";[71] thus, to move from judging others in terms of their attributes to judging them in terms of their reputations is "to have moved from questions of identity to those of value and opinion";[72] in this narrow space between attribute and reputation questions of trust problematically arise.

Does Achilles know who he is? The rhetorical tricks of

Ulysses are intended to bring him to such self-awareness, but this turns out to be impossible until the death of Patroclus makes a genuine impact on him. Thus, knowing oneself is bound up with knowledge of others, and this knowledge is to pose a profound dilemma for Troilus. His recognition of Cressida's infidelity is not simply a newly discovered awareness of what others are capable of, but directly challenges the knowledge on which his own identity is based, and this places him on the edge of despair, in existential doubt. Distrust and treason frame Troilus's initial confidence in his own perceptions: The transfer of Cressida to the Greek camp has been arranged by Calchas, a traitor. At this stage, however, Troilus cannot know that Cressida will prove faithless. The news that she must be exchanged for Antenor is received by Troilus as a "hateful truth"[73] and Cressida herself makes fidelity a matter of will in her determination to announce to the world:

> Make Cressida's name the very crown of falsehood
> If ever she leave Troilus! Time, force, and death,
> Do to this body what extremes you can;
> But the strong base and building of my love
> Is the very centre of the earth,
> Drawing all things to it.[74]

What Ulysses terms the "mystery in the soul of state" now crudely requires that Troilus and Cressida are parted. Troilus's realization that it is a political truth that brooks no argument, that "rudely beguiles our lips / Of all rejoindure, forcibly prevents / Our locked embrasures, strangles our dear vows / Even in the birth of our own labouring breath"[75] gives their love urgency, so increasing the risks of trust. Cressida's "a woeful Cressid 'mongst the merry Greeks!"[76] hints at erotic reward and prompts Troilus's "be thou but true of heart"[77] and the exchange of tokens of mutual faithfulness. Troilus is aware of the changing character of love over time but not of the possibility of real betrayal. The teasing nature of Cressida's responses during their parting does not alert him to risk. Their love may be a victim of political morality, but to Troilus it remains internally complete and secure and for him this must be so. In Ulysses' world deceit, cunning, craft, and guile reign, engaged in constant renewal in the effort to keep political and temporal uncertainties at bay. For Troilus, on the other hand, trust and love are intrinsic to his being. They ingrain his sense of identity:

> . . . it is my vice, my fault:
> While others fish with craft for great opinion,
> I with great truth catch mere simplicity;
> Whilst some with cunning guild their copper crowns,
> With trust and plainness I do wear mine bare.
> Fear not my truth; the moral of my unit
> Is plain, and true; there's all the reach of it.[78]

Cressida's arrival at the Greek camp is elaborately staged and culminates in the exaggerated kissing ritual in which all take part, except Ulysses who, in snubbing Cressida, manages to insult Menelaus and show Cressida for a whore: "Her foot speaks; her wanton spirits look out / At every joint and motive of her body . . . wide unclasp the tables of their thoughts . . . set them down / For sluttish spoils of opportunity / And daughters of the game."[79] The formal entry of the Trojans shifts the focus from private to public concerns, places the impending duel at the center of events, and leads to the physical confrontation between Achilles and Hector in which risks and rewards have a more direct presence. Achilles' pride in his martial ability and disdain for his opponent make him ask brutally "in which part of his body shall I destroy him? whether there, or there, or there? / That I may give the local wound a name, / And make distinct the very breach whereout / Hector's great spirit flew."[80] Goodness and civility are seriously at issue here, but trust is not. What draws trust together with the problem of recognition is the conversation between Ulysses and Troilus, who remain as the others leave to prepare for the impending fight. Ulysses, ever willing to make mischief out of another's vulnerability, informs Troilus that Diomed "neither looks upon the heaven nor earth, / But gives all gaze and bent of amorous view / On the fair Cressid."[81] His mock innocent question, "this Cressida in Troy? / Had she no lover there / That wails her absence?"[82] hints at lechery and betrayal without needing to name Troilus directly as the man betrayed. The repetitive response – "She was belov'd, she lov'd; she is, and doth"[83] – is all Troilus can manage, given his love, his nature, and the circumstances. He is alarmed and anxious, and at this point unaware that later he will actually witness Cressida's infidelity.

Ulysses puts infidelity into words. Troilus hears but does not believe or even fully understand that it can be Troilus who is betrayed. What is open to damage from a broken promise is not a legal contract or a business agreement but sexual love. It is often the case that desire bears a less than straightforward relation to affection. That love makes its object seem unique is a significant and troublesome aspect of its power, but this does not arise exclusively from desire. For J. L. Stocks, desire is "essentially transferable or vagrant as between individuals of the appropriate kind, and its valuations are necessarily relative."[84] By contrast, affection individuates, manifesting the intrinsic "delight in contemplating the characteristic motions of the beloved object, the care for it, the absorption in the life of the lover."[85] Trust in human attachments of devotion or love is not an instrumental policy that is merely useful to the truster but is essential to the feelings involved. If this is true, we have returned to an earlier question: Is the trust in the truster, the value in the valuer? Troilus in love with Cressida is not the Troilus who had argued so vehemently with Hector that "what is aught but as tis valued."[86] In love with Cressida he thinks he has recognized an object of intrinsic value, something that is "precious of itself":[87] She is worthy of trust. Trust is now inherent in the way Troilus sees, and because this is so, it is not *external* to his character in the way that it is to Ulysses. Does this establish a boundary between love and politics? Trust is a feature of Troilus's inner life and so he cannot stand apart from it, testing its strengths and weaknesses as an instrument of policy. To Ulysses a failure of trust signifies an unsuccessful move in the game. To Troilus it marks not an error of policy but a fundamentally flawed vision. Transgression, therefore, is not just a challenge to contractual integrity, undesirable because of its disutility, but an assault on being. When Philoctetes interprets Neoptolemus's keeping the bow as treachery, it is not simply because the bow rightly belongs to him that he is so completely distraught. Similarly, when Troilus observes Cressida's infidelity, what shatters him is not simply the fact that she has broken a promise. The crucial question then becomes, Is the transgression in the truster? Hegel's view of love as a necessarily unstable and insecure attachment places a premium on trust:

> The first moment in love is that I do not wish to be a self-subsistent and independent person and that, if I were, then I would feel defective and incomplete. The second moment is that I find myself in another person, that I count for something in the other, while the other in turn comes to count for something in me. Love, therefore, is the most tremendous contradiction."[88]

In Kant the vagaries of love receive greater emphasis; as a feeling it is almost idiosyncratic in origin and object. Infidelity is construed by Kant from the universal point of view; as such, it is a transgression because it breaches the moral rights of the transgressed, which should be protected and reasserted. The fault in Kant's terms lies squarely with the transgressor, but he is aware that human affections, as opposed to desires, are not easily open to ethical command – we cannot will to love our neighbor or do so as a result of rational argument or persuasion. Nevertheless, as rational beings we can protect ourselves against infidelity by developing institutional structures of agreed reciprocal rights and duties. Marriage in Kant's view is a contractual relation that is freely and equally entered upon, even if the rights and duties are not equally distributed.[89] Kant is conscious of the contingencies of character and circumstance that make praise and blame difficult when human emotions are at stake, but he insists that these are still to be understood in terms of the sharp distinction between reason and desire that grounds his ethical philosophy. Thus, rationality gives rise in human attachments to rights and duties mutually acknowledged by autonomous beings, whereas desire reflects an animal sexuality that, Kant thinks, brings humanity "closer to the animal kingdom than any other of its properties."[90]

Lovers in Kant's understanding possess each other as property is possessed, including property rights over each other's genitalia. The implausibilities in Kant's discussion of the erotic no doubt derive from dualisms deeply ingrained in his metaphysics and they appear in his discussion of the crimes of sexual and military honor – infanticide by the mother of an illegitimate child, whose arrival is, Kant states, as if it has "found its way into the commonwealth by stealth, so to speak, like contraband goods,"[91] and an officer who kills an opponent in a duel, one who "risks losing his own life in order to prove his martial courage."[92] Kant's solution is to retain the death penalty for these crimes in accordance with "the categorical imperative of penal justice" even though "public justice as dispensed by the state is *injustice* in the eyes of the people."[93] Both good and evil, however, seem too powerful for rewards and punishments to be administered with complete justice. Lieut D'Hubert in Conrad's *The Duel* – "a cool head, a warm heart, open as the day. Always correct in his behaviour. One had to trust him,"[94] – regularly risks his life after being forced into a series of duels by a fellow officer who believes himself to have been insulted. Then under no obligation, need, or want, he is able to say of his opponent who has taunted him, made his life a misery – "we can't let him starve. He has lost his pension and he is utterly incapable of doing anything in the world for himself. We must take care of him secretly, to the end of his days."[95] Kant's advice to Maria von Herbert, too, reveals his view that love, though distant from reward, is subordinate to rational morality.[96] She has lied to a new lover about an earlier relationship, but when she eventually discloses this, love weakens. For Kant, concealment in love is understandable, but his main concern is that she shows true repentance for having lied rather than receive the reward of peace of mind.

The tension in Kant's liberalism between public rationality and private feeling is readily apparent. In Zola's *Thérèse Raquin*, we approach a landscape of betrayal that is recognizably modern. Here trust is secular, unrepressed passion now ruthless in its demands, sexuality at odds with institutional constraints, and public and private valuations in disarray. Risk and reward, aspiration and frustration, are here at play in the context of bourgeois valuations. The house as a private sanctuary is breached by infidelity; the violation of Camille's trust is compounded by his illness, dependence, and powerlessness. Laurent exploits rituals of guest privilege as a disguise; his friendship with Camille he uses as a shield to conceal true motives. In the early stages of their adultery Thérèse and Laurent assess risk and reward in terms dictated by their passion. Prudence is subsidiary to desire, their affrontery and recklessness governed only by the fear of disclosure. Zola portrays Laurent's sexual nature as hedonistic, complicated not by duty but the utilitarian need to balance the strengths and weaknesses of one feeling against those of another; the language of mechanistic psychology is not accidental – Laurent's "fears and misgivings could not stand up to his desires,"[97] his "passion had not yet stifled his peasant caution."[98] Motivation is here an exercise in felicific calculation; sexual physiognomy is described scientifically, almost as a nineteenth-century case study in criminology. By contrast, Thérèse has a more complex state of mind. To herself she represents her situation as that of a natural spirit stunted by society. What repels her about Camille, therefore, is not his illness, but his unnatural invalidism; his treatment has *perpetuated* his disease. Conscious, however, that she is "doing wrong,"[99] Thérèse locates her hypocrisy in her upbringing. What has turned her into a liar is a refinement that is contrary to her nature, so her adultery arises from need frustrated by convention and is not within the remit of responsibility. However, both role playing and cruelty require a degree of detachment, of independent determination. Laurent's deceit means that now he must perform the part of Camille's friend:

> Never before had he enjoyed such gratification of his appetites . . . he felt neither anger nor remorse as he talked to Camille in the language of intimate friendship. He did not even watch his words and gestures, so certain was he of his own prudence and self-control, for the selfishness with which he enjoyed his bliss saved him from making any slip.[100]

The dominant sanction in Laurent's behavior is fear of discovery. Moral concern for Camille or Madame Raquin is absent, and he thinks only that he is "acting as anybody else would have done in his position, namely as a poor and hungry man."[101] It is impossible for us to ignore Thérèse's cruelty – "she derived a bitter enjoyment from deceiving Camille and Madame Raquin"[102] – and her persistent humiliation of them is a notable feature of her adultery.

In *Thérèse Raquin* faithlessness derives from desire. It is not a function of the weaknesses that some claim are inherent in the very idea of marital promising – that love cannot logically be promised or that a temporally unrestricted commitment is actually inconsistent with changes in character.[103] Public confidence – "You would have thought it was a gathering of old friends who knew the very secrets of each others' hearts and who confidently entrusted themselves to the good faith of their friendship"[104] – protects a private, undisclosed opposition; adultery is an opportunity for deceit and cruelty that changes the adulterers and places their wrongdoing on the edge of evil. Laurent's plan to murder Camille originates in necessity. Passion ruthlessly demands the removal of obstacles that stand in its way; Laurent's work threatens to interfere – but for him "this woman was a necessity of life, like food and drink,"[105] and the risks that they will be discovered increase. So "in the frenzy of his adultery he had begun to entertain the thought of murder";[106] he had "put this man's death into words."[107] Laurent's way of justifying the crime to himself reflects his character. Both material interest and personal advantage point to Camille's murder. Rewards do outweigh risks. What Zola calls Laurent's "brutal peasant logic"[108] tells him that murder is less risky than kidnap or any other way of achieving his ends, as long as the crime remains undetected. No moral scruple or reservation interrupts these crude reflections. Risk and reward are calculated entirely in terms of personal advantage. Tony Tanner remarks on the tensions signified by the title of George Eliot's *The Mill on the Floss*: "tensions between the obligations of property and the importunities of passion; between familial and social bonds and ties and unanticipated and unpatterned private promptings of desire; between culture, law and nature; ultimately between life and death."[109]

Eliot's novel, as Tanner says, "begins and ends with an embrace in the river."[110] In Zola, it is the Seine that sets the scene for Camille's final embrace, in a staged boating accident in which Thérèse and Laurent brutally drown him. Camille's death is publicly believed to be an accident. Laurent is safe; he has committed a crime and avoided retribution; as Zola puts it, "he was free of his crime. He had killed Camille. The matter had been closed and no more would be heard of it."[111] Laurent's need to know that Camille's body has been discovered causes him little anxiety; he does not recognize his obsessive visits to the morgue as a sign of dangers to come. Indeed, when he does finally see Camille's putrefying corpse, his only reaction is that his worries are at an end. He seems now to be at peace: "From now on Laurent was at peace, and joyfully threw himself into the task of forgetting his crime and the annoying and painful scenes which had followed."[112] In murder, as Hegel remarks, "it is not a piece of flesh, as something isolated, which is injured, but life itself";[113] such a crime requires public rectification. While Camille's murder passes unrecognized by the community, it proves less easy for Laurent to forget. Our attention is drawn, therefore, to the inner life, to how Laurent and Thérèse, murderer and accomplice, recognize their guilt. This perception is a necessary condition of remorse, of shame, of ethical punishment and forgiveness.

The utilitarian stress on consequentialist criteria in deciding whether it is justifiable to harm the few to protect the many results in a highly abstract moral philosophy usually illustrated by thinly defined examples. However, moral dilemmas, conflicts between morality, political urgencies, and sexual desires invite reflection on the inner life and how its relation to the public world might be explored in terms of concealment, transparency, or transgression. The consciousness of the agent here embraces wrongdoing in the name of politics or love. From the utilitarian point of view the risks and rewards involved in such situations are external to character in the way that the courage of mountaineers, for example, lies in their willingness to risk injury and possible death in the face of external hazards. By contrast, what is risked in dirty hands cases is the possibility that courage in the fulfillment of good ends may be transferred to the satisfaction of bad ones, and that actions conditionally justifiable in one set of circumstances may be unconditionally excused in others. How agents understand themselves in these circumstances bears significantly on a public moral sense in related ways. As Simone Weil argues, attachment to the moral end in question must be such as to limit the wrongdoing its name can justify. She writes:

> It is quite possible for one to become a double-acting secret service agent out of patriotism, in order the better to serve one's country by deceiving the enemy. But if the efforts expended in this form of activity are in excess of the energy supplied by the patriotic motive, and if one later on acquires a taste for this form of activity for its own sake, there comes a time almost inevitably when one no longer knows oneself whom one is serving and whom one is deceiving, when one is ready to serve or to deceive anybody.[114]

Further, trust in those who may have to act badly on our behalf is related to the feelings they reveal in taking such decisions. Peter Winch refers to a play that has as its theme "the forced repatriation of a group of Russian prisoners of war in British hands in consequence of a political deal between the British and Soviet governments."[115] He is concerned with the portrayal of the moral feelings of the soldiers involved in the repatriation: "The commandant's disgust might be expressed in the judgement that he has done something squalid in betraying these human beings who trusted him."[116] Do moral repugnance and self-disgust rescue trust? This would require that agents not only look forward to the consequences of their actions but reflect morally on what they have done. So the self-reflective values – remorse and shame – will play a part in the way a community restores a moral balance that has been disturbed; they will have an important place in the way a community sustains trust. Neoptolemus in returning the bow redeems himself in relation to Philoctetes, but this necessarily means that the oracle cannot now be fulfilled. Without the bow Troy will not be defeated. How then can Neoptolemus redeem himself to politics? Troilus's commitment to Cressida is made in ignorance of real betrayal. How are we to understand the political transformation that he then undergoes as a result of his realization of this? In a secular and less determined context, in *Thérèse Raquin*, how is it possible for the moral community to survive as long as serious transgression remains unrecognized and therefore unresolved?

Chapter 6

Forgetting and forgiveness

What is it, fundamentally, that allows us to recognise *who has turned out well?* . . . he honours by *choosing,* by *admitting,* by *trusting* . . . He believes neither in "misfortune" nor in "guilt": he comes to terms with himself, with others; he knows how to *forget* – he is strong enough; hence everything *must* turn out for his best.

Friedrich Nietzsche, Ecce Homo

Without being forgiven, released from the consequences of what we have done, our capacity to act would, as it were, be confined to one single deed from which we could never recover; we would remain the victims of its consequences forever, not unlike the sorcerer's apprentice who lacked the magic formula to break the spell.

Hannah Arendt, The Human Condition

Raven, the contract killer in Graham Greene's *A Gun for Sale,* associates distrust with solipsism and despair – "there was no one outside your own brain whom you could trust: not a doctor, not a priest, not a woman."[1] Greene's choice of subjects is not accidental. Medicine, religion, and love do seem to offer distinctive sources of hope because trustworthiness is essential to their nature. Without faithfulness these human activities would not be what they are. Betrayal in these contexts, therefore, is especially destructive of trust, and the moral balance is correspondingly more difficult to restore. Political disloyalties, too, undermine a communal trust. When these appear as crime or corruption, public rectification in the form of legal proceedings such as indictment or impeachment is appropriate, but in political morality the issues are more

ambiguous and the process of moral restoration more difficult. Of course, political morality is not alone in this respect.
Moral conduct, too, involves retrospective judgments in
which individuals elaborate their past actions to themselves
and to others. Such judgments depend upon recognition, on
the identification of conduct as worthy of praise or blame, and
they have a significant public connotation. How moral and
political decisions are remembered or forgotten matters to a
society because it is through such a process of self-reflection
that trust is secured and renewed.

We might change the focus here slightly to look at institutional checks on dirty hands, with the object of asking if dirty
hands might be constrained by these formal means. In its
institutional form retrospective limitation of dirty hands decisions is perhaps most acute and most necessary in cases
where publicity would defeat the purpose; secrecy and concealment are, therefore, essential if the policy is to succeed. If
this is so, dirty hands will persist (which is not to say that
there is any necessary connection between secrecy and dirty
hands as such). Here, as Dennis Thompson comments, "Officials must do wrong in order to do right, and they cannot
claim that citizens endorse what they do because citizens
cannot know what they do."[2]

Thompson offers the methods of retrospective review, generalization, and mediation as ways of "reconciling secrecy
with democracy."[3] If these are successful, dirty hands are
dispelled. If not, then the choice is between dirty hands and
democracy. The idea of citizens later reviewing a policy that
at the time they did not know about is highly problematic not
least because when the opportunity for consideration eventually arrives harm may have already been inflicted. As Thompson points out, concealed political decisions not only may
involve direct injury, even death, to individuals, or changes
of government in other states, but also indirect consequences
in the form of commitments which citizens may be forced to
continue even though they would not have approved them
originally. Further, a retrospective review of a decision may
be too late to be of any real political significance, particularly

if concealment persists long after the need for it has expired. For Thompson governments should conceal things only for the achievement of specific ends, and when these either succeed or fail, the "license to deceive expires."[4]

Of course, the major difficulty of retrospection as a method of limiting dirty hands is that it seems empty of political effect, as Thompson expresses it: "For many decisions, especially those that cause major irreversible changes, judgement after the fact often leaves citizens with the opportunity to express regrets, not with a chance to influence events."[5] Although Thompson's reference to regret is instructive, it does not sufficiently expose the difficulties involved here. Even if a policy that necessarily involves secrecy is later justified retrospectively, this means not that dirty hands have been abolished but only that they have been transferred. Democratic accountability does not expunge guilt but redirects it to a collectivity, so inviting us to ask how collectivities can be blamed. We need to raise further questions, too, about what distinguishes regret from shame and remorse. These are not moral refinements of interest only to the individual who experiences them, but feelings that have a significant public role in the way a community comes to terms with actions that have been performed on its behalf.

Thompson's second mode of accountability in dirty hands cases concerns generalization, according to which the general policy involving concealment can be publicly discussed beforehand and rules governing conduct agreed to without limiting either the freedom of officeholders actually to make decisions or their practical effectiveness in applying policy in contingent circumstances. But, as Thompson himself points out, generalization can only cover relatively straightforward cases in which "the target of enforcement is not critical";[6] further, in, for example, the use of unmarked police cars to detect speeding or drunken-driving infringements, the offenses involved can be agreed to in advance and stated with a considerable degree of objectivity. In political morality, however, the identification of both offender and offense is much more hazardous, and even if a particular end is agreed to, it does not follow that citizens will permit governments to employ any means for its achievement. The uncertainties to which politics is unavoidably subject make it difficult to circumscribe political decisions by a moral framework agreed to in advance. This means for Thompson that "officials will dirty their hands on their own, and citizens will not be able to call them to account, except after the fact."[7]

Mediation is the attempt to combine political effectiveness with moral accountability. Policy is made subject to the oversight of legislators acting as "surrogates for citizens,"[8] and political debate on dirty hands issues is thereby made semi-public. As the institutional embodiment of a Kantian publicity requirement, mediation suffers from the instability inevitably involved in shifting from a criterion of moral judgment that determines the minimum conditions of moral discourse to its expression in substantive moral and political debate. Thus, while Kant's publicity requirement is intended to preclude this, actual legislative scrutiny of dirty hands cases may be affected by considerations of interest and consequential political advantage. As Thompson tellingly recounts, speaking about congressional examination of CIA activity in Chile, trust between committee and agency may collapse to the point where the agent "did not trust the members of the committee to keep the secrets they asked him to reveal."[9] The indirect consequences of disclosure may be so harmful that officials are deterred from openness and omit to divulge information that otherwise should be made publicly available; officials may be cautious with the truth for fear of giving ammunition to the ill-intentioned. Quite clearly, the risk here is that both well- and ill-intentioned will suffer from concealment and secrecy. As Thompson admits, the methods of controlling dirty hands – retrospection, generalization, and mediation – do not cover "the whole class of secret dirty-handed decisions, and for those left uncovered, the traditional problem of dirty hands persists."[10]

It is clear, then, that the notion of an institutional restraint is not by itself sufficient to establish a satisfactory limit on the problematic nature of political morality, and retrospective review may or may not have the effect of limiting immoral actions done in secret, may or may not make secret action compatible with democracy, but nevertheless does not render dirty hands any less dirty. This means that it is necessary to probe more deeply if the relation between trust and dirty hands is to be adequately elucidated.

What notion of reflective judgment is at work here? Consider two examples in which immoral actions are performed for political reasons. The first concerns Marx's discussion in *The Civil War in France* of the execution by the Communards during the 1871 Paris Commune of hostages, including the archbishop of Paris and other priests.[11] Marx is sensitive to the moral difficulties involved in the taking of hostages – that in terms of its intrinsic character it is morally objectionable that the innocent should be forced to answer for the behavior of others – but he argues that the circumstances in which these hostages were taken represented a certain kind of necessity; their taking was not an act of gratuitous cruelty, blackmail, or kidnapping, but a response to the army's policy of executing Communard prisoners in their control. Marx writes that "the Commune again and again had offered to exchange the archbishop and ever so many priests in the bargain, against the single Blanqui, then in the hands of Thiers,"[12] but that Thiers, officer in command of the army, "had obstinately refused."[13] Marx's argument certainly suggests a degree of moral refinement and reluctance present in the reflections of the Commune, which is absent in Thiers. It is just about possible to interpret this whole incident as a straightforward case of utilitarian thinking, balancing one set of considerations against another with a view to achieving the more desirable end, though clearly such brutal instrumentalism cannot do justice to all the moral complexities involved. According to this interpretation, however, Thiers emerges as the "better instrumentalist." It might be thought that this description says something about Thiers's future trustworthiness (always to be counted on as a "good instrumentalist"). But this runs up against an immovable obstacle: How can anyone ever trust an instrumentalist. Marx resists a straightforward means–ends analysis insofar as he gives the innocence of the hostages an independent moral weight. Equally, he recognizes that the moral problem is not solvable only by reference to the relative historical positions of the classes involved.

For Marx, outcomes defined either instrumentally or historically are not sufficient to ground a retrospective judgment of morality. How individuals come to recognize what they have done, come to accept moral responsibility for it, and possibly see in it a reason for guilt and remorse cannot be explained in this way. It is noteworthy that while Marx felt a certain degree of moral reservation about this case, he did argue nevertheless that the ultimate responsibility for the death of the archbishop was Thiers of whom he concludes that: "He knew that with Blanqui he would give to the Commune a head, while the archbishop would serve his purpose best in the shape of a corpse."[14] Marx's view here seems to be that the balance of instrumentalist argument is found on Thiers's side, whom he blames not only for his crimes, through *what* he has done or not done, but because of Thiers' attempt – as the "better instrumentalist" – to establish a false distance between himself and his actions, thus blocking out both external and internal criticism and judgment. Although Marx does not analyze in detail the moral responses of the Communards themselves to what they have done or the extent to which their actions will diminish their capacity to inspire trust, he does imply that they at least did not attempt to protect themselves by presenting their action as other than it was. Some notion of reflective judgment is clearly required, the emergence of which is prevented by an exclusive stress on consequentialist and historical considerations. Simone Weil brings out the complexity of what is involved here when she singles out for attention the inclinations of the agent and the potentially good–bad consequences.

> If you kill German soldiers in order to serve France and then at the end of a certain time you acquire a taste for assassinating human beings, it is clearly an evil thing.

> If, in order to serve France, you offer your assistance to work-
> men avoiding transportation to Germany and then at the end
> of a certain time you acquire a taste for helping those in misfor-
> tune, it is clearly a good thing.[15]

Self-awareness seems to be the key to future conduct here
and thus to the issue of trust: If I come to like doing something (e.g., helping those in misfortune) and am to go on
doing that thing (and am to be trusted to do that thing), then
I must surely be aware of myself as a person who likes doing
that thing.

Weil's example seems to show not only how wrongs that
issue from good motives can become wrongs per se, but
also how the risks of trust may be involved. Does the process that prevents the conversion of good into evil also provide grounds for the renewal of trust?

The notion of distance at work in Marx's critique of instrumentalism is explored further in a different sort of example in
comments made by Mary McCarthy on the massacre at My
Lai:

> Though it would have changed nothing for the victims, most
> of us would prefer to think that those women and babies and
> old men had died in a raid rather than been singled out, one
> by one, for slaughter. Logic here is unpersuasive: the deliber-
> ate killing of unresisting people *is* more repugnant than the
> same result effected by mechanical means deployed at a dis-
> tance and without clear perception of who or what is below.[16]

But the danger of this way of thinking is its tendency to
construe political morality as solely a technical exercise in
abstract rationality whose application is supposed to diminish the guilt of those involved. Here the distance between the
agent and the performance of morally repugnant actions is
defined psychologically rather than morally. But if it is simply a psychological fact that proximity determines moral reluctance, then moral questions of responsibility and blameworthiness are of limited relevance and to that extent agents

who act badly for political ends are prevented from coming to terms with what they have done.

Further, the claim that distance is established psychologically neglects the complexities involved in how individuals recognize their conduct as morally wrong, how they come to such a recognition, and how they are prepared to admit blame. Thus, the human capacity to act wrongly for the sake of other moral ends is limited not by reluctance construed psychologically but morally in terms of shame or remorse. For Hannah Arendt it is the inconsistent nature of deception itself that constitutes one constraint on political morality; "the mysteries of government" can so confuse "the minds of the actors themselves that they no longer know or remember the truth behind their concealments and their lies."[17] Arendt's point is her familiar one that truth has a necessary primacy over falsehood because the efficiency of lying and deceit "depends entirely upon a clear notion of the truth that the liar and the deceiver wishes to hide."[18] In *Ecce Homo*, Nietzsche draws our attention to the difficulties involved in analyzing the notion of forgetting; its meanings are various, and some have a crucial bearing on dirty hands and on how a society comes to terms with the identification of wrongdoing. We are familiar with attempts to subject history and memory to political control, but we are also aware that such enforced amnesia is impossible to sustain. Brute terror cannot completely eradicate the evidence of an inherited past, and there is a public perception that recognizes the inherent failure of propaganda to eliminate internal contradiction and empirical error. By contrast, Nietzsche categorizes forgetting as the determination not to be restrained by the past. Forgetting is required if earlier transgressions are to be put aside; no society can live on memory alone. Previous wrongs are not merely subject to the accidents of memory but are subdued almost by an effort of will. But is a society in which moral stains are recklessly forgotten worthy of continued trust? The risk of dependency on those who may have to dirty their hands on our behalf is increased when earlier transgressions are erased in the belief that their recollection will weaken resolve.[19]

The moral and psychological burden of repression may be too great for individuals to bear. Forgetting can be a means of evading moral guilt, an attempt to construct a temporary respite from feelings of shame and the recognition of blameworthiness. In Zola's *Thérèse Raquin*, for example, Thérèse and Laurent after the murder of Camille both strive to avoid those persons and objects that remind them of their victim in the illusion that their responsibility can be successfully avoided:

> Soon they found Thursday evenings very much preferable to these intimate family ones. Alone with Madame Raquin they could not entirely forget about themselves; the thin trickle of their aunt's voice and her affectionate gaiety could not drown their inner cries of anguish. They felt bedtime getting nearer and shuddered when their eyes happened to glance at the bedroom door, and this wait for the moment when they would be alone became more and more painful as the evening wore on. But on Thursdays they could forget themselves in silliness, forget each other's presence, and suffer less.[20]

Does forgetting as a form of moral evasion have a more ambiguous import in politics? The fact that some societies are unwilling to remember their past does not cancel out the claim that there are certain crimes, outrages against humanity, for example, which ought not to be forgotten. It has been persuasively argued that the conditions of individual moral responsibility are transferable to the actions of collectivities, and that within specific constraints these are open to moral blame. For Peter French: "The only justifiable reason for morally blaming a whole population is that the population merits moral blame, and the determination of blameworthiness is first a question of standards and then one of abilities and opportunities."[21] For J. Glenn Gray "the greater the possibility of free action in the communal sphere, the greater the degree of guilt for evil deeds done in the name of everyone."[22] But the attempt to locate guilt in morality and politics is based on the premise that it is open to recognition, and, as Judith Shklar forcibly argues, in political trials this may not be so clear-cut: "It is not the trial itself that is important, but the political values involved."[23] An exclusive legalistic emphasis on guilt and responsibility does not capture the moral difficulties involved here. It is a feature of human conduct that actions often entail consequences that were not intended. Neoptolemus's decision to give up the bow to Philoctetes risks unintended harm to the Greeks whose possession of it will secure their victory over the Trojans. Commitments and promises are meant to protect trust from such uncertainties. After the event individuals employ "pleas, explanations, justifications, and other modifiers"[24] that enable them to redeem conduct when it has gone tragically wrong. Such moral discourse characteristically takes place in conversation between individuals, but it is not merely private. It has a significant public reverberation as a mode of renewing trust and it requires a degree of awareness and concern, which can be slow to develop because it has been obstructed, as we have seen, by deliberate forgetting and inattention. The moral end game in Sophocles' *Philoctetes* charts individuals' use of such language in the ways they respond to the gravity of their decisions. How is the moral balance restored? What process of rectification is involved?

Neoptolemus's first task after returning the bow is to dispel Philoctetes' well-grounded mistrust. Significantly, Philoctetes' response to Odysseus's retreat shows how he understands the limits of political morality: "Well, well it's easy to see what cowards they are, / These officers, self-styled ambassadors, / When it comes to a fight, for all their mighty talk."[25] Odysseus is a "political moralist"; his skill is words, his deviousness and cunning are no match for Philoctetes in an open confrontation. By contrast Neoptolemus has asked for and received Philoctetes' forgiveness for his earlier deceptions – the return of the bow seems to have established a basis for trust, but Neoptolemus still faces the demands of loyalty to his fellow Greeks. How then can he persuade Philoctetes to return voluntarily to Troy? In his argument, Neoptolemus appeals to a number of distinct considerations. He tries to convince Philoctetes that his suffering is self-inflicted and, as such, is a rebuff to all those who have tried to help him. Philoctetes certainly has moral right on his side, but not even this can compensate for his now self-imposed exile and his determination to refuse aid and support: "There is no excuse, / Nor pity, for those who choose to cling to suffering / And hardship of their own making, as you would do."[26] Neoptolemus appeals, too, to Philoctetes' need for public and private goods. Return to Troy will mean political glory and private well-being – a cure for his terrible wound, for it is *only* by going to Troy that his affliction can be removed. Finally, he tries to prove to Philoctetes that the outcome is guaranteed – the fall of Troy will be Philoctetes' triumph: "How do I know it / We have a Trojan prisoner, / Helenus, a notable prophet, who has pronounced, / That this must come to pass."[27]

The moral dilemma Philoctetes is placed in is a complex association of moral claims, political imperatives, and trust. He acknowledges that now Neoptolemus is a sincere friend and that "he cannot turn deaf ears / To my kind counsellor";[28] but how can he rejoin those who have caused him such great distress, let alone contribute to their success? Philoctetes' demands cannot be accommodated by material reward, and also he suspects his enemies of hostility toward him and further treachery, "the soul that has conceived one wickedness / Can nurse no good thereafter."[29] Distrust is so deeply rooted in Philoctetes that he rejects reconciliation and the word of Neoptolemus whom he does now recognize as a friend. There is, too, in Philoctetes' speech a moral skepticism not only toward motivation and action, but about the very possibility of goodness in the world he was forced to leave: "Can eyes of mine, / Seeing such things as they have seen, see this, / My meeting again, Those two, my murderers."[30] More important, Philoctetes cannot understand how Neoptolemus, as the son of Achilles, can actually want him to go to Troy to give support to those who have caused him so much pain. In this respect, there is an absolute disagreement between them as to how the moral balance can be restored. Trust plays a significant part here because, as Philoctetes claims, Neoptolemus has sworn "a solemn oath"[31] to take him home. But Philoctetes' demand for vengeance is so uncompromising that he feels that with his enemies destroyed "I could believe my torture ended."[32] As Blundell writes perceptively of Philoctetes:

> He cannot conceive of Achilles' son failing to agree that a single injury means unremitting hatred at whatever cost to oneself. The injury that he himself sustained was extraordinarily severe, involving betrayal, dishonour and severe physical hardship. The resulting thirst for vengeance is so fierce that he is prepared to forgo the rectification of both dishonour and hardship in order to deny satisfaction to his enemies. . . . He would rather remain an outcast from society than re-enter it on terms that compromise his hatred.[33]

Philoctetes' question to Neoptolemus, therefore – "Do you want to brand yourself with the villainy to which you lend your aid?"[34] – amounts to a challenge to his moral integrity. Neoptolemus's counterrequest that Philoctetes trust both in the gods and in his promises as a friend is too weak to resolve Philoctetes' dilemma. Neoptolemus' friends are Philoctetes' enemies and this fact nothing can alter. Indeed, Philoctetes so far returns to his old distrust and suspicion that Neoptolemus is on the point of giving up, of accepting that on its own terms the dilemma is unsolvable:

> What is the use, then,
> If all my talking, if nothing I can say
> Will change your mind? I'd better say no more,
> And you must go on living, as you are,
> This hopeless, helpless life."[35]

It is an existential moment. Philoctetes makes one more plea. Trust must now be given or withheld. Both Philoctetes and Neoptolemus agree that this cannot be decided solely on consequentialist lines, although for Neoptolemus success in the Trojan War does represent a beneficial end that outweighs the harm suffered by Philoctetes. After a brief hesitation, it is Neoptolemus who agrees to take Philoctetes home. Friendship and compassion stemming from Neoptolemus's struggle to maintain moral consistency and self-respect are to him more important than military glory, obligations to his fellow Greeks, and his reputation amongst them; his fear that "the Achaeans will make it hot for me"[36] is allayed by Philoctetes' reciprocal offer of the bow as mutual protection.

At this stage of events the restoration of a moral balance is clearly incomplete. Trust between friends has been recovered; Philoctetes' exile has ended on terms he finds morally acceptable, but the cost is a political one and it is Neoptolemus who must bear it. Morality and politics remain tragically disunited. In Sophocles, however, the dilemma ends with the intervention of the gods in the form of Heracles, whose authority enables him to convince Philoctetes that he should accompany Neoptolemus to Troy. When Heracles commands Philoctetes "to seek out Paris, / First cause of all this wickedness and destroy him / With those, my weapons; you are to sack the city / And carry home the spoils, the award of honour,"[37] his disinterestedness carries considerable weight – here is a judgment Philoctetes can trust. Heracles' is

> The very voice
> That I have longed to hear!
> The face
> As once I knew it!
> I shall not disobey.[38]

For MacIntyre the intervention of Heracles does not resolve the dilemma but "rescues the characters from their impasse."[39] Heracles' decision is authoritative and final, but what it signals is not the resolution of the conflict but simply its end. This means on MacIntyre's reading that: "It leaves unbridged the gap between the acknowledgement of authority, of a cosmic order and of the claims to truth involved in the recognition of the virtues on the one hand and our particular perceptions and judgements in particular situations on the other."[40] This does not imply that the tragedy derives from the flaws present in individual character, that it resides in Philoctetes' stubbornness and intransigence, Odysseus's trickery, or Neoptolemus's moral inexperience. Rather, in MacIntyre's view, tragedy is found in the unavoidable conflict of one moral value with another, in the collision of one mode of human existence with another, and is, therefore, independent of the contingent attributes of character. In Sophocles the realm of the gods is a realm of moral certainty, the nature of which human perceptions can never fully disclose.

However, as Blundell well points out,[41] the intervention of Heracles is not simply a device to bring the narrative to its end, but a way of showing the ethical positions involved in sharper relief. For Philoctetes the obligations of friendship do not outweigh the need for vengeance, but to divine authority he is willing to defer. Neoptolemus's failure to persuade Philoctetes to return with him to Troy later reveals the altruism in his offer to take him home. Philoctetes' readiness to trust is bound up with his recognition that Neoptolemus's motives are pure, his self-reflection has run its course. Neoptolemus has come to realize what he is capable of doing or not doing to another. His sincerity now provides a basis for trust that his earlier attempts at political persuasion failed to create. The claims of friendship are shown to be prior to the need for revenge, and only an authentic trust establishes a solid ground for mutual benefit. The intervention of Heracles reminds them that their stalemate can be removed only through a mutual renunciation in which it is right that Neoptolemus should be the first mover: "You cannot conquer Troy without his help, / Nor he without you."[42] As Blundell comments: "The onus is on Neoptolemus to prove beyond any doubt this commitment to their *philia*. Only this can create the trust in which a true friendship of mutual support may flourish, a friendship that can finally afford to disregard the threats of its enemies."[43]

The recovery of trust in the closing moments of the *Philoctetes* arises from a mutual recognition whose essential simplicity stands in sharp contrast to the painful misunderstandings and rejections that have preceded it. Moral perplexity is not removed crudely by a deus ex machina, but through a process of mutual exploration and discovery. Philoctetes remains for a long time wary of Neoptolemus's previous deception and he is unwilling to forget it completely until convinced by Neoptolemus' conduct and the stages through which it passes that his words are now worthy of trust. Forgiveness for Neoptolemus's earlier transgression, his theft of the bow, is clearly a necessary condition of this regaining of confidence. Forgiveness means that some actions no longer need to be remembered; trust can be renewed and a future project, the expedition to Troy, rejoined in aspiration and hope. During the *Philoctetes* Neoptolemus grows in moral stature and authority; his initial naïveté is slowly overcome by a more realistic self-assessment of his ethical nature. Moral perplexity here signifies not a failure of rationality but a gradual loss of innocence, which eventualy allows Neoptolemus a clearer recognition of who he is and how he is bound to others. In *Troilus and Cressida,* by contrast, the loss of innocence is more brutal, the first perception of betrayal leaving character devastated and so frustrating the rebirth of trust. The end game of Shakespeare's play charts the psychological complexities of betrayal primarily from the standpoint of the betrayed. Cressida's faithlessness is a "soul-murder"[44] of Troilus; it robs him of his sense of worth, leaves him dislocated, distraught, no longer capable of trust, driven only by disillusionment. What experience does Troilus undergo when he sees himself betrayed?

What he sees is not a casual attempt at seduction by Diomed, but an infidelity that attracts Cressida's active complicity: When Diomed – "a false-hearted rogue, a most unjust knave; I will no more trust him when he leers than I will a serpent when he hisses"[45] – demands a surety for Cressida's promise, what she offers, "in faith, I will, la; never trust me else,"[46] is Troilus's sleeve, the token of his own love and trust now easily parted with, its value nothing except how it is valued by the present mood. When Cressida and Diomed leave, Troilus remains, determined to "make a recordation to my soul"[47] of what he has seen and heard, Cressida "now turn'd whore."[48] Now his being is divided between what he thinks and what he has seen. What he has witnessed he refuses to believe:

> . . . there is a credence in my heart,
> An esperance so obstinately strong,
> That doth invent the attest of eyes and ears,
> As if those organs had deceptious functions,
> Created only to calumniate.[49]

Thus, his despairing question, "Was Cressid here?"[50] Troilus is the victim of a broken promise, but what causes his suffering is not the violation of his rights but the injury to his love. Simone Weil remarks that "rights have no direct connection with love";[51] when love is betrayed, the language of rights is simply inappropriate and cannot capture what is at stake. Rights may be put aside, outweighed, or insisted upon. They can stand apart from issues central to human identity in ways that love cannot. Troilus's experience, therefore, is both an emotional and an intellectual crisis. When Ulysses responds that Cressida most certainly was there, Troilus's reply reflects his intellectual dilemma:

> Let it not be believed from womanhood.
> Think, we had mothers; do not give advantage
> to stubborn critics, apt, without a theme
> For depravation, to square the general sex
> By Cressid's rule: rather, think this not Cressid.[52]

This division penetrates Troilus's being. His mind and intellect tell him that what he sees cannot be. But what he sees is. The purity of his love cannot be contradicted by the reality of Cressida's infidelity. He cannot see how it is possible to will the good, to make commitments of mutual faithfulness, *and* choose the worse. How is it possible to know the good and yet act otherwise? Is Cressida weak-willed? Did the transgression lie in himself as truster? Is trust closed to trust? Better to deny that Cressida was there. For Troilus the moment is a nightmare that threatens to deracinate his being. But Troilus does possess the primary Aristotelian virtue of self-control to realize that the direction pointed to by "think this not Cressid"[53] is the way madness lies. He does have the residual capacity to distance himself from his anxieties and in so doing he recognizes the "madness of discourse"[54] with which he is engaged. "This is, and is not, Cressid"[55] is unsustainable both in logic and in life; in his deepest disillusion Troilus has come to see faithlessness for what it is: "The bounds of heaven are slipp'd, dissolv'd, and loos'd."[56] With that Cressida's memory can be contemptuously put aside, she is scornfully forgotten; "The fractions of her faith, arts of her love, / the fragments, scraps, the bits, and greasy reliques / Of her o'er-eaten faith, are bound to Diomed."[57]

In *Troilus and Cressida* nothing is settled, motivation is of the moment, consumption is all, plans count for little, time and chance for much. Troilus's love and the Greek search for glory at Troy are portrayed devoid of religious consolation and support. But does this give Cressida too little significance? Is she merely shallow, a function of the desires of others, valuable only because others value her? For John Bayley, Cressida lacks any will of her own:

> She has no sense of, does not want to know, what has taken place: pleasure, boredom and infidelity are alike unsorted phenomena of the moment for her, and she is denied past and future awareness to the point where she is no more than a voice speaking lines in the theatre. Someone said of Marilyn Monroe that she was "discontinuous with any idea of personality." It is the same with Cressida. She becomes her words.[58]

Trust in the context of Thersites' view of life – "lechery, lechery; still, wars and lechery: nothing else holds fashion"[59] – has neither place nor voice, but *Troilus and Cressida* cannot be reduced to a nihilistic posture and, indeed, may be read as a direct parody of such. Will, power, and appetite are categories too crude to identify Cressida's characterlessness. She is a creation of the needs and values of others. She has, therefore, no consistency, no certainty of self, no assured sense of who she is. At times helpless, indecisive, exasperating, and weak, at others, distrustful, willful, and independent, she is, as John Bayley writes, "in a continual state of inadvertancy and division."[60] Troilus's conclusion that Cressida is a nature split confines his future; he seems to have accepted that character cannot provide a stable security because judgment, love, character, and language itself do not provide a safe refuge for trust, and when he destroys Cressida's letter he does so with, "words, words, mere words."[61] Troilus has not been required to test his own moral self-estimation – it is Cressida who has betrayed him. He reacts by transforming love betrayed into public hate, the fragilities of his inner life he replaces with public commitment:

> . . . as much as I do Cressid love,
> So much by weight hate I her Diomed:
> That sleeve is mine that he'll bear on his helm;
> Were it a casque composed by Vulcan's skill,
> My sword should bite it.[62]

The lover has become the warrior.

Hector, too, the invincible, the source of honor and moral rectitude, is vulnerable to the momentary and the transitory. He reverses his decision to return Helen to the Greeks, and yet rejects the pleas of Cassandra, and his wife, Andromache, that he should not fight because the gods have prophesied "bloody turbulence" and "shapes and forms of slaughter."[63] Andromache's appeal is expressed in arguments that Ulysses would have understood. It is the moral nature of the end that counts. If Hector's life requires that he break a promise, which, as a "hot and peevish vow"[64] is not, as Cassandra claims, binding in any case and would not be thought so by the gods, then what moral objection could there be? Why should this one breach of trust diminish Hector's trustworthiness? Why should this single exercise of political morality devalue the polity's deepest aspiration? Andromache argues:

> O! be persuaded: do not count it holy
> To hurt by being just: it is as lawful,
> For we would give much, to use violent thefts,
> And rob in the behalf of charity.[65]

The choice that faces Hector involves trust, and it is Cassandra who makes its meaning plain – "it is the purpose that makes strong the vow; / But vows to every purpose must not hold. / Unarm, sweet Hector"[66] – to which Hector's reply is that of the man of honor. Without his trust his life has no value – "the dear man / Holds honour far more precious-dear than life."[67] The debate between sacrificial honor and prudential policy continues in an emotionally and politically heightened form in the exchange between Hector and Troilus that immediately follows. Hector's determination to fight "in the vein of chivalry"[68] is regarded by Troilus as signifying nothing more than the "vice of mercy."[69] The vengeance that sparks Troilus's anger here is precisely the reason why Hector warns him not to fight. Troilus at war has placed himself beyond restraint – "who should withold me? / Not fate, obedience, nor the hand of Mars";[70] no moral rule or filial appeal can stop Troilus in his rush to slaughter. In the grip of revenge Troilus cannot forget his betrayal. He becomes the embodiment of power, fighting in a mood described by Ulysses as one of "careless force and forceless care."[71] These final moments in *Troilus and Cressida* mark a military engagement in which decency is eliminated. There is no sight of reconciliation here – it is a world of unrelenting brutality and force.

In her reflections on Homer's *Iliad*,[72] which has a significant bearing on Shakespeare's treatment of the Trojan theme, Simone Weil reads the poem politically as a commentary on the fall of France in 1940 following the German invasion. She defines force as that which "turns anybody who is subject to it into a *thing*."[73] We see this manifested in the capacity, first, to kill, to turn a human being literally into a corpse, and, second, to destroy what is distinctively human – choice, the ability to consent or refuse. In war there are many who are obliterated in this way, but force can also have a terrible effect on those who possess it. She writes: "Force is as pitiless to the man who possesses it, or thinks he does, as it is to its victims; the second it crushes, the first it intoxicates."[74] Troilus is already a being whose sense of moral location is lost. Achilles becomes one with the death of Patroclus; now he wants battle with Hector, "know what it is to meet Achilles angry."[75] Hector's death in Shakespeare is portrayed as a savage contract killing, uncomplicated by considerations of morality or honor. An un-Homeric Achilles orders his Myrmidons to "in fellest manner execute your aims,"[76] and it is an unarmed Hector whom they kill. Hector's murder is carried out by Achilles' mercenaries, whom he then instructs to announce "Achilles hath the mighty Hector slain."[77]

Achilles' singular brutality – "Come tie his body to my horse's tail; / Along the field I will the Trojan trail"[78] – is productive only of multiplying calls for vengeance in return. Troilus's "hope of revenge shall hide our inward woe"[79] leaves crime in the forefront of his memory and imagination, so leaving the moral balance unrestored. The negativity of Troilus's last speech derives from the emptiness of revenge and is entirely consistent with the bleak logic of his actions since his betrayal. This is in tune with Simone Weil's reading of the *Iliad:* "But the auditors of the *Iliad* knew that the death of Hector would be but a brief joy to Achilles, and the death of Achilles but a brief joy to the Trojans, and the destruction of Troy but a brief joy to the Achaeans."[80] Remembering only the need to repay crime with crime, to return injury with injury, distrust with distrust is in effect a kind of forgetting. Displaced by inhumanity the retrospective virtues of reconciliation and forgiveness are hard to recover. Troilus cannot see what he has become. For Simone Weil, "At least a suppliant, once his prayer is answered, becomes a human being again, like everybody else. But there are other, more unfortunate creatures who have become things for the rest of their lives."[81] Unlike Philoctetes who regains his humanity in his realization that he can trust once more, and Neoptolemus who discovers what it is like to repay trust with trust, Troilus in his disillusion, scorn, and hate is closer to Weil's "more unfortunate creatures."

What is at stake here is not encompassed by the conventional language of political morality. Consequential gain, legal uncertainty, moral complexity, and doubt are familiar ingredients and are, in fact, present in Shakespeare – in, for example, the killing of the French prisoners in *Henry V.*[82] But for those like Troilus, whose moral natures have been transformed by betrayal, the question arises as to how goodness can be recovered. What must be identified for this to take place? Can forgiveness figure as a public as well as a private means of redeeming trust? In *Troilus and Cressida* what complicates these questions is Shakespeare's reversal of our moral expectations. There is no sure moral foundation or inner life of virtue to which we can turn when faced by moral difficulty. Nothing is substantial. The characters speak to each other in moral terms, but their words lack a permanent integrity. Moral language is used in a vacuum. As John Bayley points out, the relation between consciousness and world in *Troilus and Cressida* contrasts with that in *Macbeth:* "For it is in Macbeth's own consciousness that coherency and purpose have become extinguished, have become a tale told by an idiot. In the world outside him the logic of time proceeds with its serene, restorative, but for him terrible assurance."[83] Troilus's world provides him with no such "outside"; no direction exists from which he can endeavor to regain his former self. In a world lacking in continuity, where past and future are collapsed into a present uninterrupted by substantial memory or deliberation, forgetting becomes the condition of life, forgiveness a logical impossibility, and trust in another person an unavoidable fragmentation of being. What Troilus sees but tries despairingly not to see is his betrayal. What Laurent and Thérèse in Zola's *Thérèse Raquin* deliberately attempt to put from their minds is their crime. Can evil be willed from the memory?

Trust in those who act badly depends on their recognizing what it is about their conduct that gives trusters a reason for concern. What Troilus experiences totally defeats his willingness to trust – "my love with words and errors still she feeds, / But edifies another with her deeds."[84] And Cressida's own response to what she has done – "this fault in us I find, / The error of our eye directs our mind,"[85] – guarantees only future willfulness. Laurent's murder of Camille cannot be redeemed by any outweighing motive or consequence. He has not killed to save the lives of others or to further a just war. In his attempt to conceal his crime from himself, he blocks punishment and forgiveness. What light does this shed on forgiveness in the public realm? Neoptolemus searches for a way of redeeming himself to Philoctetes for deceiving him. But Laurent struggles to negate his crime and, like Troilus's "this is, and is not, Cressid," he discovers that his obsession to erase what he has done is a logical impossibility – responsibility for crime cannot be removed by willing the crime undone. For Simone Weil those "who are so estranged from the good that they seek to spread evil everywhere can only be reintegrated with the good by having harm inflicted on them."[86] In Simone Weil's view this *is* the ethical function of punishment – it enables the criminal to identify his crime. But Laurent has escaped punishment; society remains ignorant of his crime, so how then is he able to recognize it himself? Arendt sees forgiveness in isolation from others as devoid of reality, signifying "no more than a role played before one's self."[87] In relation to public offenses, this gives the community a crucial moral place. Laurent's determination to avoid punishment ensures only that his moral blindness will continue and he cannot, therefore, approach the forgiveness that gives crime the opportunity to recover from itself; he remains a victim "of its consequences for ever."[88]

Strategies of avoidance are adopted by the protagonists in *Thérèse Raquin,* which in fact make their condition worse. They find themselves led into emotional blind alleys and psychological inconsistencies from which there is no escape. Initially, they dread meeting Madame Raquin not for reasons of compassion but from the fear that they might reveal their guilt. They find that crime has killed sexual passion – "when the killers thought they had brought off the murder and could give themselves up in peace to the pleasures of their love, their victim rose from the dead and turned their bed to ice."[89] The tactics they use to disguise their crime from themselves simply lead to increased torments and anxieties. A Nietzschean appeal to strength of will leads only to further cruelty and nervous exhaustion. Laurent's utilitarianism – he speaks throughout in the language of self-interest and advantage – exists in uncontrolled tension with the logic of his inner life:

> He tried to think of still more advantages, and was delighted when he thought he had delved into his self-interest and found a new argument for marrying the drowned man's widow. But try as he would to find hope, dream as he might about a future glutted with slothful delights, he still felt sudden chills run over his skin, and there were still moments when a feeling of dread choked the joy in his throat.[90]

Through his dreams his moral sense follows a nightmarish equation of its own. When Laurent takes up art, Zola describes it as working almost independently of his will. His imagination needs to exorcise itself in spite of his attempts to repress and control it. Laurent's paintings of different subjects – old men and young girls – reveal a spontaneity and passion unknown in his previous work, and yet "they're all the same, like Camille."[91] Laurent's continual reference to his motives in terms of interests obstructs remorse – "he would have committed the murder over again had he thought his interests required it"[92] – prevents renewal and forces him to live a double life. Thérèse, too, loses "any clear conception of what she was herself, and lived in a cruel state of indecision."[93] The avoidance of the reality of their crime takes different forms. Both attempt to persuade themselves that their motives are different from what they actually are. Public and private life are now in disjunction: "Their public faces never hinted at the agonies that had just been torturing them in private; they looked calm and happy, instinctively concealing their sufferings."[94] Trust is superficial, maintained through hypocrisy and lies. In their private moments, too, the murder takes on a dominating presence that renders all other aspects of their life banal, empty of meaning, of use only as a distraction, a futile attempt to evade the truth. When Madame Raquin falls ill, they nurse her, finding in it "a means of forgetting, a rest to the spirit which spurred them on to renewed efforts."[95] Forgetting and remembering play a crucial role in the end game of *Thérèse Raquin*. The stroke that leaves Madame Raquin mute and powerless immediately precedes her realization that those she had loved and trusted are actually the murderers of her son. In terror she denies value. If she could have been mistaken in trusting *their* goodness, then love, friendship, and decency cannot exist – "Nothing existed but murder and lust."[96] This recognition drives away the goodness in her life; she is now obsessed with vengeance, but in her agonized muteness she lacks a language through which denunciation can be expressed. She resorts to sign, to communication by tapping out the letters in the murderers' names, but her painful efforts are misunderstood. Public recognitions have been so penetrated by falsehood that imagination is weakened and truth misinterpreted.

Between Laurent and Thérèse mutual hatred and resentment does not take long to grow. Their refusal to recognize the truth about themselves leads them to blame one another and stems from a "passionate egoism,"[97] which now gives them nothing but frustration and pain. They face the problem of the radical egoist described by Bernard Harrison – the engagements and attachments that matter to human beings in their lives are unavailable to radical egoists because they are excluded by self-concern. So for Harrison:

> So far as (the radical egoist) keeps up an appearance of involvement in such relationships, that practice must have as its object some set of goals which lie beyond the charade of seeming trust and seeming concern: it cannot be *the marriage* and its shared goals, *the friendship* and its companiable pleasures which interest (the radical egoist); it has to be *something else*. But what can this *something else* be?[98]

Egoism and the associated need for concealment force Thérèse and Laurent to treat their public behavior as a charade, but they soon discover that they have nothing to hide but their crime. Now aware that Camille's murder has brought them nothing, their attention turns to mutual recrimination, denials of responsibility, and protestations of innocence. Thérèse adopts the posture but not the substance of the penitent. She displays feelings of shame, not out of regret for her offense but from cowardice and fear. In Thérèse's mind "there was calculation in her remorse,"[99] and she *uses* Madame Raquin as "a sort of prayer-stool"[100] before which she ostentatiously and relentlessly begs forgiveness. Her half-recognition that her crime can be expiated only through repentance is treated by Laurent with contempt and suspicion. Cruelty and hatred now become their methods for obliterating the truth; the decline of their lives into a despairing debauchery of body and spirit reflects a futile attempt at forgetting. And so when Laurent and Thérèse independently plan each other's death "the logical consequences of Camille's murder run their course, which was to end with the killing of the killers themselves."[101] But their mutual realization of what they have become does finally allow for something approaching human tenderness, even if their suicide is an acknowledgment as much of psychological and emotional exhaustion as genuine remorse; their crime remains unrepudiated, Madame Raquin unforgiving, "unable to feast her eyes enough, eyes that crushed them with brooding hate."[102]

What is absent in the concluding sections of Zola's novel is any sense of the healing power and recuperative value of repentance. Devoid of either punishment or forgiveness, crime remains unrectified and the corrosive effect this has on trust left unrestored. The overwhelming moral negativity of the ending of *Thérèse Raquin*, the gradual movement of Thérèse and Laurent to a literal and ethical dead end, illuminates by its absence the potentially close relation between forgiveness and trust. For Aurel Kolnai, forgiveness "expresses that attitude of *trust* in the world which, unless it is vitiated by hare-brained optimism and dangerous irresponsibility, may be looked upon, not to be sure as the starting-point and the very basis, but perhaps as the epitome and culmination of morality."[103] This is not to deny that forgiveness is a response to wrongdoing, to which punishment and resentment may be no less just reactions. Equally, it should not obscure the differences between forgiveness appropriate in

personal relations and pardon, which commonly involves remission in the public sphere.[104] Philoctetes' forgiveness of
Neoptolemus restores friendship and encourages some renewal of trust – though the connection between trust and forgiveness is not necessarily simple or direct: forgiveness (of
trespass and/or trespasser) is no absolute *guarantee* of future
trust. For David Heyd, "acts of pardon may lead to the
strengthening of social cohesion, to the reduction of (unjusti-
fied) resentment of the convict towards his society, and to the
promotion of trust."[105] Forgiveness may be thought especially
applicable in dirty hands cases where offenses do not involve
malicious intent and may be performed in circumstances of
emergency by well-intentioned political agents acting under
moral duress, experiencing the full force of intractable dilemmas from which they cannot escape without moral loss. A
sense of remorse absent in Troilus whose resentment violently
overcomes his capacity for forgiveness and in Laurent whose
egoism blinds him can play a significant role in the capacity of
moral and political agents to inspire continued trust following
a necessary transgression. By contrast, the special fear of
those who have suffered the costs of dirty hands' decisions
may make forgiveness inappropriate and trust merely an encouragement to more serious and severe wrongdoing. To
deny forgiveness a place in politics at all, however, seems
possible only on the basis of a comfortable hypocrisy or the
illusion that politics is the only mode of human existence in
which such hard decisions have to be made or where individuals are morally trapped by their wants and desires. Further, an
attitude of unrelenting suspicion can defeat both its object and
trust; by comparison, the magnanimous will not only refuse to
deceive others but will wish "necessarily to liberate [them-
selves] from the oppressive fear of being deceived and . . .
from the fear of being seen or thought to be deceived."[106]

Forgiveness is in Jeffrie Murphy's words a "forswearing of
resentment,"[107] in which the often powerful feelings of anger
or hatred for someone who has inflicted moral damage are
actually overcome. An offense or injury is not merely, but
virtuously, forgotten. Arendt gives forgiveness as a moral

notion a crucial political bearing that derives from her distinctive understanding of political morality. Arendt's writings are an attempt to reconstitute politics as a region of human aspiration and fulfillment. Her notion of this region's autonomy involves mutual engagement and shared understanding, and she defends it against its enemies whether these are bureaucratic instrumentalism or even the moral good. The conventional view of political morality as a moral accountancy, a utilitarian calculation of benefit, is rejected on the grounds that the lesser evil may soon be seen as not evil at all, that the possibility that evil will be done only when it is necessary soon translates into the probability that it will be done when it is not, and that in any case a great and neglected danger to politics comes not from evil alone, but from specific forms of the good. Against this background her view of promise keeping and forgiveness has a significance that is lost in utilitarian and contractualist accounts. Both faculties play a part in political morality and both derive from the primary obligation to a public world in which political action becomes possible. They are, therefore, values predicated of communities, expressive of both trust and the need for common action and disclosure. In *The Human Condition* Arendt places forgiveness in relation to her triadic understanding of human undertakings. Whereas labor and work can be redeemed only from outside their respective natures, action provides the hedge against irreversibility and the unforeseen from within its own potentialities. Forgiving is, in Arendt's view, the remedy to the human predicament of irreversibility, promise keeping to the dilemmas created by uncertainty and unpredictability. Through forgiveness, past misdeeds may be undone, so protecting new generations from the moral blight resulting from actions for which they have no responsibility. As W. H. Walsh comments:

> If my children or my contemporaries perpetrate shameful deeds I can perhaps be saddled with some share of the blame, since it is at least possible that I might have taken steps to prevent their acting in that way. But what action of mine

could have altered my great-grandfather's regrettable addiction to the bottle, or prevented the Opium War with China in the early 1840s?[108]

Whereas Walsh is concerned with the logical conditions of shame and guilt, Arendt goes a step further. Without remission, past conduct might confine future projects. Unframed by repentance or forgiveness, action cannot inspire trust and so loses the capacity to create and discover. For Arendt both forgiveness and promise keeping necessarily "depend on plurality";[109] they depend on others in ways that sharpen their connection with trust and which show the impossibility of their being exercised in isolation. By contrast with the Platonic notion of rule in which the self is "writ large"[110] the morality of forgiveness belongs to politics understood as action in concert, one that "rests on experiences which nobody could ever have with himself."[111] Utilitarianism, the language of means and ends, can never provide a remedy for irreversibility because its power for change is also in Arendt's view a power to destroy; as it construes "acting in the mode of making,"[112] it must be a dangerous *ignoratio*. Arendt identifies Jesus as the discoverer of forgiveness in the public realm and, although she stresses its religious origins in Christianity, this does not for her diminish its secular power. Transgression needs forgiveness for life to progress: "Only through this constant mutual release from what they do can men remain free agents, only by constant willingness to change their minds and start again can they be trusted with so great a power as that to begin something new."[113]

Forgiveness stands directly opposed to vengeance, which, as we saw in *Troilus and Cressida*, blights and negates. Of their many differences, forgiveness alone has the capacity to create something new – it is freely given and also frees its recipient from the just resentment and retribution that have been put aside. Arendt is aware that forgiveness is normally understood as a personal, though not only a private or individual, virtue whose exercise matters both to the one who gives and to the one who receives. In this sense, the willingness to forgive appears most dramatically in the context of love, which, indeed, for Arendt removes the distance between individuals created by politics and on which it depends. Love in its striking need for immediacy is for Arendt "the most powerful of all antipolitical human forces."[114] In rejecting love is she not also removing one of the most potent sources of forgiveness and the regeneration of trust? But it is not true, Arendt argues, that only love has the capacity for forgiveness. For her "what love is in its own, narrowly circumscribed sphere, respect is in the larger domain of human affairs."[115] Respect allows distance *and* mutuality – an understanding of the predicaments of others without which forgiveness would be impossible.

Arendt's attempt to give clemency a place in politics that includes and yet goes beyond the juridical is only half-successful. Forgiveness as a moral response seems to depend for both its entitlement and virtue on coming uniquely from the individual who has suffered wrong. Can a state exercise this moral function? There are, of course, some political crimes that, as Arendt herself powerfully and controversially draws to our attention, must not be forgiven. Is radical evil closed to forgiveness and punishment? In relation to forgiveness particularly George Kateb's point holds good – that "moral traits from private life, indeed from the best in private life, must be mixed with the political virtues for the sake of drawing some of the poison out of action."[116] Nevertheless, what is valuable in Arendt's account is her view that forgiveness is deeply dependent on plurality and that its exercise is paralyzed when "the self-coercion of totalitarian logic destroys man's capacity for experience and thought just as certainly as his capacity for action."[117] Shakespeare's question – "wilt thou make trust a transgression?"[118] – is answered negatively by Arendt:

> What makes loneliness so unbearable is the loss of one's own self which can be realized in solitude, but confirmed in its identity only by the trusting and trustworthy company of my equals. In this situation, man loses trust in himself as the

partner of his thoughts and that elementary confidence in the world which is necessary to make experiences at all.[119]

In Arendtian terms, to be entrusted politically means that "care for the world takes precedence over care for the self,"[120] even if in the effort to resist evil wrongdoing is committed. Those whose preoccupation with their moral purity displaces concern for the world cannot inspire trust. Political action, in concert with others, is performed "by the trusting and trust-worthy company of my equals."[121] Arendt's radical revision of politics means that trust is not a weakness, a sign of fragility, easily transgressed, exploited, and enfeebled by cunning and deceit, but an ethical disposition of inherent and independent strength, which is capable of self-renewal through forgive-ness but not forgetting. To think of trust as a potential weak-ness or an error is to confuse trust with reliance; misplaced trust signifies not a failure of judgment by the truster, but a moral breach by the individual in whom trust is placed.[122] For Kierkegaard, "the cunning deceiver, who moves with the most supple, most ingratiating flexibility of craftiness – he does not perceive how clumsily he proceeds. He imagines himself to be superior; he smiles in self-satisfaction; . . . he does not suspect that the lover is the infinitely superior one."[123]

Conclusion

Trust is diverse both in value and location. As a relational good, it calls attention to the attributes of truster and trusted. It may be understood as a precondition of human cooperation and a distinct policy available in specific circumstances. Trust may be inspired by the speaker or the speech, by character or action; as a feature of public institutions whose rules are open to alteration, trust may be construed as an artifact, a device that human beings can control and adjust to changing needs and demands. Trust may be a conditional value, justifying praise only on specific occasions, or it may express an unqualified trustworthiness signifying fidelity or mutual faithfulness. Love, an exclusive loyalty or affection, may make trust blind; equally, trust can attract trust in return. Hobbes takes an uncompromising view of these ambiguities and equivocations. To the man who thinks himself confident of the trustworthiness of others, he asks "what opinion he has of his fellow-subjects, when he rides armed; of his fellow citizens, when he locks his doors; and of his children, and servants, when he locks his chests. Does he not there as much accuse mankind by his actions, as I do by my words?"[1]

But Hobbes's starting point is too severe and can only generate further mutual misapprehension and fear. It is true, of course, that human societies sometimes disintegrate to the point where mutual trust is impossible and citizens face each other as potential enemies. Thucydides describes such a situation as existing after the revolution at Corcyra:

Conclusion

> The simplicity which is so large an element in a noble nature was laughed to scorn and disappeared. An attitude of perfidious antagonism everywhere prevailed; for there was no word binding enough, nor oath terrible enough to reconcile enemies. Each man was strong only in the conviction that nothing was secure; he must look to his own safety and could not afford to trust others.[2]

Between the extremes of unreserved trust and mutual distrust, it is possible to so locate trust that it is not always required to defend itself or apologize. In the uncertain ground between attribute and reputation trust finds a vulnerable but discernible reference. If attributes were determined solely by objective classification, trust would be redundant. If, on the other hand, judgments were based on reputation alone, it would be impossible. In a similar way trust is rendered fragile by time but is not completely destroyed by it. External misfortune and hazards internal to character threaten trust by exposing it to different kinds of outcome. Moral reservations with regard to a specific project and which emerge gradually over a course of time relocate the risks and rewards of trust. What is regarded as worthy of trust at one moment may be unreliable at another. The benefits and burdens that apply to both truster and trusted are not open to understanding in abstraction from the contexts that shape them, but this unavoidable relativity does not make either the exercise or receipt of trust merely contingent. Temporal language relates past, present, and future through anticipation and hope as well as expectation and prediction. Trust is not only a function of calculable risk. It emerges in distinct human contexts in relation to specific human goods and, in refined and subtle ways, draws on recollection and memory to safeguard its present expressions, which can as much signify a serious gesture of faith in a moral or political future as indicate recklessness or foolhardiness. Choice concentrates the risks and rewards of trust. Here our concern has been with choice in relation to the interstices of conduct – with how it arises, with its determinants in particular public and private contexts, with moral character changing and unfolding under the impact of events and the constraints they involve, and most significantly with trust as a feature of character in passage and context in transition.

When individuals are faced by moral and political dilemmas, choice is placed under severe strain. Who bears the burden of hard moral and political choices has been a constant theme. The Kantian claim that in morality and politics trust is most securely located when these activities are formulated in terms of their basic rules may dominate to the point where we lose sight of what it is to trust a stranger, a friend, or an enemy. Trust in those whose actions are right in utilitarian terms but leave them guilty of a moral wrong is not automatically blameworthy or incautious, but requires further analysis of both character and the goods that are put at risk by the exercise of trust. In both public and private life there are occasions where secrecy may be justified; some desirable projects would be defeated if they were to be made public. The idea of a moral cost, too, is understood in both public and private contexts; some admirable conduct involves consequences where the damage to others cannot be retrieved. The presence of such considerations is not sufficient to make trust unwise, although its future exercise may be more constrained as a result. A trusted individual who commits an act of wrongdoing under severe moral duress is not automatically rendered unworthy of trust. But the risk remains that criminal means once tolerated are very often soon preferred and that the good once entangled with the corrupt will become corrupt itself. Trust, however, does offer a way of drawing the sting from dirty hands cases, a way untouched by utilitarianism and unexamined by a concentration on rights. Trust is a feature of a moral vocabulary used by those who know that rule may be corrupted by private interest *and* that in the exercise of rule good may not be a sufficient barrier to evil; they also know that there is a moral difference between these. The shared practice of judging character provides a ground for trust and distrust. It provides a basis for public estimation and judgment, for the recognition that trust has been abused when political ambition "disjoins remorse from power."[3] The resulting moral leeway between discretion and deceit offers a space for trust that gives rules a necessary freedom and citizens a frame of public reference. On an Aristotelian view the various senses of trust in such a practice exist in delicate balance. Public law and moral character together establish grounds for rational deliberation and provide an enclosure of moderation that protects the polity against harmful disturbance and renews trust through the reflective moral responses of shame and regret, punishment and forgiveness.

This double emphasis on the mutuality of well-grounded institutions and moral character revises our understanding of the relation between public and private virtue. When Hume asks, "what proportion these two species of morality bear to each other?"[4] his answer is in terms of general human experience and interest. It is because human beings have an interest in the well-being resulting from a peaceful political order that they are prepared to relax their moral code and reconcile themselves "more easily to any transgressions of justice among princes."[5] But the language of interest speaks only in terms of gains and losses and cannot, therefore, fully embrace the consciousness involved in seeing one's hands dirty, the attempts to evade guilt by washing it away, or the perspectives of those who are victims of such decisions. Aristotle, by contrast, while recognizing trust as a feature of agreements of reciprocal exchange, emphasizes friendship as an intrinsic bond of states[6] and gives greater prominence to the redemptive values that allow a community to restore a moral balance that has been disturbed. Aristotle does not deny the existence of substantial conceptual differences between public and private values, but he stresses that if trust is to be maintained and renewed, they should not drift too far apart. As we have seen, what actually constitutes the closeness of public and private existence is a matter of some complexity, which both sustains and challenges trust. The bow in Sophocles' *Philoctetes* is emblematic of the multiple associations and dissociations that surround trust in the overlap between public and private concerns. The bow is Philoctetes' lifeline, a necessary means of his subsistence and support in which he must trust if he is to survive. It is also a military artifact, a weapon that gives its possessor the power to determine the fate of cities. As both a domestic tool and an instrument of war, it is an object of moral and political argument. Disputes center on how it is transferred from one to another – whether it is bestowed freely as a gift or stolen by force and cunning. Ownership is a fundamental that involves obligations recognized by all. To Philoctetes, however, the bow is not only an item of property but a means of rejoining a public world. Conflict over its possession reveals features common to both public and private realms. In both we find conflicts of moral character – between Philoctetes and Odysseus, between Odysseus and Neoptolemus; and conflicts of value between Philoctetes' individual resentment at having been wronged and Odysseus's belief that a purposive political life is rendered impossible if a single act of wrongdoing is allowed to block a desirable collective aspiration. Neoptolemus discovers that the bow takes on a variety of meanings for him, whether he sees it as an instrument of political morality, a piece of property owned by another, a sign of his ill-treatment of Philoctetes, a source of shame for having broken a trust, evidence of his regard for him, or a weapon potentially injurious to Odysseus. Later, Neoptolemus gradually identifies the bow as an indicator of Philoctetes' feelings toward him. Its status, then, is neither uniquely public nor private, but represents the good of a friendship trust that cuts across the public–private divide.

Here the language of dirty hands is intelligible because it contains nuances and references that are already in place in individual moral vocabulary. We know what it is like to see private as well as public projects made uncertain by external luck or flaws internal to character or the goal itself. Our familiarity with asymmetries of power includes private as well as public relationships. Our experience of the vulnerability involved in trusting another permits an insight into the dangers of political trust, which are exposed on a larger scale. Human attachments and allegiances in both public and private life involve a possible surrender to as yet unnoticed harm. Troilus declares his love for Cressida in complete ignorance of real betrayal. Hector in Shakespeare's play commits himself politically in the "vein of chivalry"[7] and is butchered. But we also know that the exercise of trust may inspire trust in return, and our fear that private existence may collapse into mutual distrust reflects the parallel concern that political life may be similarly diminished. One remedy for this state of affairs is the location of trust in a public authority whose rules and procedures serve to protect individuals from harm of which they may be unaware. In this way governments may be issued with provisional and highly conditional "licenses to deceive,"[8] so allowing the achievement of necessary, specific political ends and the continuation of faith in well-grounded rules and constraints. Paradoxically, however, the shift to institutional trust may weaken the perception of those characteristics that provide a basis for individual trust or distrust. It would be ironic if a preoccupation with the rational basis of system trust resulted only in the encouragement of a more calculating disposition and an inability to act in the public domain unless securely supported by sanctions, insurance policies, or safety procedures.

In this way the move to institutional trust risks individuals' losing sight of moral attributes close to the giving or withholding of trust.[9] To counter this difficulty, trust has here been construed as a problem of recognition. Understanding trust as a way of seeing does not abolish questions concerning its utility, but it means that they no longer have a primary significance. This understanding encourages the exploration of how trust as the expression of inner regard is related to public expectation, how character sets limits on itself and comes into conflict with a public role. In both *Troilus and Cressida* and *Thérèse Raquin*, this allows us to examine complex modes of concealment and transparency in which the relation between truster and trusted closely parallels that between valuer and valued. Here the notion of a test for trust has a crucial place because through it we ascertain how trust may or may not be squared with the moral decency of trust relationships, and we can also establish the boundaries between trust and other distinguishable attachments such as love in which trust may be involved. This attempt to recover the public sense of personal trust is desirable because an institutional trust says little about moral character and disposition so long as its requirements are met. If public trustworthiness is guaranteed only by vanity or fear of rebuke, by the desire for gain or the dread of sanctions, it is not surprising that the allegiance it inspires is correspondingly shallow.

In Dickens's *Bleak House* Lady Dedlock is asked if there is a particular person whom she fears and she replies that there is one who lacks the feeling to be either a friend to her or an enemy. He is Sir Leicester Dedlock's lawyer, who is "mechanically faithful without attachment, and very jealous of the profit, privilege, and reputation of being master of the mysteries of great houses."[10] He is described as lacking all human emotion, "indifferent to everything but his calling . . . the acquisition of secrets,"[11] and when asked if she could place her trust in him Lady Dedlock replies "I shall never try."[12] The inability of such a mechanical, but no doubt efficient, guardian of interest to inspire trust is hardly surprising, but it implies, too, the existence of an untrustworthiness that is closed to forgiveness and renewal. Troilus lashing out in revenge at his betrayal is illustrative of a different kind of foreclosure of trust. Of course, trust may be withheld when past wrongs committed by whose who ask for trust cannot be forgotten, when past moral stains cannot be ignored. But as a permanent state of mind, such distrust, as Nicolai Hartmann comments, only leads to disintegration and impotence. Trust, by contrast, "imposes an obligation"[13] – hence, "the unequalled depth of moral indignation which a deliberate breach of faith calls forth even in those who are not betrayed by it."[14]

In complex moral and political circumstances we have shown how trust can survive its transgression and retain an independent but not risk-free moral worth. Trust is not to be seen as uniquely the territory of the sentimental or the calculating; both in and out of politics it claims its own special province of merit. If we can agree that trust finally is neither celestial nor hard-faced, then this might go a long way toward its restoration as a virtue that repays the close attention of the assiduous individual's steady gaze.

Notes

CHAPTER 1

1. David Hume, *Essays, Moral, Political and Literary*, 40.
2. Christopher Ricks, *T. S. Eliot and Prejudice*, 80.
3. Martin Hollis, "Dirty Hands," *British Journal of Political Science* 12 (October 1982): 393.
4. Annette Baier, "Trust and Antitrust," *Ethics* 96 (January 1986): 239.
5. Machiavelli, *The Discourses*, ed. Bernard Crick, 393–4.
6. Ibid., 393.
7. Ibid.
8. Ibid., 394.
9. Machiavelli, *The Prince*, ed. Quentin Skinner and Russell Price, 62.
10. Ibid.
11. Ibid.
12. Plato, *The Republic*, 389c.
13. Michael Walzer, "Political Action: The Problem of Dirty Hands," *Philosophy and Public Affairs* 2 (1973): 167–8.
14. Ibid., 161.
15. Stuart Hampshire, "Public and Private Morality," in Stuart Hampshire (ed.), *Public and Private Morality*, 49; see also idem, *Innocence and Experience*, for further discussion of his views.
16. Hampshire, "Public and Private Morality," 50.
17. Dennis F. Thompson, *Political Ethics and Public Office*, 23.
18. Ibid., 24.
19. Sophocles, *Antigone*, in *The Theban Plays*, trans. E. F. Watling, 321.

20. Edmund Burke, *Reflections on the Revolution in France,* edited and with an introduction by Conor Cruise O'Brien, 240.
21. Ibid., 176–7.
22. Walzer, "Political Action," 165.
23. Ibid.
24. Ibid., 176.
25. Ibid., 166.
26. Ibid.
27. A. Baier, "Trust and Antitrust," 235.
28. Richard Swinburne, *Faith and Reason,* 111.
29. Ibid.
30. Aristotle, *The Politics,* 1307b, trans. B. Jowett, in *Works of Aristotle,* vol. 10.
31. John Donne, "To the Countess of Bedford," in John Donne, *Complete Poetry and Selected Prose,* ed. John Hayward, 166.
32. Jean-Paul Sartre, *Three Plays,* trans. Kitty Black, 85.
33. Brian Vickers, *Towards Greek Tragedy,* 224.
34. Ibid.
35. John Dunn, "Trust and Political Agency," in Diego Gambetta (ed.), *Trust, Making and Breaking Cooperative Relations,* 85.
36. Diego Gambetta, "Can We Trust Trust?" in Gambetta, *Trust,* 221.
37. Ibid.
38. Geraint Parry, "Trust, Distrust and Consensus," *British Journal of Political Science* 6 (1976): 142.
39. Gambetta, "Can We Trust Trust?" in Gambetta, *Trust,* 224.
40. Ibid.
41. Max Beloff (ed.), *The Federalist,* with an introduction and notes by Max Beloff, 204; and see Mortimer R. Kadish and Sanford H. Kadish, *Discretion to Disobey, A Study of Lawful Departures from Legal Rules.*
42. Lance Banning, "Some Second Thoughts on Virtue and the Course of Revolutionary Thinking," in Terence Ball and J. G. A. Pocock (eds.), *Conceptual Change and the Constitution,* 207.
43. John Rawls, *A Theory of Justice,* 454.
44. Judith Shklar, *Ordinary Vices,* 184.
45. Ibid., 161.
46. Alan Ryan, "Hobbes, Toleration, and the Inner Life," in David Miller and Larry Siedentop (eds.), *The Nature of Political Theory,* 215–6.

47. Shklar, *Ordinary Vices*, 162.
48. Bernard Harrison, "Moral Judgement, Action and Emotion," *Philosophy* 59 (1984): 310.
49. Ibid.
50. Bernard Williams, *Morality: An Introduction to Ethics*, 93.
51. See Charles Fried, "The Lawyer as Friend: The Moral Foundations of the Lawyer–Client Relation," *Yale Law Journal* 85 (1976): 1060–89; Bernard Williams, "Politics and Moral Character," in Hampshire, *Public*, 55–73, esp. 65–8; Charles Fried, *Right and Wrong*, 167–94; Richard Wasserstrom, "Lawyers as Professionals: Some Moral Issues," *Human Rights* 5 (1975): 2–24; Andreas Eshete, "Does a Lawyer's Character Matter?" in David Luban (ed.), *The Good Lawyer*, 270–85; and Sissela Bok, "Can Lawyers Be Trusted?" *University of Pennsylvania Law Review* 138, no. 3 (January 1990): 913–33.
52. Machiavelli, *The Letters of Machiavelli*, edited and translated by Allan Gilbert, letter no. 225, p. 249.
53. Hannah Arendt, *On Revolution*, 290.
54. John Stuart Mill, *Utilitarianism*, 21.
55. A. Baier, "Trust and Antitrust," 252.
56. Sissela Bok, "Distrust, Secrecy, and the Arms Race," *Ethics* 95 (April 1985): 722.
57. Shklar, *Ordinary Vices*, 160.
58. Burke, *Reflections*, 125.
59. Hollis, "Dirty Hands," 397.
60. Machiavelli, *The Prince*, 74.

CHAPTER 2

1. G. W. F. Hegel, *The Philosophy of Right*, translated and with notes by T. M. Knox, 230.
2. Ibid., 229.
3. Nancy Sherman, *The Fabric of Character, Aristotle's Theory of Virtue*, 1.
4. Kurt Baier, "Justice and the Aims of Political Philosophy," *Ethics* 99 (July 1989): 789.
5. Ibid.
6. William Shakespeare, *Julius Caesar*, in *The Complete Works*, ed. W. Craig, V v 73–5.

7. Ibid., II i 10–15.
8. Ibid., 18–19.
9. Ibid., 21.
10. Ibid., 30–1.
11. Ibid., 32–4.
12. Ibid., 132–40.
13. Ibid., III i 181–3.
14. Ibid., 224–6.
15. Ibid., 236–9.
16. Ibid., III ii 56.
17. Bernard Williams, "Politics and Moral Character," in Stuart Hampshire, *Public and Private Morality*, 64.
18. Richard Rorty, *Contingency, Irony and Solidarity*, 188.
19. F. W. Winterbotham, *The Ultra Secret*, 61. There is some measure of disagreement among historians regarding the location and extent of responsibility in this case; see Martin Gilbert, *Winston S. Churchill*, vol. 6, *The Finest Hour, 1939–1941*, 913–14: "No thought of protecting the source of the knowledge of the target inhibited these defensive measures." See also N. E. Evans, "Air Intelligence and the Coventry Raid," *Journal of the Royal United Services Institute* 121 (September 1976): 66–74; as Martin Hollis comments, in "Dirty Hands," *British Journal of Political Science* 12 (October 1982), if "Churchill was given no such information . . . certainly those who deciphered the German signals did know; so the case can stand, even if Churchill is not the focus of it" (391).
20. R. F. Holland, *Against Empiricism*, 136.
21. Robert Rhodes James (ed.), *Chips: The Diaries of Sir Henry Channon*, 167.
22. Oscar Wilde, *Plays*, 156.
23. Ibid., 177.
24. Ibid.
25. Ibid., 203.
26. Ibid., 243.
27. Aristotle, *Politics*, 1284b.
28. Ibid., 1260a.
29. Ibid., 1277b.
30. Aristotle, *Nicomachean Ethics*, 1134a, trans. W. D. Ross, in *The Works of Aristotle*, vol. 9.
31. Martha Craven Nussbaum, *The Fragility of Goodness*, 352.
32. T. H. Irwin, *Aristotle's First Principles*, 443.

33. Aristotle, *Nicomachean Ethics*, 1163b; see also R. G. Mulgan, *Aristotle's Political Theory*, 78–101.
34. Aristotle, *Politics*, 1307b; see Irwin, *Aristotle's First Principles*, 638; for a discussion of Aristotle on dirty hands, see Michael Stocker, *Plural and Conflicting Values*, 51–84; and for an extensive recent discussion of an Aristotelian view of the relation between practical reasoning, ruling, and trust, see Martha Craven Nussbaum, *Love's Knowledge, Essays on Philosophy and Literature*, esp. 97–105: "We need formal procedures and codified rules in the public sphere for a number of reasons: to speed up the working-through of complex material that could not be surveyed by perception in the available time; to guard against corruption in situations where bias could easily distort judgement; and, in general, to provide a context of choice for those whose reasoning we do not really trust" (*Love's Knowledge*, 99): see also idem, *Aristotle's De Motu Animalium*, Essay 4, esp. 212.
35. William Cobbett, *Sermons*, 42–3.
36. Aristotle, *Nicomachean Ethics*, 1110a.
37. Friedrich Meinecke, *Machiavellism*, trans. Douglas Scott, 6.
38. Ibid., 7.
39. See Aristotle, *Nicomachean Ethics*, 1124a–1125a.
40. John Casey, "The Noble," in A. Phillips Griffiths (ed.), *Philosophy and Literature*, 137; see also idem, *Pagan Virtue: An Essay in Ethics*.
41. Machiavelli, *The Discourses*, ed. Bernard Crick, 393.
42. Ibid., 464.
43. William Shakespeare, *Coriolanus*, in *The Complete Works*, ed. W. Craig, II ii 5–6; for further discussion of Coriolanus, see my *Politics, Innocence and the Limits of Goodness*, 86–99.
44. Shakespeare, *Coriolanus*, I i 261.
45. Ibid., IV vii 35.
46. Machiavelli, *The Discourses*, 408–9.
47. For further discussions of Machiavelli's views on ambition, see Russell Price, "Ambizione in Machiavelli's Thought," *History of Political Thought* 3, no. 3 (November 1982): 383–445; see also John Leonard, "Public versus Private Claims: Machiavellianism from Another Perspective," *Political Theory* 12, no. 4 (November 1984): 491–506.
48. Thomas Hobbes, *Human Nature, The English Works of Thomas Hobbes*, ed. Sir William Molesworth, vol. 4, 52.

49. Ibid.
50. Aristotle, *Politics*, 1284a.
51. Machiavelli, *The Discourses*, 472.
52. Harvey C. Mansfield, Jr., *Machiavelli's New Modes and Orders*, 385. I am indebted to Mansfield's discussion in this section.
53. Ibid.
54. Machiavelli, *The Prince*, ed. Quentin Skinner and Russell Price, 28–9; see the discussion of authority and trust in Hannah Pitkin, *Fortune Is a Woman: Gender and Politics in the Thought of Niccolo Machiavelli*, 77.
55. Shakespeare, *Coriolanus*, I i 29–30.
56. Mansfield, *Machiavelli's New Modes and Orders*, 54–5.
57. Machiavelli, *The Discourses*, 444.
58. Shakespeare, *Coriolanus*, V iii 35–7.
59. Ibid., III iii 133.
60. Shklar, *Ordinary Vices*, 145.
61. Ibid.
62. Thomas Hobbes, *De Cive, The English Version*, ed. Howard Warrender, 139; for an extended modern discussion of this theme, see Stanley Cavell, "Coriolanus and Interpretations of Politics," in his *Discovering Knowledge in Six Plays of Shakespeare*, 143–77.
63. Machiavelli, *The Discourses*, 444.
64. Mansfield, *Machiavelli's New Modes and Orders*, 359.
65. Thomas Hobbes, *Leviathan*, edited and with an introduction by Michael Oakeshott, 60.
66. Ibid., 45.
67. For example, by Michael Oakeshott in "The Moral Life in the Writings of Thomas Hobbes," in his *Rationalism in Politics*, 248–300; Dorothea Krook, *Three Traditions of Moral Thought*, 122–31; and M. M. Goldsmith, *Hobbes's Science of Politics*, 79–83, 244–5; for the conventional view, see, for example, Frederick D. Weil, "The Stranger, Prudence and Trust in Hobbes's Theory," *Theory and Society* 15 (1987): "the growth of trust – which now appears as the reduction or redirection of fear under the social contract – results from the success of the sovereign in (1) assuring security and (2) reducing extreme conflict by a prudential policy of establishing certain minimal practices in the public realm and of banishing the most controversial points from the arena of public decision to the private realm" (779).
68. Hobbes, *Leviathan*, 461.

69. Ibid.
70. Ibid., 92.
71. Oakeshott, "The Moral Life," 291.
72. Ibid., 293.
73. Aristotle, *Politics*, 1284a; for a discussion of Aristotle's views on magnanimity in relation to Coriolanus, see John Alvis, "Coriolanus and Aristotle's Magnanimous Man Reconsidered," *Interpretation* 7–8 (1978): 4–28.
74. David Hume, *A Treatise of Human Nature*, ed. L. A. Selby-Bigge, 601.
75. Edmund Burke, *Reflections on the Revolution in France*, edited and with an introduction by Conor Cruise O'Brien, 93.
76. Quentin Skinner, "The State," in Terence Ball, James Farr, and Russell L. Hanson (eds.), *Political Innovation and Conceptual Change*, 126.
77. Juliet Du Boulay, *Portrait of a Greek Mountain Village*, 190.
78. Jane Austen, *Pride and Prejudice*, 263.
79. Bernard Harrison, "Moral Judgement, Action and Emotion," *Philosophy* 59 (1984): 311–12.
80. See Skinner, "The State," 124; and Deborah Baumgold, *Hobbes's Political Theory*, 113–4.
81. Hobbes, *Leviathan*, 159–60; see Baumgold, *Hobbes's Political Theory*, 86.
82. Hobbes, *Leviathan*, 92.
83. See Kenneth Minogue, "Loyalty, Liberalism and the State," in George Feaver and Frederick Rosen (eds.), *Lives, Liberties and the Public Good*, 207.

CHAPTER 3

1. Machiavelli, *The Discourses*, ed. Bernard Crick, 238.
2. Ibid., 238–9.
3. John Dunn, "Trust and Political Agency," in Diego Gambetta (ed.), *Trust and Making and Breaking Cooperative Relations*, 74.
4. Thomas Nagel, "Ruthlessness in Public Life," in Stuart Hampshire (ed.), *Public and Private Morality*, 75.
5. John Dunn, "Trust," 85–7.
6. Ibid., 86; for discussion of the philosophical and historical aspects of *raison d'état*, see Gaines Post, *Studies in Medieval*

Legal Thought, Public Law and the State 1100–1322, 241–310; William F. Church, *Richelieu and Reason of State;* C. J. Friedrich, *Constitutional Reason of State;* Ernst Kantorowicz, "Mysteries of State," *Harvard Theological Review* 48 (1955): 65–91; Roman Schnur (ed.) *Staats räson;* see also Peter S. Donaldson, *Machiavelli and Mystery of State.*

7. Church, *Richelieu*, 46.
8. Quentin Skinner, *The Foundations of Modern Political Thought*, vol. 1, *The Renaissance*, 249.
9. Giovanni Botero, *The Reason of State*, trans. P. J. Waley and D. P. Waley, 41.
10. For full accounts of the importance of trust in Locke's political thought, see John Dunn, *The Political Thought of John Locke*, 120–87; idem, " 'Trust' in the Politics of John Locke," in his *Rethinking Modern Political Theory*, 34–55; and idem, "Trust," 73–93; see also Geraint Parry, *John Locke;* Richard Ashcraft, *Locke's Two Treatises of Government;* and A. W. Sparkes, "Trust and Teleology: Locke's Politics and His Doctrine of Creation," *Canadian Journal of Philosophy* 3, no. 2 (December 1973): 268. For discussion of the notion of trusteeship in its legal and political sense, see Michael Lessnoff, *Social Contract;* J. W. Gough, *The Social Contract;* and idem, *John Locke's Political Philosophy*, 136–72.
11. Brian Barry, *Political Argument*, 226–9.
12. William James, "The Will to Believe," in *Selected Papers on Philosophy*, 119.
13. Geraint Parry, "Trust, Distrust and Consensus," *British Journal of Political Science* 6 (1976): 140; for basically the same point in an unrelated context, see Stephen Parsons, "On the Logic of Corporatism," *Political Studies* 36 (1988): 515–23: "If workers are basically untrusting, where does this initial trust arise from? It cannot emerge from corporatist arrangements but must exist prior to them" (519). "Why is trust a resource of associational arrangements when it must already exist in order for associations to form? (519 n. 23).
14. N. Luhmann, *Trust and Power*, ed. T. Burns and G. Poggi, 55–6.
15. Ibid., 83.
16. Immanuel Kant, *Lectures on Ethics*, trans. Louis Infield, 227.
17. Ibid.
18. For Kant's views, see his "On a Supposed Right to Tell Lies

from Benevolent Motives," in Kant, *Critique of Practical Reason*, trans. Thomas Kingsmill Abbott, 361–5.

19. Roger J. Sullivan, *Immanuel Kant's Moral Theory*, 175.
20. Kant, *Lectures on Ethics*, 228.
21. Alf Ross, *Directives and Norms*, 23.
22. Sissela Bok, *Lying*, 181.
23. Ibid., 145.
24. Sissela Bok, "Blowing the Whistle," in Joel L. Fleishman, Lance Liebman, and Mark H. Moore (eds.), *Public Duties: The Moral Obligations of Government Officials*, 211; see also Amy Gutman and Dennis Thompson (eds.), *Ethics and Politics*, 61–77; see Charles Fried's discussion of justified lying in his *Right and Wrong*, 69–78: "Where another initiates an encounter (as by asking a question) intending to *force* such a fact out of me, and thus force me to do wrong or to yield a right to him against my will, it is he, not I, who abuses the mutual institution of truth-telling" (77).
25. Kenneth Minogue, "Loyalty, Liberalism and the State, George Feaver and Frederick Rosen (eds.), *Lives, Liberties, and the Public Good*, 216.
26. Kant, *Perpetual Peace*, in *Kant's Political Writings*, ed. Hans Reiss, trans. H. B. Nisbett, 125–30; for modern discussions in relation to political morality, see Bok, *Lying*, 90–4; and Dennis F. Thompson, *Political Ethics and Public Office*, 116–22.
27. Kant, "The Metaphysic of Morals," 168.
28. Susan Mendus, "The Serpent and the Dove," *Philosophy* 63 (1988): 333.
29. Christine M. Korsgaard, "The Right to Lie: Kant on Dealing with Evil," *Philosophy and Public Affairs* 15 (1986): 327.
30. Kant, *Perpetual Peace*, 116.
31. Mendus, "Serpent," 342.
32. Kant, *The Metaphysic of Morals*, 139.
33. Ibid.
34. Bernard Williams, "Politics and Moral Character," in Stuart Hampshire (ed.), *Public and Private Morality*, 65.
35. See further, Charles Fried, *Right and Wrong*, 189–94; Bernard Williams, "Professional Morality and Its Dispositions," in David Luban (ed.), *The Good Lawyer* 259–69; and Andreas Eshetle, "Does a Lawyer's Character Matter?" in David Luban (ed.), *The Good Lawyer*, 275–6.

36. Thomas Hobbes, *Leviathan*, edited and with an introduction by Michael Oakeshott, 184.
37. Ibid.
38. Ibid.
39. William Cobbett, *Sermons*, 97–120.
40. Ibid., 97 (Micah, 7 iii).
41. Ibid., 114.
42. Ibid., 104; for a discussion of the concept of secret trust in Roman law, see David Johnston, *The Roman Law of Trusts*, 42–75.
43. Williams, "Politics and Moral Character," in Hampshire, *Public and Private Morality*, 68.
44. Mendus, "Serpent," 334.
45. See Bernard Williams, *Moral Luck*, 20–39.
46. For further discussion, see Andreas Eshetle, "Character, Virtue and Freedom," *Philosophy* 57 (1982): 495–513.
47. Martha Craven Nussbaum, "The Discernment of Perception: An Aristotelian Conception of Private and Public Morality," in J. Cleary (ed.), *Proceedings of the Boston Area Colloquium in Ancient Philosophy*, 168.
48. Martin Hollis, "Dirty Hands," *British Journal of Political Science* 12 (October 1982): 389.
49. Ibid.
50. Ibid., 397.
51. Ibid.
52. Ibid., 393.
53. William Shakespeare, *Macbeth*, in *The Complete Works*, ed. W. Craig, I vii 12–16.
54. Cicero, *De Officiis*, trans. Walter Miller, 375; see also Martin Hollis, *The Cunning of Reason*, 173–93.
55. Ibid., 377.
56. Ibid.
57. Ibid., 391.
58. Ibid., 389.
59. Alan Silver, "'Trust' in Social and Political Theory," in G. D. Suttles and M. N. Zald (eds.), *The Challenge of Social Control*, 60.
60. Annette Baier, "Trust and Antitrust," *Ethics* 96 (January 1986): 239.
61. On this point, see Virginia Held, *Rights and Goods*, 62–85; and

idem, "On the Meaning of Trust," *Ethics* 78 (1968): 156–9; see also Barry, *Political Argument*, 253–6.

62. A. Baier, "Trust and Antitrust," 240.
63. Ibid., 251.
64. Michael Slote, *Goods and Virtues*, 65.
65. Ibid.
66. Ibid.
67. D. O. Thomas, "The Duty to Trust," *Proceedings of the Aristotelian Society* 79 (1978–9): 100.
68. Ibid., 93.
69. Bernard Harrison, "Moral Judgement, Action and Emotion," *Philosophy* 59 (1984): 310–11.
70. A. Baier, "Trust and Antitrust," 255.
71. Hannah Arendt, *The Human Condition*, 190.

CHAPTER 4

1. John Rawls "The Sense of Justice," *Philosophical Review* 62 (1963): 291.
2. Ibid.
3. Michael Oakeshott, *Rationalism in Politics*, 129.
4. G. W. F. Hegel, *The Philosophy of Right*, 164; for a recent discussion of Hegel's recognition of the political dangers of excessive mistrust, see Stephen Houlgate, *Freedom, Truth and History: An Introduction to Hegel's Philosophy*, 121–2.
5. G. W. F. Hegel, *Aesthetics: Lectures on Fine Art*, trans. T. M. Knox, vol. I, 204.
6. Alasdair MacIntyre, *After Virtue*, 143.
7. Adrian Poole, *Tragedy, Shakespeare and the Greek Example*, 212.
8. Tony Tanner, *Adultery in the Novel*, 27.
9. Hegel, *Aesthetics*, 206.
10. See Martha Craven Nussbaum, "Consequences and Character in Sophocles' *Philoctetes*," *Philosophy and Literature* 1, pt. 1 (1976–7): 30–1.
11. Sophocles, *Philoctetes*, trans. E. F. Watling, in *Electra and Other Plays*, 172–86.
12. Poole, *Tragedy*, 191.
13. Ibid., 192.

14. Ibid., 193.
15. Nussbaum, "Consequences," 30; see also Mary Whitlock Blundell, "The Moral Character of Odysseus in *Philoctetes*," *Greek, Roman and Byzantine Studies* 28 (1987): 307–29.
16. N. Luhmann, *Trust and Power*, ed. T. Burns and G. Poggi, 83.
17. Hegel, *Philosophy of Right*, 106.
18. Sophocles, *Philoctetes*, 116–19.
19. See my *Politics, Innocence and the Limits of Goodness*, for discussion of the impact of innocence on politics.
20. Sophocles, *Philoctetes*, 166.
21. Søren Kierkegaard, *The Concept of Dread*, translated and with an introduction and notes by Walter Lowrie, 33.
22. Poole, *Tragedy*, 199.
23. Sophocles, *Philoctetes*, 521–3.
24. Mary Whitlock Blundell, *Helping Friends and Harming Enemies: A Study in Sophocles and Greek Ethics*, 202.
25. Poole, *Tragedy*, 189–90.
26. John Bayley, *Shakespeare and Tragedy*, 102.
27. Ibid.
28. William Shakespeare, *Troilus and Cressida*, ed. Kenneth Palmer, I iii 375–9.
29. Ibid., II ii 21–4.
30. Ibid., 174–7.
31. Ibid., 56–7.
32. Ibid., 53.
33. Ibid., 81–2.
34. Ibid., 200–3.
35. For a discussion of Aristotle on this problem, see John M. Cooper, "Aristotle on the Goods of Fortune," *Philosophical Review* 94, no. 2 (April 1985): 173–96.
36. Shakespeare, *Troilus and Cressida*, II iii 207–8.
37. Bayley, *Shakespeare and Tragedy*, 111.
38. Shakespeare, *Troilus and Cressida*, III ii 83–5.
39. In his introduction to the Arden edition of the play: Shakespeare, *Troilus and Cressida*, 51.
40. Ibid., III ii 89–91.
41. Ibid., 180.
42. Ibid., 185–7.
43. Ibid., 126.
44. Bayley, *Shakespeare and Tragedy*, 115.

45. Ibid., 111.
46. Shakespeare, *Troilus and Cressida*, III ii 146–8.
47. Hegel, *Philosophy of Right*, 262.
48. Ibid., 111.
49. Ibid., 263.
50. John Stuart Mill, *Autobiography*, edited and with a preface by John Jacob Coss, 118–19.
51. Emile Zola, *Thérèse Raquin*, translated and with an introduction by Leonard Tancock, 31.
52. Ibid., 36.
53. Ibid.
54. Ibid., 38.
55. Ibid., 39.
56. Ibid., 40.
57. Ibid., 41.
58. Ibid., 50.
59. Hegel, *Philosophy of Right*, 115.
60. Tanner, *Adultery*, 11.
61. Ibid., 375.
62. Zola, *Thérèse Raquin*, 74.
63. Annette Baier, "Trust and Antitrust," *Ethics* 96 (January 1986): 253.
64. Ibid.
65. Zola, *Thérèse Raquin*, 60.
66. Hegel, *Philosophy of Right*, 265.
67. A. Baier, "Trust and Antitrust," 255.
68. Ibid.
69. Ibid.
70. Ibid., 255–6.
71. Ibid., 256.
72. Ibid.
73. Ibid., 259–60.
74. Ibid., 256.
75. Peter Jones, *Philosophy and the Novel*, 110.
76. Henry James, *Lord Beaupré and Other Tales*, 255–310.
77. S. Gorley Putt, *The Fiction of Henry James*, 255.
78. Judith Shklar, *Ordinary Vices*, 143.
79. For a discussion of the variety of lies and liars in Shakespeare, see Inga-Stina Ewbank, "Shakespeare's Liars," *Proceedings of the British Academy* 69 (1983): 137–68.

CHAPTER 5

1. Niklas Luhmann, "Familiarity, Confidence, Trust: Problems and Alternatives," in Diego Gambetta (ed.), *Trust, Making and Breaking Cooperative Relations*, 100.
2. Shelly Kagan, *The Limits of Morality*, 89.
3. Simone Weil, *The Need for Roots*, trans. Arthur Wills, with a preface by T. S. Eliot, 32.
4. Ibid., 33.
5. Annette Baier, "Trust and Antitrust," *Ethics* 96 (January 1986): 252.
6. Geoffrey Hawthorn, "Three Ironies in Trust," in Diego Gambetta, *Trust, Making and Breaking Cooperative Relations*, 115.
7. Ibid.
8. John Dunn, *Political Obligation in Its Historical Context: Essays in Political Theory*, 271.
9. Gilbert Harman, "Relativistic Ethics: Morality as Politics," *Midwest Studies in Philosophy* 3 (1978): 118.
10. Ibid.
11. David Hume, *A Treatise of Human Nature*, ed. L. A. Selby-Bigge, 569.
12. David Hume, *Enquiries Concerning the Human Understanding and Concerning the Principles of Morals*, ed. L. A. Selby-Bigge, 186; see also Knud Haakonssen, *The Science of a Legislator: The Natural Jurisprudence of David Hume and Adam Smith*, 39–44.
13. David Hume, *Essays, Moral, Political and Literary*, 474; see also Jonathan Harrison, *Hume's Theory of Justice*, 203–10.
14. See Mill's Letter to William Thornton, 17 April 1863, John Stuart Mill, *The Later Letters of John Stuart Mill, 1849–1873*, ed. Francis E. Mineka and Dwight N. Lindley, 854.
15. Ibid.
16. Ibid.
17. See John Skorupski, *John Stuart Mill*, 412.
18. Mill, *Later Letters*, 854.
19. In Euripides, *Hecabe*, in *Medea and Other Plays*, translated and with an introduction by Philip Vellacott, 883.
20. Cicero, *De Officiis*, trans. Walter Miller, 361.
21. Skorupski, *Mill*, 331.
22. Thucydides, *The Peloponnesian War*, trans. Rex Warner, with an introduction and notes by M. I. Finley, 414–29.

23. Ibid., 415.
24. Ibid.
25. Ibid., 417.
26. Ibid.
27. Judith Shklar, *Ordinary Vices*, 174.
28. Thucydides, *Peloponnesian War*, 421.
29. Ibid., 422.
30. Ibid., 419.
31. Christopher Ricks, *T. S. Eliot and Prejudice*, 84.
32. Ibid., 84–5; Diego Gambetta employs a similar example for slightly different effect: "If one group of soldiers for some reason believes itself to be facing a mob of unrestrained warriors and trusts neither the latter's time preferences nor their rationality, 'peaceful' signals are more likely to be interpreted as a trap" (Diego Gambetta, "Can We Trust Trust?" in Diego Gambetta [ed.], *Trust, Making and Breaking Cooperatives*, 227).
33. Ricks, *T. S. Eliot and Prejudice*, 85.
34. Michael Slote, *Goods and Virtues*, 48–9.
35. George Orwell, *Nineteen Eighty-Four*, 23.
36. Ibid.
37. Ibid.
38. William Shakespeare, *Measure for Measure*, in *The Complete Works*, ed. W. Craig, II iv 145.
39. Ibid., 150–2.
40. Søren Kierkegaard, *Purity of Heart Is to Will One Thing*, trans. Douglas V. Steere, 69.
41. Ludwig Wittgenstein, *Tractatus Logico-Philosophicus*, trans. D. F. Pears and B. F. McGuiness, 6.422, p. 147; see Peter Winch, *Ethics and Action*, 210–17.
42. Sophocles, *Philoctetes*, in *Electra and Other Plays*, trans. E. F. Watling, 909–10.
43. Ibid., 659–61.
44. Mary Whitlock Blundell, *Helping Friends and Harming Enemies, A Study in Sophocles and Greek Ethics*, 204–5.
45. Sophocles, *Philoctetes*, 838–41.
46. C. M. Bowra, *Sophoclean Tragedy*, 281.
47. Sophocles, *Philoctetes*, 900–1.
48. Ibid., 927–8.
49. Bowra, *Sophoclean Tragedy*, 278.
50. Sophocles, *Philoctetes*, 957–8.

51. Ibid., 932–3.
52. Ibid., 972–5.
53. Ibid., 1015–19.
54. Ibid., 1023–4.
55. Ibid., 1029–37.
56. Ibid., 1058–60.
57. Blundell, *Helping Friends*, 211.
58. Sophocles, *Philoctetes*, 1024–31.
59. Ibid., 1246.
60. Ibid., 1250.
61. Ibid., 1245–9.
62. Blundell, *Helping Friends*, 212–13.
63. Sophocles, *Philoctetes*, 1310–11.
64. William Shakespeare, *Troilus and Cressida*, ed. Kenneth Palmer, III iii 9.
65. Ibid., ii 205.
66. Ibid., iii 150–3.
67. Ibid., 153.
68. John Bayley, *Shakespeare and Tragedy*, 101.
69. Shakespeare, *Troilus and Cressida*, II iii 164–9.
70. Kenneth Palmer in his introduction to Shakespeare, *Troilus and Cressida*, 76.
71. Shakespeare, *Troilus and Cressida*, III iii 80–3.
72. Palmer, introduction to Shakespeare, *Troilus and Cressida*, 76.
73. Shakespeare, *Troilus and Cressida*, IV iv 31.
74. Ibid., ii 106–12.
75. Ibid., iv 35–8.
76. Ibid., 55–6.
77. Ibid., 57.
78. Ibid., 102–8.
79. Ibid., v 55–63.
80. Ibid., 240–5.
81. Ibid., 279–82.
82. Ibid., 287–8.
83. Ibid., 291.
84. J. L. Stocks, *Morality and Purpose*, 38.
85. Ibid., 50.
86. Shakespeare, *Troilus and Cressida*, II ii 52.
87. Ibid., 55.
88. Hegel, *The Philosophy of Right*, translated and with notes by T. M. Knox, 261.

89. For a discussion of Kant's views on marriage, see Howard Williams, *Kant's Political Philosophy*, 114–24.
90. Kant, "Reflections on the Philosophy of Right," cited in Williams, *Kant's Political Philosophy*, 115.
91. Kant, *Political Writings*, ed. Hans Reiss, trans. H. B. Nisbett, 158.
92. Ibid.
93. Ibid.
94. Joseph Conrad, *A Set of Six*, 176.
95. Ibid., 233.
96. See Kant, *Philosophical Correspondence*, edited and translated by Arnulf Zweig, 188–90.
97. Emile Zola, *Thérèse Raquin*, translated and with an introduction by Leonard Tancock, 65.
98. Ibid., 68.
99. Ibid., 73.
100. Ibid., 72.
101. Ibid.
102. Ibid., 73.
103. For a discussion and criticism of this view, see Susan Mendus, "Marital Faithfulness," *Philosophy* 59 (1984): 243–52; and for a discussion of Hume's views on chastity, see Annette Baier "Good Men's Women: Hume on Chastity and Trust," *Hume Studies* 5 (1979): 1–19; and Marcia Baron, "Hume's Noble Lie: An Account of His Artificial Virtues," *Canadian Journal of Philosophy* 12 (3 September 1982): 539–55.
104. Zola, *Thérèse Raquin*, 74.
105. Ibid., 77.
106. Ibid., 81.
107. Ibid.
108. Ibid., 82.
109. Tony Tanner, *Adultery in the Novel*, 67.
110. Ibid., 66.
111. Zola, *Thérèse Raquin*, 105.
112. Ibid., 113.
113. Hegel, *Philosophy of Right*, 82.
114. Simone Weil, *The Need for Roots*, trans. Arthur Mills, with a preface by T. S. Eliot, 203–4.
115. Peter Winch, *Trying to Make Sense*, 167.
116. Ibid., 167–8.

CHAPTER 6

1. Graham Greene, *A Gun for Sale*, 236.
2. Dennis F. Thompson, *Political Ethics and Public Office*, 23.
3. Ibid., 24.
4. Ibid., 26.
5. Ibid.
6. Ibid.
7. Ibid., 29.
8. Ibid.
9. Ibid., 30.
10. Ibid., 32.
11. Karl Marx, "The Civil War in France," in Lewis S. Feuer (ed.), *Marx and Engels, Basic Writings on Politics and Philosophy*, 422–30; I would like to thank Steve Buckler for the many discussions I have had with him about the importance of this example; for his own views, see N. E. Buckler, "Political Action and Moral Judgement" (Ph.D. diss., University of Southampton), ch. 8, esp. pp. 207–8 and 233–8.
12. Ibid., 426.
13. Ibid.
14. Ibid.
15. Simone Weil, *The Need for Roots*, trans. Arthur Mills, with a preface by T. S. Eliot, 203.
16. As quoted by Jonathan Glover, *Causing Death and Saving Lives*, 288, during his discussion of moral distance (286–97).
17. Hannah Arendt, *Crises of the Republic*, 30; and for further discussion of forgiveness and forgetting, see Michael Oakeshott, *On Human Conduct*, 83, and Benedetto Croce, *The Conduct of Life*, 46–51.
18. Ibid., 30.
19. See John R. S. Wilson, "In One Another's Power," *Ethics* 88 (1978–9); 299–315.
20. Emile Zola, *Thérèse Raquin*, translated and with an introduction by Leonard Tancock, 187.
21. Peter French, "Morally Blaming Whole Populations," in Virginia Held, Sidney Morgenbesser, and Thomas Nagel (eds.), *Philosophy, Morality and International Affairs*, 285.
22. J. Glenn Gray, *The Warriors: Reflections on Men in Battle*, 199.
23. Judith Shklar, *Legalism*, 220.

24. Hanna Pitkin, *Wittgenstein and Justice*, 149–50.
25. Sophocles, *Philoctetes*, in *Electra and Other Plays*, trans. E. F. Watling, 1313–15.
26. Ibid., 1325–7.
27. Ibid., 1337–9.
28. Ibid., 1350–1.
29. Ibid., 1359–60.
30. Ibid., 1352–4.
31. Ibid., 1368.
32. Ibid., 1043.
33. Mary Whitlock Blundell, *Helping Friends and Harming Enemies: A Study in Sophocles and Greek Ethics*, 217.
34. Sophocles, *Philoctetes*, 1373–4.
35. Ibid., 1393–7.
36. Ibid., 1409.
37. Ibid., 1458–61.
38. Ibid., 1444–7.
39. Alasdair MacIntyre, *After Virtue*, 132.
40. Ibid., 143.
41. Blundell, *Helping Friends*, 220–5; I am greatly indebted to Blundell's interpretation at this stage of the argument.
42. Sophocles, *Philoctetes*, 1434–5.
43. Blundell, *Helping Friends*, 225.
44. The term is Strindberg's; see Inga-Stina Ewbank, "Shakespeare's Liars," *Proceedings of the British Academy* 69 (1983): 155.
45. William Shakespeare, *Troilus and Cressida*, ed. Kenneth Palmer, v i 98–100.
46. Ibid., ii 57.
47. Ibid., 113.
48. Ibid., 108.
49. Ibid., 117–21.
50. Ibid., 122.
51. Simone Weil, "Human Personality," in *An Anthology*, edited and with an introduction by Sian Miles, 83; for an illuminating discussion of Simone Weil's view of the limitation of the language of rights, see Peter Winch, *Simone Weil: "The Just Balance,"* 179–82.
52. Shakespeare, *Troilus and Cressida*, V ii 126–30.
53. Ibid., 130.
54. Ibid., 139.
55. Ibid., 143.

56. Ibid., 152–3.
57. Ibid., 154–7.
58. John Bayley, *The Uses of Division*, 191–2.
59. Shakespeare, *Troilus and Cressida*, V ii 192–4.
60. Bayley, *Uses*, 206.
61. Shakespeare, *Troilus and Cressida*, V iii 109.
62. Ibid., ii 164–8.
63. Ibid., V iii 10–12.
64. Ibid., 16.
65. Ibid., 19–22.
66. Ibid., 23–5.
67. Ibid., 27.
68. Ibid., 32.
69. Ibid., 37.
70. Ibid., 51–2.
71. Ibid., v 40.
72. Simone Weil, *The Iliad or the Poem of Force*, trans. Mary McCarthy.
73. Ibid., 3.
74. Ibid., 11.
75. Shakespeare, *Troilus and Cressida*, V v 46.
76. Ibid., vii 6.
77. Ibid., viii 14.
78. Ibid., 21–2.
79. Ibid., x 31.
80. Frederick D. Weil, *The Iliad or the Poem of Force*, 19.
81. Ibid., 8.
82. William Shakespeare, *Henry V*, in *The Complete Works*, ed. W. Craig, IV vi 7.
83. Bayley, *Uses*, 191.
84. Shakespeare, *Troilus and Cressida*, V iii 112–13.
85. Ibid., ii 108–9.
86. Simone Weil, *Selected Essays 1934–43*, trans. Richard Rees, 31.
87. Hannah Arendt, *The Human Condition*, 237.
88. Ibid.
89. Zola, *Thérèse Raquin*, 177.
90. Ibid., 141.
91. Ibid., 196.
92. Ibid., 172.
93. Ibid., 122.
94. Ibid., 189.

95. Ibid., 188.
96. Ibid., 206.
97. Ibid., 215.
98. Bernard Harrison, "Moral Judgement, Action and Emotion," *Philosophy* 59 (1984): 316.
99. Zola, *Thérèse Raquin*, 223.
100. Ibid.
101. Ibid., 254.
102. Ibid., 256.
103. Aurel Kolnai, *Ethics, Value and Reality*, 223.
104. See David Heyd, *Supererogation*, 154–64.
105. Ibid., 162.
106. K. J. Dover, *Greek Popular Morality in the Time of Plato and Aristotle*, 194.
107. Jeffrie G. Murphy, "Forgiveness and Resentment," *Midwest Studies in Philosophy*, ed. Peter French et al., vol. 7, 504; for a criticism, see Norvin Richards, "Forgiveness," *Ethics* 99 (October 1988): 76–97. For further discussion, see Jeffrie G. Murphy and Jean Hampton, *Forgiveness and Mercy*; and for a discussion of the relations between forgiveness and pardon, see Kathleen Dean Moore, *Pardons – Justice, Mercy and the Public Interest*.
108. W. H. Walsh, "Pride, Shame and Responsibility," *Philosophical Quarterly* 20, no. 78 (January 1970): 1–13.
109. Arendt, *Human Condition*, 237.
110. Plato, *The Republic*, trans. F. M. Cornford, for example, 441C.
111. Arendt, *Human Condition*, 238.
112. Ibid.
113. Ibid., 240.
114. Ibid., 242.
115. Ibid., 243.
116. See George Kateb, *Hannah Arendt, Politics, Conscience, Evil*, 36.
117. Hannah Arendt, *The Origins of Totalitarianism*, 474.
118. William Shakespeare, *Much Ado About Nothing*, in *The Complete Works*, ed. W. Craig, II i 234.
119. Arendt, *Origins of Totalitarianism*, 477.
120. Hannah Arendt, *Lectures on Kant's Political Philosophy*, edited and with an interpretative essay by Ronald Beiner, 50.
121. Arendt, *Origins of Totalitarianism*, 477.
122. For an excellent discussion drawing on Wittgenstein's argument in *On Certainty*, see Lars Hertzberg, "On the Attitude of

Trust," *Inquiry* 31 (1989): 307–22. The article by Olli Lagen-spetz, "Legitimacy and Trust," *Philosophical Investigations* 15, no. 1 (January 1992): 1–21, raises important questions, but unfortunately appeared too late for me to give it the consideration it deserves. I hope to address the points it makes at some future date. See also D. Z. Phillips, "My Neighbour and My Neighbours," *Philosophical Investigations*, 12, no. 2 (April 1989): 112–33.

123. Søren Kierkegaard, *Works of Love*, trans. Howard Hong and Edna Hong, 227.

CONCLUSION

1. Thomas Hobbes, *Leviathan*, edited and with an introduction by Michael Oakeshott, 82–3.
2. Thucydides, *History of the Peloponnesian War*, trans. Benjamin Jowett, vol. 1, 244.
3. William Shakespeare, *Julius Caesar*, in *The Complete Works*, ed. W. Craig, II i 18–19.
4. David Hume, *A Treatise of Human Nature*, ed. L. A. Selby-Bigge, 569.
5. Ibid.
6. Aristotle, *Nicomachean Ethics*, trans. W. D. Ross, *The Works of Aristotle*, vol. 11, 1155a 23–5.
7. William Shakespeare, *Troilus and Cressida*, ed. Kenneth Palmer, V iii 32.
8. Dennis F. Thompson, *Political Ethics and Public Office*, 26.
9. See the interesting discussion of what it means to lose a moral concept in Cora Diamond, "Losing Your Concepts," *Ethics* 98 (January 1988): 255–77.
10. Charles Dickens, *Bleak House*, 410.
11. Ibid.
12. Ibid.
13. Nicolai Hartmann, *Ethics*, trans. Stanton Coit, vol. 2, *Moral Values*, 295; and see Raimond Gaita, *Good and Evil: An Absolute Conception:* "Trust is not surrender: to trust is both to judge something worthy of our trust and ourselves to be worthily trusting" (273).
14. Hartmann, *Ethics*, 292.

Bibliography

Alvis, John. "Coriolanus and Aristotle's Magnanimous Man Reconsidered." *Interpretation* 7–8 (1978): 4–28.

Arendt, Hannah. *The Human Condition.* Chicago: University of Chicago Press, 1958.

On Revolution. London: Faber & Faber, 1963.

Crises of the Republic. Harmondsworth: Penguin Books, 1973.

The Origins of Totalitarianism. New edition with added prefaces. San Diego, Calif.: Harcourt Brace Jovanovitch, 1973.

Lectures on Kant's Political Philosophy. Edited and with an interpretive essay by Ronald Beiner. Chicago: University of Chicago Press, 1982.

Aristotle. *Nicomachean Ethics.* Translated by W. D. Ross. *The Works of Aristotle.* Vol. 11. Oxford: Oxford University Press (Clarendon Press), 1940.

The Politics. Translated by B. Jowett. *The Works of Aristotle.* Vol. 10. Oxford: Oxford University Press (Clarendon Press), 1946.

Ashcraft, Richard. *Locke's Two Treatises of Government.* London: Unwin Hyman, 1987.

Austen, Jane. *Pride and Prejudice.* London: Spring Books, 1966.

Baier, Annette. "Good Men's Women: Hume on Chastity and Trust." *Hume Studies* 5 (1979): 1–19.

"Trust and Antitrust." *Ethics* 96 (January 1986): 231–60.

Baier, Kurt. "Justice and the Aims of Political Philosophy." *Ethics* 99 (July 1989): 771–91.

Ball, Terence, and J. G. A. Pocock (eds.). *Conceptual Change and the Constitution.* Lawrence: University Press of Kansas, 1988.

Ball, Terence, James Farr, and Russell L. Hanson (eds.). *Political Innovation and Conceptual Change.* Cambridge University Press, 1989.

Bibliography

Banning, Lance. "Some Second Thoughts on Virtue and the Course of Revolutionary Thinking." In Terence Ball and J. G. A. Pocock (eds.), *Conceptual Change and the Constitution*. Lawrence: University Press of Kansas, 1988.

Baron, Marcia. "Hume's Noble Lie: An Account of His Artificial Virtues." *Canadian Journal of Philosophy* 12, no. 3 (September 1982): 539–55.

Barry, Brian. *Political Argument*. London: Routledge & Kegan Paul, 1965.

Baumgold, Deborah. *Hobbes's Political Theory*. Cambridge University Press, 1988.

Bayley, John. *The Uses of Division*. London: Chatto & Windus, 1976.
Shakespeare and Tragedy. London: Routledge & Kegan Paul, 1981.

Beloff, Max (ed.). *The Federalist*. Oxford: Blackwell Publisher, 1948.

Blundell, Mary Whitlock. "The Moral Character of Odysseus in *Philoctetes*." *Greek, Roman and Byzantine Studies* 28 (1987): 307–29.
Helping Friends and Harming Enemies A Study in Sophocles and Greek Ethics. Cambridge University Press, 1989.

Bok, Sissela. *Lying*. London: Quartet, 1980.
"Blowing the Whistle." In Joel L. Fleishman, Lance Leibman, and Mark H. Moore (eds.). *Public Duties: The Moral Obligations of Government Officials*. Cambridge: Harvard University Press, 1981, 204–20.
"Distrust, Secrecy and the Arms Race." *Ethics* 95 (April 1985): 712–27.
"Can Lawyers Be Trusted?" *University of Pennsylvania Law Review* 138, no. 3 (January 1990): 913–33.

Botero, Giovanni. *The Reason of State*. Translated by P. J. and D. P. Waley. London: Routledge & Kegan Paul, 1956.

Bowra, C. M. *Sophoclean Tragedy*. Oxford: Oxford University Press (Clarendon Press), 1944.

Buckler, N. E. "Political Action and Moral Judgement." Ph.D. diss., University of Southampton, 1989.

Burke, Edmund. *Reflections on the Revolution in France*. Edited and with an introduction by Conor Cruise O'Brien. Harmondsworth: Penguin Books, 1982.

Casey, John, "The Noble." In A. Phillips Griffiths (ed.), *Philosophy and Literature*. Royal Institute of Philosophy Lecture Series, 16. Cambridge University Press, 1984, 135–53.
Pagan Virtue: An Essay on Ethics. Oxford: Oxford University Press (Clarendon Press), 1990.

Bibliography

Cavell, Stanley. *Discovering Knowledge in Six Plays of Shakespeare.* Cambridge University Press, 1987.

Church, William F. *Richelieu and Reason of State.* Princeton, N.J.: Princeton University Press, 1972.

Cicero. *De Officiis.* Translated by Walter Miller. London: Heinemann, 1951.

Cobbett, William. *Sermons.* London: C. Clement, 1822.

Conrad, Joseph. *A Set of Six.* London: Methuen & Co., 1931.

Cooper, John M. "Aristotle on the Goods of Fortune." *Philosophical Review* 94, no. 2 (April 1985): 173–96.

Croce, Benedeto. *The Conduct of Life.* London: Harrap (n.d.).

Diamond, Cora. "Losing Your Concepts." *Ethics* 98 (January 1988): 255–77.

Dickens, Charles. *Bleak House.* London: Chapman & Hall, 1900.

Donaldson, Peter S. *Machiavelli and Mystery of State.* Cambridge University Press, 1988.

Donne, John. *Complete Poetry and Selected Prose.* Edited by John Hayward. London: Nonesuch Press, 1936.

Dover, K. J. *Greek Popular Morality in the Time of Plato and Aristotle.* Oxford: Blackwell Publisher, 1974.

Du Boulay, Juliet. *Portrait of a Greek Mountain Village.* Oxford: Oxford University Press (Clarendon Press), 1974.

Dunn, John. *The Political Thought of John Locke.* Cambridge University Press, 1969.

Political Obligation in Its Historical Context, Essays in Political Theory. Cambridge University Press, 1980.

"'Trust' in the Politics of John Locke." In his *Rethinking Modern Political Theory.* Cambridge University Press, 1985.

"Trust and Political Agency." In Diego Gambetta (ed.), *Trust, Making and Breaking Cooperative Relations.* Oxford: Blackwell Publisher, 1988, 73–93.

Eshetle, Andreas. "Character, Virtue and Freedom." *Philosophy* 57 (1982): 495–513.

"Does a Lawyer's Character Matter?" In David Luban (ed.), *The Good Lawyer.* Totowa, N.J.: Rowman & Allenheld, 1983, 270–85.

Euripides. *Medea and Other Plays.* Translated and with an introduction by Phillip Vellacott. Harmondsworth: Penguin Books, 1963.

Evans, N. E. "Air Intelligence and the Coventry Raid." *Journal of the Royal United Services Institute* 121 (September 1976): 66–74.

Bibliography

Ewbank, Inga-Stina. "Shakespeare's Liars." *Proceedings of the British Academy,* 69 (1983): 137–68.

Feaver, George, and Frederick Rosen. *Lives, Liberties and the Public Good.* London: Macmillan Press, 1987.

Fleishman, Joel L., Lance Leibman, and Mark H. Moore (eds.). *Public Duties: The Moral Obligations of Government Officials.* Cambridge: Harvard University Press, 1981.

French, Peter. "Morally Blaming Whole Populations." In Virginia Held, Sidney Morgenbesser, and Thomas Nagel (eds.), *Philosophy, Morality and International Affairs.* New York: Oxford University Press, 1974, 266–85.

Fried, Charles. "The Lawyer as Friend: The Moral Foundations of the Lawyer–Client Relation." *Yale Law Journal* 85 (1976): 1,060–89.

Right and Wrong. Cambridge: Harvard University Press, 1978.

Friedrich, C. J. *Constitutional Reason of State.* Providence, R.I.: Brown University Press, 1957.

Gaita, Raimond. *Good and Evil: An Absolute Conception.* London: Macmillan Press, 1991.

Gambetta, Diego. "Can We Trust Trust?" In Diego Gambetta (ed.), *Trust, Making and Breaking Cooperative Relations.* Oxford: Blackwell Publisher, 1988, 213–37.

(ed.). *Trust, Making and Breaking Cooperative Relations.* Oxford: Blackwell Publisher, 1988.

Gilbert, Martin. *Winston S. Churchill.* Vol. 6, *The Finest Hour.* London: Heinemann, 1983.

Glover, Jonathan. *Causing Death and Saving Lives.* Harmondsworth: Penguin Books, 1977.

Goldsmith, M. M. *Hobbes's Science of Politics.* New York: Columbia University Press, 1966.

Gough, J. W. *The Social Contract.* Oxford: Oxford University Press (Clarendon Press), 1936.

John Locke's Political Philosophy. Oxford: Oxford University Press (Clarendon Press), 1950.

Gray, J. Glenn. *The Warriors: Reflections on Men in Battle.* New York: Doubleday, 1967.

Greene, Graham. *A Gun for Sale.* London: Heinemann, 1936.

Gutman, Amy, and Dennis Thompson (eds.). *Ethics and Politics.* Chicago: Nelson-Hall, 1984.

Haakonssen, Knud. *The Science of a Legislator: The Natural Jurispru-*

dence of David Hume and Adam Smith. Cambridge University Press, 1981.

Hampshire, Stuart. "Public and Private Morality." In Stuart Hampshire (ed.), *Public and Private Morality.* Cambridge University Press, 1978, 25–53.

Innocence and Experience. London: Lane, 1989.

Harman, Gilbert. "Relativistic Ethics: Morality as Politics." *Midwest Studies in Philosophy* 3 (1978): 109–21.

Harrison, Bernard. "Moral Judgement, Action and Emotion." *Philosophy* 59 (1984): 295–321.

Harrison, Jonathan. *Hume's Theory of Justice.* Oxford: Oxford University Press (Clarendon Press), 1981.

Hartmann, Nicolai. *Ethics.* 3 vols. Translated by Stanton Coit. London: Allen & Unwin, 1932.

Hawthorn, Geoffrey. "Three Ironies in Trust." In Diego Gambetta (ed.), *Trust, Making and Breaking Cooperative Relations.* Oxford: Blackwell Publisher, 1988, 111–26.

Hegel, G. W. F. *The Philosophy of Right.* Translated and with notes by T. M. Knox. Oxford: Oxford University Press (Clarendon Press), 1967.

Aesthetics: Lectures on Fine Art. Vol. 1. Translated by T. M. Knox. Oxford: Oxford University Press (Clarendon Press), 1975.

Held, Virginia. "On the Meaning of Trust." *Ethics* 78 (1968): 156–9.

Held, Virginia, Sidney Morgenbesser, and Thomas Nagel (eds.). *Philosophy, Morality and International Affairs.* New York: Oxford University Press, 1974.

Rights and Goods. New York: Free Press, 1984.

Hertzberg, Lars. "On the Attitude of Trust." *Inquiry* 31 (1989): 307–22.

Heyd, David. *Supererogation.* Cambridge University Press, 1982.

Hobbes, Thomas. *Human Nature, The English Works of Thomas Hobbes.* Vol. 4. Edited by Sir William Molesworth. London: 1839–44.

Leviathan. Edited and with an introduction by Michael Oakeshott. Oxford: Blackwell Publisher, 1960.

De Cive, The English Version. Edited by Howard Warrender. Oxford: Oxford University Press (Clarendon Press), 1983.

Holis, Martin. "Dirty Hands." *British Journal of Political Science* 12 (October 1982): 385–98.

The Cunning of Reason. Cambridge University Press, 1987.

Holland, R. F. *Against Empiricism.* Oxford: Blackwell Publisher, 1980.

Bibliography

Houlgate, Stephen. *Freedom, Truth and History: An Introduction to Hegel's Philosophy.* London: Routledge & Kegan Paul, 1991.

Hume, David. *Essays, Moral, Political and Literary.* London: Grant Richards, 1903.

A Treatise of Human Nature. Edited by L. A. Selby-Bigge. Oxford: Oxford University Press (Clarendon Press), 1949.

Enquiries Concerning the Human Understanding and Concerning the Principles of Morals. Edited by L. A. Selby-Bigge. Oxford: Oxford University Press (Clarendon Press), 1951.

Irwin, T. H. *Aristotle's First Principles.* Oxford: Oxford University Press (Clarendon Press), 1988.

James, Henry. *Lord Beaupré and Other Tales.* London: Macmillan Press, 1923.

James, Robert Rhodes (ed.). *Chips: The Diaries of Sir Henry Channon.* London: Weidenfeld & Nicolson, 1967.

James, William. "The Will to Believe." In *Selected Papers on Philosophy.* London: Dent, 1917, 99–125.

Johnson, Peter. *Politics, Innocence and the Limits of Goodness.* London: Routledge, 1988.

Johnston, David. *The Roman Law of Trusts.* Oxford: Oxford University Press (Clarendon Press), 1988.

Jones, Peter. *Philosophy and the Novel.* Oxford: Oxford University Press (Clarendon Press), 1975.

Kadish, Mortimer R., and Sanford H. Kadish. *Discretion to Disobey: A Study of Lawful Departures from Legal Rules.* Stanford University Press, 1973.

Kagan, Shelly. *The Limits of Morality.* Oxford: Oxford University Press (Clarendon Press), 1989.

Kant, Immanuel. "On a Supposed Right to Tell Lies from Benevolent Motives." In *Critique of Practical Reason,* translated by Thomas Kingsmill Abbott. London: Longman Group, 1959.

Philosophical Correspondence. Edited and translated by Arnulf Zweig. Chicago: University of Chicago Press, 1967.

Kant's Political Writings. Edited by Hans Reiss, translated by H. B. Nisbett. Cambridge University Press, 1970.

Lectures on Ethics. Translated by Louis Infield. London: Methuen & Co. 1979.

Kantorowicz, Ernst. "Mysteries of State." *Harvard Theological Review.* 48 (1955): 65–91.

Kateb, George. *Hannah Arendt, Politics, Conscience, Evil.* Oxford: Martin Robertson, 1984.

Bibliography

Kierkegaard, Søren. *Purity of Heart Is to Will One Thing.* Translated by Douglas V. Steere. New York: Harper & Row, 1956.

The Concept of Dread. Translated and with an introduction and notes by Walter Lowrie. Princeton, N.J.: Princeton University Press, 1957.

Works of Love. Translated by Howard and Edna Hong. London: Collins, 1962.

Kolnai, Aurel. *Ethics, Value and Reality.* London: Athlone, 1977.

Korsgaard, Christine M. "The Right to Lie: Kant on Dealing with Evil." *Philosophy and Public Affairs* 15 (1986): 325–49.

Krook, Dorothea. *Three Traditions of Moral Thought.* Cambridge University Press, 1959.

Leonard, John. "Public versus Private Claims: Machiavellianism from Another Perspective." *Political Theory* 12 no. 4 (November 1984): 491–506.

Lessnoff, Michael. *Social Contract.* London: Macmillan Press, 1986.

Locke, John. *Two Treatises of Government.* Edited and with a critical introduction and notes by Peter Laslett. Cambridge University Press, 1967.

Luhmann, N. *Trust and Power.* Edited by T. Burns and G. Poggi. Chichester: Wiley, 1979.

"Familiarity, Confidence, Trust: Problems and Alternatives." In Diego Gambetta (ed.). *Trust, Making and Breaking Cooperative Relations.* Oxford: Blackwell Publisher, 1988, 94–107.

Lukes, Steven. *Marxism and Morality.* Oxford: Oxford University Press (Clarendon Press), 1985.

Machiavelli, N. *The Letters.* Edited and translated by Allan Gilbert. New York: Carpricorn Books, 1961.

The Discourses. Edited by Bernard Crick, Harmondsworth: Penguin, 1979.

The Prince. edited by Quentin Skinner and Russell Price. Cambridge University Press, 1988.

MacIntyre, Alasdair. *After Virtue.* 2nd ed. London: Duckworth, 1985.

Mansfield, Harvey C., Jr. *Machiavelli's New Modes and Orders.* Ithaca, N.Y.: Cornell University Press, 1979.

Marx, Karl. "The Civil War in France." In Lewis S. Feuer (ed.), *Marx and Engels, Basic Writings on Politics and Philosophy,* London: Collins, 1974, 389–431.

Meinecke, Friedrich. *Machiavellism.* Translated by Douglas Scott. London: Routledge & Kegan Paul, 1957.

Bibliography

Mendus, Susan. "Marital Faithfulness." *Philosophy* 59 (1984): 243–52.

"The Serpent and the Dove." *Philosophy* 63 (1988): 331–43.

Mill, John Stuart. *Autobiography.* Edited and with a preface by John Jacob Coss. New York: Columbia University Press, 1960.

Utilitarianism. London: Dent, 1964.

The Later Letters, 1849–1873. Edited by Francis E. Mineka and Dwight N. Lindley. London: University of Toronto Press, Routledge and Kegan Paul, 1972.

Minogue, Kenneth. "Loyalty, Liberalism and the State." In George Feaver and Frederick Rosen (eds.), *Lives, Liberties, and the Public Good.* London: Macmillan Press, 1987, 203–27.

Moore, Kathleen Dean. *Pardons – Justice, Mercy and the Public Interest.* New York: Oxford University Press, 1989.

Mulgan, R. G. *Aristotle's Political Theory.* Oxford: Oxford University Press (Clarendon Press), 1977.

Murphy, Jeffrie G. "Forgiveness and Resentment." *Midwest Studies in Philosophy.* 7 (1982): 503–16.

Murphy, Jeffrie G., and Hampton Jean. *Forgiveness and Mercy.* Cambridge University Press, 1988.

Nagel, Thomas. "Ruthlessness in Public Life." In Stuart Hampshire (ed.), *Public and Private Morality.* Cambridge University Press, 1978, 75–91.

Nussbaum, Martha Craven. "Consequences and Character in Sophocles' *Philoctetes.*" *Philosophy and Literature* 1, pt. 1 (1976–7): 25–53.

Aristotle's De Motu Animalium. Princeton, N.J.: Princeton University Press, 1985.

"The Discernment of Perception: An Aristotelian Conception of Private and Public Morality." In J. Cleary (ed.), *Proceedings of the Boston Area Colloquium in Ancient Philosophy.* New York: University Press of America, 1985, 151–201.

The Fragility of Goodness. Cambridge University Press, 1986.

Love's Knowledge, Essays on Philosophy and Literature. Oxford: Oxford University Press, 1990.

Oakeshott, Michael. *Rationalism in Politics.* London: Methuen & Co., 1962.

On Human Conduct. Oxford: Oxford University Press (Clarendon Press), 1975.

Orwell, George. *Nineteen Eighty-Four.* Harmondsworth: Penguin Books, 1960.

Bibliography

Palmer, Kenneth. Introduction to William Shakespeare, *Troilus and Cressida*. London: Methuen & Co. 1982.

Parry, Geraint. "Trust, Distrust and Consensus." *British Journal of Political Science* 6 (1976): 129–42.

John Locke. London: Allen & Unwin, 1978.

Parsons, Stephen. "On the Logic of Corporatism." *Political Studies* 36 (1988): 515–23.

Phillips, D. Z. "My Neighbour and My Neighbours." *Philosophical Investigations* 12, no. 2 (April 1989): 112–33.

Pitkin, Hannah. *Wittgenstein and Justice*. Berkeley and Los Angeles: University of California Press, 1972.

Fortune Is a Woman: Gender and Politics in the Thought of Niccolo Machiavelli. Berkeley and Los Angeles: University of California Press, 1984.

Plato. *The Republic*. Translated by F. M. Cornford. Oxford: Oxford University Press, 1961.

Poole, Adrian. *Tragedy, Shakespeare and the Greek Example*. Oxford: Blackwell Publisher, 1987.

Post, Gaines. *Studies in Medieval Legal Thought, Public Law and the State 1100–1322*. Princeton N.J.: Princeton University Press, 1964.

Price, Russell. "Ambizione in Machiavelli's Thought." *History of Political Thought* 3, no. 3 (November 1982): 383–445.

Putt, S. Gorley. *The Fiction of Henry James*. Harmondsworth: Penguin Books, 1968.

Rawls, John. *A Theory of Justice*. Oxford: Oxford University Press, 1972.

Ricks, Christopher. *T. S. Eliot and Prejudice*. London: Faber & Faber, 1988.

Rorty, Richard. *Contingency, Irony and Solidarity*. Cambridge University Press, 1989.

Ross, Alf. *Directives and Norms*, London: Routledge & Kegan Paul, 1968.

Ryan, Alan. "Hobbes, Toleration and the Inner Life." In David Miller and Larry Siedentop (eds.), *The Nature of Political Theory*. Oxford: Oxford University Press (Clarendon Press), 1983, 197–218.

Sartre, Jean-Paul. *Three Plays*. Translated by Kitty Black. London: Hamish Hamilton, 1949.

Schnur, Roman (ed.). *Staats räson*. Berlin: Duncker & Humblot, 1979.

Bibliography

Shakespeare, William. *The Complete Works.* Edited by W. Craig. Oxford: Oxford University Press, 1964.

Troilus and Cressida. Edited by Kenneth Palmer. London: Methuen & Co., 1982.

Sherman, Nancy. *The Fabric of Character: Aristotle's Theory of Virtue.* Oxford: Oxford University Press (Clarendon Press), 1989.

Shklar, Judith. *Legalism.* Cambridge: Harvard University Press, 1964.

Ordinary Vices. Cambridge: Harvard University Press, 1984.

Silver, Alan. "'Trust' in Social and Political Theory." In G. D. Suttles and M. N. Zald (eds.), *The Challenge of Social Control.* Norwood, N.J.: Ablex Publishing, 1985, 52–67.

Skinner, Quentin. *The Foundations of Modern Political Thought,* vol. 1, *The Renaissance.* Cambridge University Press, 1978.

"The State." In Terence Ball, James Farr, and Russell L. Hanson (eds.), *Political Innovation and Conceptual Change.* Cambridge University Press, 1989.

Skorupski, John. *John Stuart Mill.* London: Routledge & Kegan Paul, 1989.

Slote, Michael. *Goods and Virtues.* Oxford: Oxford University Press (Clarendon Press), 1983.

Sophocles. *The Theban Plays.* Translated by E. F. Watling. Harmondsworth: Penguin Books, 1956.

Philoctetes. In *Electra and Other Plays.* Translated by E. F. Watling. Harmondsworth: Penguin Books, 1967.

Sparkes, A. W. "Trust and Teleology: Locke's Politics and His Doctrine of Creation." *Canadian Journal of Philosophy* 3, no. 2 (December 1973): 263–73.

Stocker, Michael. *Plural and Conflicting Values.* Oxford: Oxford University Press (Clarendon Press), 1990.

Stocks, J. L. *Morality and Purpose.* London: Routledge & Kegan Paul, 1969.

Sullivan, Roger J. *Immanuel Kant's Moral Theory.* Cambridge University Press, 1989.

Swinburne, Richard. *Faith and Reason.* Oxford: Oxford University Press (Clarendon Press), 1981.

Tanner, Tony. *Adultery in the Novel.* Baltimore: Johns Hopkins University Press, 1979.

Thomas, D. O., "The Duty to Trust." *Proceedings of the Aristotelian Society* 79 (1978–9): 89–101.

Bibliography

Thompson, Dennis F. *Political Ethics and Public Office.* Cambridge: Harvard University Press, 1987.

Thucydides. *History of the Peloponnesian War.* Translated by Benjamin Jowett. 2nd ed. Oxford: Oxford University Press (Clarendon Press), 1900.

The Peloponnesian War. Translated by Rex Warner, with an introduction and notes by M. I. Finley. Harmondsworth: Penguin Books, 1979.

Vickers, Brian. *Towards Greek Tragedy.* London: Longman Group, 1973.

Walsh, W. H. "Pride, Shame and Responsibility." *Philosophical Quarterly* 20, no. 78 (January 1970): 1–13.

Walzer, Michael. "Political Action: The Problem of Dirty Hands." *Philosophy and Public Affairs* 2 (1973): 160–80.

Wasserstrom, Richard. "Lawyers as Professionals: Some Moral Issues." *Human Rights* 5 (1975): 2–24.

Weil, Frederick D. "The Stranger, Prudence and Trust in Hobbes's Theory." *Theory and Society* 15 (1987): 761–96.

Weil, Simone. *The Need for Roots.* Translated by Arthur Mills, with a preface by T. S. Eliot. London: Routledge & Kegan Paul, 1952.

The Iliad or the Poem of Force. Translated by Mary McCarthy. Wallingford, Penn.: Pendle Hill, 1970.

Selected Essays 1934–43. Translated by Richard Rees. London: Oxford University Press, 1962.

An Anthology. Edited and with an introduction by Sian Miles. London: Virago Press, 1985.

Wilde, Oscar. *Plays.* Harmondsworth: Penguin Books, 1963.

Williams, Bernard. *Morality: An Introduction to Ethics.* Cambridge University Press, 1972.

"Politics and Moral Character." In Stuart Hampshire (ed.), *Public and Private Morality.* Cambridge University Press, 1978, 55–73.

Moral Luck. Cambridge University Press, 1981.

"Professional Morality and Its Dispositions." In David Luban (ed.), *The Good Lawyer.* Totowa, N.J.: Rowman & Allenheld, 1983, 259–69.

Williams, Howard. *Kant's Political Philosophy.* Oxford: Blackwell Publisher, 1983.

Wilson, John R. S. "In One Another's Power." *Ethics* 88 (1978–9): 299–315.

Winch, Peter. *Ethics and Action.* London: Routledge & Kegan Paul, 1972.

Bibliography

Trying to Make Sense. Oxford: Blackwell Publisher, 1987.

Simone Weil: "The Just Balance." Cambridge University Press, 1989.

Winterbotham, F. W. *The Ultra Secret*. London: Weidenfeld & Nicolson, 1974.

Wittgenstein, Ludwig. *Tractatus Logico-Philosophicus*. Translated by D. F. Pears and B. F. McGuiness. London: Routledge & Kegan Paul, 1966.

Zola, Emile. *Thérèse Raquin*. Translated and with an introduction by Leonard Tancock. Harmondsworth: Penguin Books, 1963.

Index

Alvis, J., 180n73
Aquinas, St. Thomas, 55–6
arcana imperii, 59
Arendt, H., 24, 52, 53, 75, 82, 136,
   143, 157, 161–5, 176n53,
   184n71, 191n17, 193n87,
   194nn109 and 111 and 117 and
   119 and 120
Aristotle, 16–17, 36–40, 46, 47, 52,
   91, 151, 169
   Nicomachean Ethics, 40, 177n30,
   178nn33 and 36 and 39, 195n6
   The Politics, 175n30, 177n27,
   179n50, 180n73
Austen, J., 48, 180n78
   Pride and Prejudice, 48

Baier, A., 15, 72–3, 74, 98, 99–101,
   174n4, 175n27, 176n55,
   183n60, 184nn62 and 70,
   186n67, 187n5, 190n103
Baier, K., 28, 176n4
Banning, L., 175n42
Baron, M., 190n103
Barry, B., 57, 181n11, 184n61
Baumgold, D., 180nn80 and 81
Bayley, J., 89, 92, 94, 152, 156,
   185nn26 and 37 and 44,
   189n68, 193nn58 and 60 and 83
Beloff, M., 175n41
Blundell, M. W., 87, 119, 123, 147,

149, 185nn15 and 24, 188n44,
   189nn57 and 62, 192nn33 and
   41 and 43
Bok, S., 60–1, 176nn51 and 56,
   182nn22 and 24 and 26
Botero, G., 56, 181n9
   The Reason of State, 56
Bowra, C. M., 120, 188nn46 and 49
Buckler, N. E., 191n11
Burke, E., 14, 47, 76, 175n20,
   176n58, 180n75

Casey, J., 41, 178n40
Cavell, S., 179n62
Channon, Sir Henry, 34, 177n21
Church, W., 56, 181nn6 and 7
Cicero, 71–2, 106, 111–12, 183n54,
   187n20
Cobbett, W., 39, 66, 178n35, 183n39
Conrad, J., 103, 130, 190n94
   The Secret Sharer, 103
   The Duel, 130
contractarianism, 8, 10, 11, 17–18,
   20, 49–50, 73, 74–5, 77–8, 162
Cooper, J. M., 185n35
Croce, B., 191n17

Diamond, C., 195n9
Dickens, C., 106, 172
   Oliver Twist, 106–7
   Bleak House, 172, 195n10